THE HEART OF THE MIDDLE EAST

The Heart of the Middle East is a classic account of the history and culture of Iraq. Written in 1925 at the height of the colonial era, it offers unique insights into a complex past that continues to influence events today, both in the region and far beyond it. Beginning with the earliest known inhabitants of what was called Mesopotamia, Coke describes Roman-Persian rivalry in the area, the collapse of both Persia and Constantinople before the onset of the Arabs, the golden age of the Abbassid Caliphate, the coming of the Turks and, with their decline, the coming of the English, the rise in the Middle East of European influence generally, and the parallel rise of a reborn Arab nationalism. Coke then focuses on the early modern period of the nation's history, detailing the emergence of Mesopotamia on the stage of modern world politics, the involvement in World War I, and its aftermath. In 1920 the British Government, having emerged from the War with a mandate for Mesopotamia, proposed to facilitate the development of the area as a self-governing State, even though there was little evidence that the native population wanted to become a nation. Describing the people of the country, Coke asks – '*Arabs, Jews, Kurds, Seljuk Turks, Persians, Assyrians, Telkaifis, Armenians – how mould such a composite collection of races into a single nation? Sunnis, Shiahs, Jews, Christians, Sabians, Yezidis – how to lessen the friction between such a variety of creeds? How to persuade the tribal sheikh to sacrifice his power for the sake of a non-existing State?*' Nonetheless, the new country was intended by the League of Nations and the British Government to be an experiment in nation-building, an exercise that would demonstrate that all such differences could be overcome by logic, reason and the application of strong political pressure from outside. Coke's account of the early years of the new state explains much about the present political, and is essential reading for all those with an interest in the history and politics of the Middle East.

THE KEGAN PAUL ARABIA LIBRARY

THE SYRIAN DESERT
Christina Phelps Grant

THE TRAGEDY OF THE ASSYRIAN
MINORITY IN IRAQ
R. S. Stafford

THE TRIBES OF THE MARSH ARABS
OF IRAQ
Fulanain

THE VANISHED CITIES OF ARABIA
Mrs. Steuart Erskine

ARABIA AND THE ISLES
Harold Ingrams

STUDIES IN ISLAMIC MYSTICISM
Reynold A. Nicholson

LORD OF ARABIA: IBN SAUD
H. C. Armstrong

AVARICE AND THE AVARICIOUS
Jim Colville

TWO ANDALUSIAN PHILOSOPHERS
Abu Bakr Muhammad ibn Tufayl
& Abu'l Walid Muhammad ibn
Rushd

THE PERFUMED GARDEN OF
SENSUAL DELIGHT
Muhammad ibn Muhammad al-
Nafzawi

THE WELLS OF IBN SAUD
D. van der Meulen

ADVENTURES IN ARABIA
W. B. Seabrook

SEAFARING IN THE ARABIAN GULF
AND OMAN
Dionisius A. Agius

POEMS OF WINE & REVELRY
Jim Colville

THE ANTHROPOLOGY OF IRAQ
Henry Field

SOUTHERN ARABIA
J. Theodore Bent

IRAQ
Philip Willard Ireland

THE SAND KINGS OF OMAN
Raymond O'Shea

THE BLACK TENTS OF ARABIA
Carl S. Raswan

BEDOUIN JUSTICE
Austin Kennett

THE ARAB AWAKENING
George Antonius

ARABIA PHOENIX
Gerald De Gaury

HOW GREEK SCIENCE PASSED TO
THE ARABS
DeLacy O'Leary

SOBRIETY AND MIRTH
Jim Colville

IN THE HIGH YEMEN
Hugh Scott

ARABIC CULTURE THROUGH ITS
LANGUAGE AND LITERATURE
M. H. Bakalla

IBN SA'OUD OF ARABIA
Ameen Rihani

IRAQ FROM MANDATE TO
INDEPENDENCE
Ernest Main

THE ANCIENT ROAD
John Guest
& Peter Gwynvay Hopkins

THE COUNTRIES AND TRIBES OF THE
PERSIAN GULF
Samuel Barrett Miles

THE EMERGENCE OF QATAR
Habibur Rahman

THE LONG ROAD TO BAGHDAD
Edmund Candler

THE HEART OF THE
MIDDLE EAST
Richard Coke

THE HEART OF THE MIDDLE EAST

RICHARD COKE

Routledge
Taylor & Francis Group

LONDON AND NEW YORK

First published in 2006 by
Kegan Paul Limited

Published 2016 by Routledge
2 Park Square, Milton Park, Abingdon, Oxfordshire OX14 4RN
711 Third Avenue, New York, NY 10017

First issued in paperback 2016

Routledge is an imprint of the Taylor and Francis Group, an informa business

© Kegan Paul, 2006

All rights reserved. No part of this book may be reprinted or reproduced or utilised in any form or by any electric, mechanical or other means, now known or hereafter invented, including photocopying or recording, or in any information storage or retrieval system, without permission in writing from the publishers.

British Library Cataloguing in Publication Data
Coke, Richard
The heart of the Middle East. – (The Kegan Paul Arabia library)
1. Iraq – History 2. Iraq – Civilization
I. Title
956.7

ISBN 13: 978-1-138-97590-3 (pbk)
ISBN 13: 978-0-7103-1143-6 (hbk)

CONTENTS

CHAPTER		PAGE
	INTRODUCTION	11
I.	EARLY DAYS	15
II.	THE ROMAN-PERSIAN RIVALRY	27
III.	THE COMING OF THE ARAB	38
IV.	THE DIVISION OF ISLAM	52
V.	THE GOLDEN AGE	65
VI.	LIFE IN THE GOLDEN AGE	78
VII.	THE COMING OF THE TURK	88
VIII.	THE COMING OF THE ENGLISH	103
IX.	THE COMING OF THE GERMAN	121
X.	THE WORLD WAR	143
XI.	THE YEAR OF HOPE	160
XII.	THE YEAR OF DISILLUSION	179
XIII.	THE PEOPLE OF THE COUNTRY	195
XIV.	THE CREATION OF THE NEW STATE	216
XV.	THE ORGANIZATION OF THE EXECUTIVE	235
XVI.	MONEY, WATER, FIELD, AND ROAD	247
XVII.	HEALTH AND EDUCATION	264
XVIII.	INDUSTRY AND BUSINESS	277
XIX.	SOCIAL LIFE	290
XX.	THE DAWN OF A TO-MORROW	301
	APPENDIX	316
	INDEX	317

LIST OF ILLUSTRATIONS

H.M. King Feisal	*Frontispiece*
	Facing page
Babylonian Statue	22
Babylonian Statuettes	22
Babylonian Books	22
The Great Arch at Ctesiphon	32
Najaf	58
A ruined tower at Samarra	100
Babylon to-day	100
Basrah	146
East Baghdad	172
Kifl	208
The Old Turkish Bridge at Baghdad	258
The Shrine of the Imams at Samarra	258
The New University of Al-al-beit at Baghdad	274
The uncompleted bridge at Mosul	282
Sir Percy Cox	308
The Tower of Nimrod, near Babylon	314

MAPS

	Page
Iraq	9
The Middle East	10
Ancient and Modern Baghdad	120

H.M. KING FEISAL

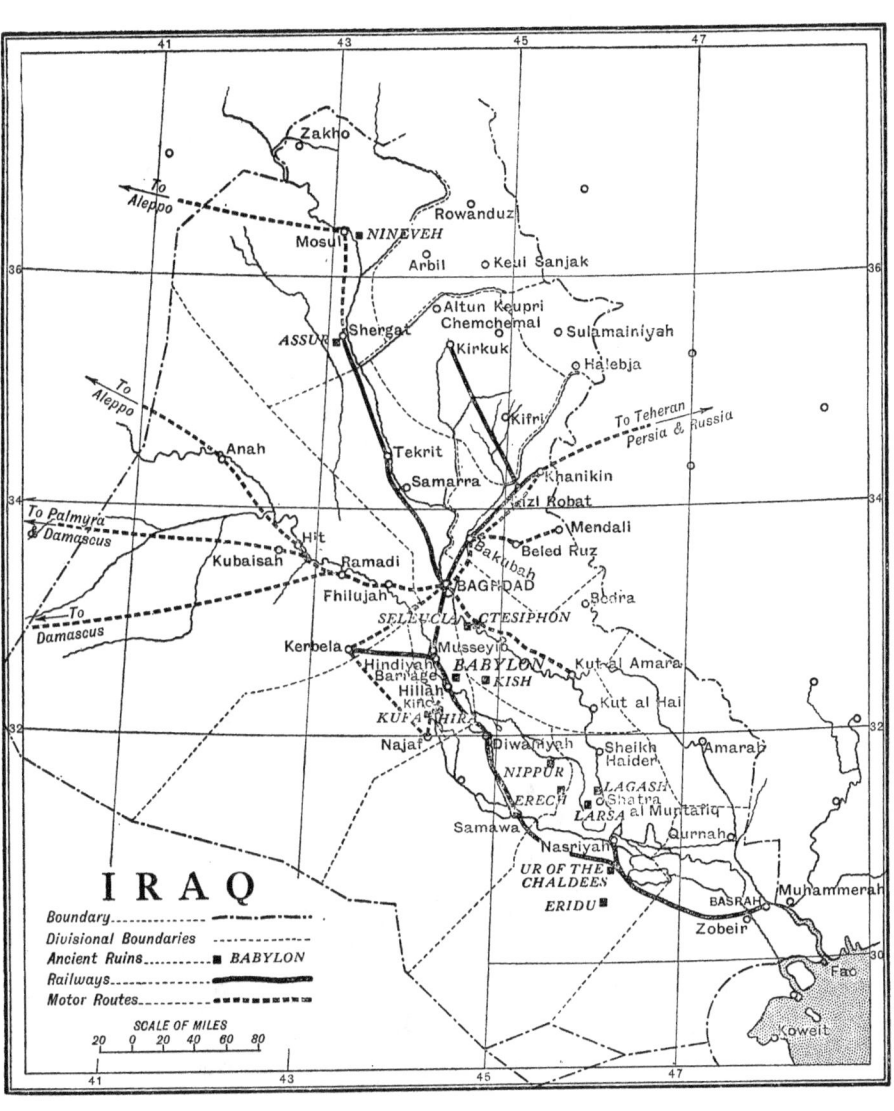

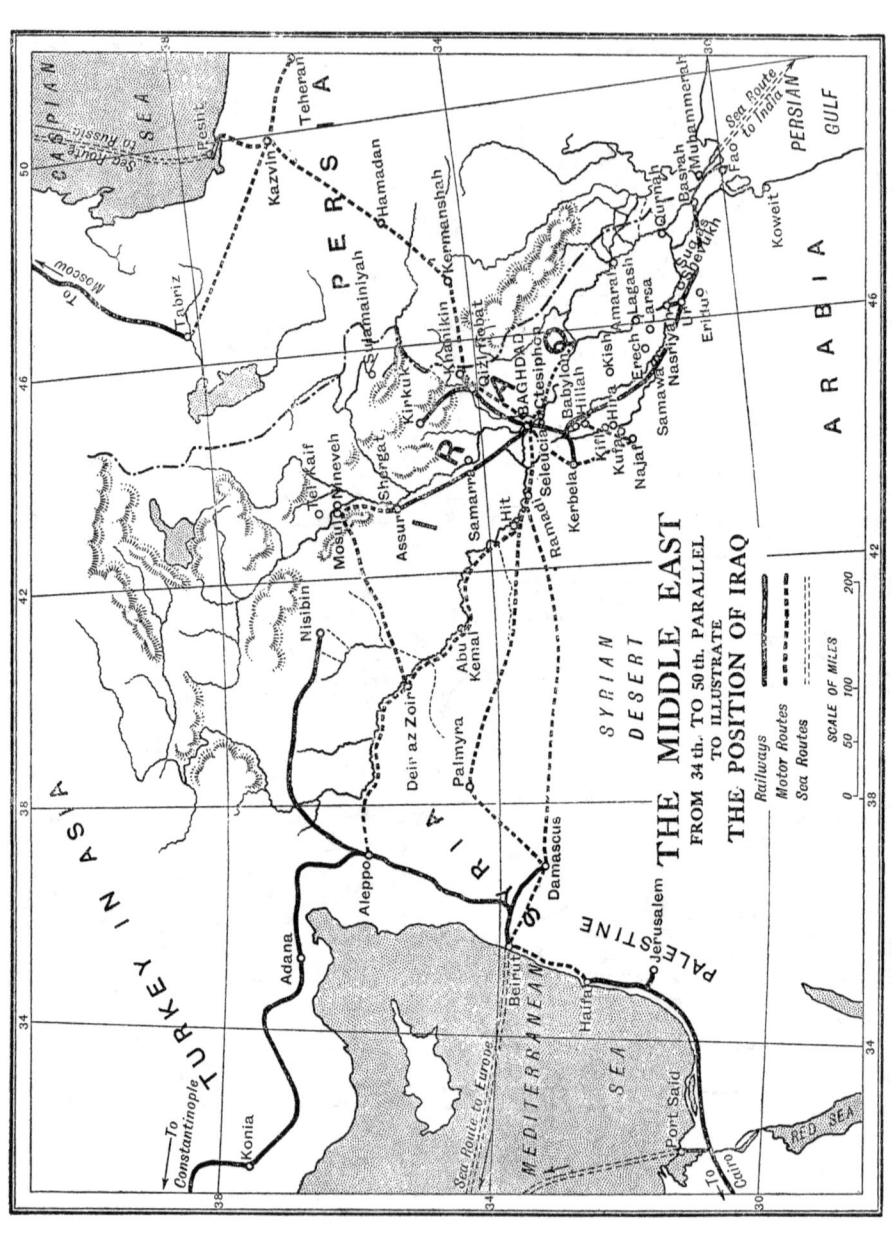

prejudiced press. Great Britain has been slowly conquering Mesopotamia for many years, and, having at last accomplished the conquest, she is in honour bound to accept the consequences of her actions. She cannot withdraw her support from the territory whose previous government she has persistently undermined and finally destroyed, without a serious reflection on her honour and her ability as a colonizing nation.

It is not, however, the object of the writer to plead the case of Mesopotamia, so much as to offer a brief and, so far as such a thing is possible, an unprejudiced account of her history, her population and her present condition. Much of Mesopotamian history is extremely confused and uncertain, and it would be impossible in a short work to attempt the discussion of all knotty historical points; as far as possible, where conflicting accounts of any historical episode occur, the writer has thought it best to adopt the version published in the *Encyclopædia Britannica*, as being the generally accepted popular authority of the day. In more recent times, where several versions of an incident exist, the writer has generally inclined towards the native version; not from any feelings of hostility towards the British officials in power in the country—who have, for the most part, faced an uphill task with courage and resource—but from the feeling that, in a country where public opinion has little restraining influence over officialdom, it is only fair, in any case where doubt exists, to give the native inhabitants the benefit of the doubt.

The name "Mesopotamia" is used to-day in the languages of Europe to describe a tract of country very much larger than, and to some extent differently situated from, the "Mesopotamia" of the Greeks, from whom the word is derived. The literal rendering of the Greek term is "The land amid the rivers," and not "The land between the rivers"; thus indicating that it was recognized that there were more than two rivers in the country, and that the modern appellation of "The land of the two rivers" would have been then, as it is now, inaccurate. Mesopotamia to the Greeks meant roughly all the country north of Hit on the Euphrates and Tekrit on the Tigris as far as the mountains of Kurdistan, which corresponded

INTRODUCTION

OF all the countries which have come prominently before the notice of the public either during or after the World War, none has evoked such discussion, or aroused such storms of alternate adulation and abuse as Mesopotamia, or, to give it its Arabic style, Iraq. From the days when this land of " untapped wealth and virgin oil " was thought to be only waiting, in the words of one enthusiastic patron, " to pay the whole cost of the war," to the days of the furious " bag and baggage " campaign, which had for its object the severance of all connection with the accursed land, might seem a far cry indeed ; but the two periods were, as a matter of fact, separated by less than forty months. That such a change in public sentiment was possible in so short a time was due in part, no doubt, to the general disappointment in the results, or lack of results, of the victory as a whole ; to a common and perfectly natural feeling of lassitude and nervousness, at times amounting almost to a form of moral cowardice ; but, in the opinion of the author, most of all to a complete ignorance of actual Mesopotamian conditions, of the past history of the country (and more particularly, perhaps, of the past history of the British connection with the country), and of its future possibilities.

Contrary to the general opinion in Great Britain, the British connection with Mesopotamia did not begin with the war ; the war was but the culmination of a series of incidents, extending over a very long period of time, in which Britain more and more assumed the right to interfere with, or to control, the internal life of the country. The British connection was an accomplished fact a hundred and fifty years ago, and may easily still remain an accomplished fact a hundred and fifty years hence ; facts are stubborn things, and such a connection will hardly be easily broken either by the enunciation of pleasing political theories, or by the rodomontades of an ignorant and to arouse in the reader a renewed interest in a much maligned and little understood country, and to create for him something of the charm and interest which Mesopotamia never fails to excite in those who come to know her more intimately, the author's object will have been attained.

to the ancient kingdom of Assyria, and in modern times to the Turkish vilayet of Mosul. The name is in any case of late appearance, and is not used by Xenophon. The dominant geographical characteristics of the country, in the shape of the two great rivers, and their tributaries and distributaries, have however impressed themselves upon the imagination of those who named the country from the earliest times, the description " naharim " (from " nahr," a river), occurring as early as the sixteenth century B.C.; and a name from the same root is to be seen in connection with Mesopotamia in the twenty-fourth chapter of Genesis. Mesopotamia proper has always been referred to by the Arabs as " Al-Gezirah " (The Island), in distinction to " Al-Iraq " (The Plain), used to describe the lower alluvial district, the Chaldea or Babylonia of the ancients, formed by the great rivers in their tortuous progress from the latitude of Baghdad (where they come comparatively close to one another) to the sea. " Al-Iraq " has to-day become the official designation of both the old Iraq and Al-Gezirah, in imitation of the modern European misuse of the word " Mesopotamia "; and throughout this work it is understood that both " Mesopotamia " and " Iraq " are used in their modern, popular sense, as including all that country bounded on the north by the mountains of Kurdistan, on the south by the Persian Gulf and Arabia, on the east by Persia, and on the west by Syria and the Syrian desert. This is the country which has since the war been formed into a single geographical and political unit, at present jointly administered by King Feisal, the third son of King Hosein of the Hedjaz, and by the British authorities.

The author is indebted to many books of reference, both ancient and modern, for much of his information; as far as possible, in order to assist the continuity of the narrative, references and foot-notes have been excluded, but a list of useful books will be found at the end of this volume, for the benefit of those who care to pursue the subject. To the authors of all these books the present writer is indebted, and he hereby wishes to express his grateful thanks.

If this short and necessarily insufficient work is able

CHAPTER I

EARLY DAYS

*"O thou River who didst bring forth all things,
When the great Gods dug thee out,
They set prosperity upon thy banks."*
SUMERIAN INSCRIPTION.

IF we pursue our studies of the lives and activities of the races of men who have preceded us upon the earth back to the dawn of history, we shall find ourselves face to face at one period with a wide gap in the course of our inquiries. We shall find that we can trace the existence of man, his whereabouts and to some extent his method of living in the prehistoric ages, as a sort of sub-man or purely animal creation ; and we shall find again that the next view which we get of him is as a member of a highly organized civilization, understanding how to read and write, making war upon his neighbour, framing and obeying laws, and generally surrounded with much of the paraphernalia of living which we associate with civilized conditions to-day. How man bridged the gulf from the sub-man stage to that of the comparatively high culture of even the earliest-known civilizations, we have as yet no certain knowledge ; we simply know that he did do it ; in the matter of accurate and reliable information of the transition period, or even of the form it took, we are still completely in the dark.

Mesopotamia, like China and Egypt, meets us at the dawn of history as a *fait accompli*. Her long story begins we know not where ; of the early struggles of her inhabitants, of whence they came, of their wanderings, of their fight with wild beast, flood and marsh, of their taming of the waters of the two great rivers, we know nothing ; when the curtain is raised before our eyes, we see them already very highly civilized, with distinct racial and local qualities of their own, and in the possession of an elaborate political organization. Small and combative city states, not unlike the later and more famous products of ancient Greece, face each other across a canal or some even more artificial boundary ; each city state possesses its own government, follows its own laws and customs, and acknowledges its own god ; each, to all intents and purposes, already forms a little world of its own. The exterior relations of these city states appear to have been very bad, for war or fighting in some shape or form were almost constant occurrences ; but internally, they were very advanced. The knowledge of reading and writing was the prerogative of the educated woman as well as the educated man ; science was cultivated, and its practical applications studied ; the laws were effective, and were evidently the result of long years of practical experience ; and the irrigation system, upon which not merely the prosperity but the very existence of the country depended, was an engineering accomplishment of the first magnitude, which even in the twentieth century is capable of exciting the admiration of the expert. The irrigation system was apparently but little disturbed by the innumerable little wars waged between one or other of the city states, which seem to have been conscious of the fact that they possessed a common interest superior to all their national bickerings and rivalries ; a point of view which is not without its lesson for the modern European. It may be noted incidentally that the irrigation system must have been in full operation as early as the year 4000 B.C., or nearly six thousand years ago.

It would appear that, in spite of the constant state of conflict between the various cities, there was a considerable intercourse between them, and a large foreign population resident in each of them ; Mesopotamia, then as now, was a land of many peoples. To the south lay the sea marshes of the Kalda, or Chaldeans, inhabited by various Aramaic tribes ; in this district would lie Eridu, the port of the country and the seat of Ea, the culture-god. Some distance north-west of Eridu would come Ur of the Chaldees, a neighbour and rival of more recent growth. The sites of both these cities now lie some hundred and thirty miles inland, and it has been proved conclusively by the study of the rate of recedence of the sea in the Persian Gulf over a given period (which is an historically known quantity), that Eridu must have been flourishing at least six thousand years ago. Farther north, in the alluvial plain of Edin (the "Eden" of the Bible), would be found the cities of Lagash, Erech, Larsa, Kish, Kutha and the two Sipparas; and, perhaps superior to them all, Nippur, the historic sanctuary of El-Lil, the original incarnation of the great god Bel. Farther north again would come Assur, the little city which was later destined to become the birthplace of the great military despotism of Assyria.

The early culture of the country appears to have been mainly derived from two cities, curiously different from each other in temperament and in the main body of ideas for which they stood. Nippur in the north was the town of the hard and terrible El-Lil, the Sun God, lord of the ghost land, and creator of a world and people of his own, the underground spirits or *jinn*; southern Eridu was the home of the culture-god Ea, the revealer of the power of knowledge, the bestower of the talent for invention, the instinct of beneficence and the desire for civilization. Writing had been one of the good god's gifts, the first book of law another. Eridu's close touch with the sea would tend to keep her sane and healthy, free from harshness and narrowness of mind; the inland struggle for existence would tend to make Nippur martial, stern and egotistical. Eridu was the mother of the first sailor, Nippur of the first soldier.

In a narrow land containing many rival and pugnacious states, it was inevitable that one amongst the number should eventually aspire to a position of overlordship or supremacy; we first hear of Lagash in this connection, as the seat of a baby empire governed by a "King of kings," a title which hints at the birth of an ambition not yet dead among mankind. The third of the Lagash dynasty that we know of, E-anna-du by name, is possibly the world's first great conqueror. We know that he subdued the whole of Babylonia including the cities of Erech and Ur, overran Elam in Persia and captured the town of Az on the Persian Gulf. But his conquests were not permanent, and his dominion fell to a priestly adventurer of Erech, whose kingdom eventually extended from the "Sea of the Tigris and Euphrates" (Persian Gulf) to the "Upper Sea" (Mediterranean).

These comparatively small affairs were soon to yield to the touch of a foreign conqueror. To the south-west of Mesopotamia lies the desert and inhospitable land of Arabia, a land whose people have always played a great part in Mesopotamian history. From time immemorial sudden irruptions of wild men have come from this land of mystery, sweeping across the rich and fruitful plains to the north of them with all the irresistible force of a tidal wave. It was so now. For the first time in history we meet the Semites, that great family of nations which was destined to produce in successive ages the Assyrians, the Phoenicians, the Jews, the Carthaginians and, last but not least, the Arabs. There had undoubtedly been Semitic residents of Mesopotamia before this time, perhaps there had even been previous invasions and floods ; but this is the first occasion actually known of a complete Semitic conquest. Characteristically, it centred round the figure of a leader who afterwards became a hero of tradition. Sargon, the Semitic founder of Akkad (3800 B.C.), was, according to tradition, born of a goddess, who concealed the babe and set it adrift in an ark of bulrushes on the Euphrates ; at an appropriate moment the boy's high parentage was discovered, and the people saluted the King of Babylonia. Whatever his real origin, Sargon was a true warrior ; four times he invaded Syria and Palestine, and images of himself were erected along the shores of the Mediterranean in memory of his conquests. Nor were his interests confined to war. He raised the level of civilization in his dominions, and he is entitled to the credit of being one of the world's first great Imperial organizers. A carefully conceived system of roads connected the principal centres of his empire, on which was maintained a regular postal service ; some of the clay seals which took the place of stamps in his time are still in existence to-day. He attempted a general survey of his dominions ; he was a patron of the arts ; and his love of books is proved by the creation of his famous library, for which, incidentally, some of the first-known astronomical observations were made and tabulated.

In a manner typically Semitic, Sargon's empire collapsed as suddenly as it had arisen, and the balance of power shifted in favour of Ur of the Chaldees. Here another Semitic dynasty ruled over a considerable stretch of territory for an extended period. Modern Europe possesses a

EARLY DAYS

large number of documents of this time, which are being continually increased by the excavations at Ur ; most of them are contracts and other business notes. The collapse of the city as a power was brought about by a series of foreign invasions, first by Elam, and later by an Arabian new-comer, by name Sumabi ("Shem is my father"). The latter is chiefly interesting to us on account of his son, who was the founder of a fortress on the banks of the Euphrates which, together with an ancient shrine adjoining it, formed the nucleus of Babylon. But on the whole the Elamites appear to have been more successful than the descendants of Sumabi, for Elamite supremacy continued more or less over the whole of the delta country until the rise of Hammurabi, famous in history for his code of laws. Hammurabi overthrew the might of Elam in one great battle in 2093 B.C., and for many years afterwards the supremacy of his dynasty and of the rapidly growing city of Babylon, which he made his capital, was never seriously threatened. If the identification of Hammurabi with the Amraphel of the book of Genesis is justifiable, it was in one of the smaller wars of this period that Lot, the nephew of Abraham, was taken prisoner, and had to be rescued by his patriarchal uncle. This was the time of Babylon's rise to power. She became now the absolute mistress of the delta country, not merely politically but spiritually. Her god was accepted as the national god, and the old tribal deities were embodied in a comprehensive mythology which acknowledged Babylon as the religious metropolis of the whole country. In all her later vicissitudes, this characteristic never deserted her. The fiercest and rudest Assyrian king was glad to resort to the holy city to obtain confirmation and legality for his rule ; the victorious Persian conquerors were at pains to recognize the special sanctity of Babylon ; and even Alexander the Great was not oblivious of the prestige to be acquired by residence in the holy city of Asia.

The laws of Hammurabi, which have come down to us, reveal a civilization and a manner of living astonishingly modern. The world had already become so complicated that minute regulation had become necessary. The laws deal with the tenure of land, house rent, the status of the wife and the widow, and the condition of hired labour; they attempt to regulate forms of payment, in money and in kind, and they establish the legality of business contract. Trade appears from the allusions to it in the code to have had wide ramifications, and it is evident that caravans travelled far beyond the confines of the empire; the waterborne traffic on the Euphrates was considerable, and its control and development were, it seems, exercising the anxious care of the authorities. In the social sphere, the laws lay down the conditions under which taverns could be opened and intoxicating drink be sold, giving due warning to the tavern-keepers (who were, apparently, usually women), of the penalties which might follow disorderly scenes on the premises. In short, there does not seem much to distinguish the Babylon of four thousand years ago, in spirit at any rate, from the London or Paris of to-day.

Although the power of Hammurabi's empire gradually declined, the Babylonian tradition succeeded in fastening itself upon the imagination of the country; and when the invasion of the Kassites from the east ended by placing them in supreme control, there still remained a king in Babylon. But the Kassites, though they might flatter the capital, were unable wholly to control the provinces; and from the small city of Assur in the north there arose in the course of the years another kingdom, the work, as usual in these times, of the local priests. This kingdom was the forerunner of the Assyrian Empire.

The first Assyrian ruler of note was Shalmeneser I (1300 B.C.), the founder of the "greater Assyria" idea and of the new capital of Calah. The failure of his dynasty caused another priestly revolution at Assur, and the new family provided in Tiglath-Pileser I, at least one figure of international fame. It was he who "hunted wild bulls in the Lebanon, and was presented with a crocodile by the King of Egypt." He established the Assyrian Empire on a firm footing, and his arms were not unknown as far afield as Armenia and Cappadocia. For several hundred years after his time the Empire continued as the great power of the Middle East; in 853 B.C., for example, we find Shalmeneser II waging war successfully against the confederacy of Syrian princes headed by Benhadad of

EARLY DAYS

Damascus and Ahab of Israel. The same king later received tribute from Jehu.

A short period of anarchy in the Imperial capital was followed by the appearance on the scene of the originator of a new idea, which was destined to bear much fruit in the later history of mankind. The man was Tiglath-Pileser III (746 B.C.), and the idea was military bureaucracy. Hitherto wars had been run largely on amateur lines. The king, the head of the army and the State, was in practice little more than a dignified brigand; at a time of the year when the crops had been gathered in and the weather was pleasant for campaigning, he would raise an army from his people, invade the territory of his neighbours, seize everything of value that was portable, levy a tribute on the conquered territory in slaves and cash, and return in triumph for the winter to his own land. No attempt was made to "consolidate" the conquests, and indeed anything in the nature of permanent occupation, except in the case of countries and towns in very close proximity to the homeland, never seems to have been desired. It is partly for this reason that the early wars of Assyria and the powers which preceded her seem, in the retrospect, so interminable. They were not in fact wars as we understand the term, so much as looting expeditions, partly executed as a form of popular sport, partly with the serious purpose of providing the national exchequer with the means of carrying on its normal function. The more successful the looting in any one season, the less the necessity for heavy taxation at home. The only political object, in the narrow sense of the word, entertained was that of possible "moral effect."

But Tiglath-Pileser was a man of constructive imagination and Imperial vision. He instituted a standing army, and supported it by an elaborate bureaucracy of permanent and semi-permanent civil servants. From his new capital of Nineveh he so organized the nation that it became little less than a vast instrument of war. The metropolis was an armed camp. The spoils of victory were ruthlessly devoted to the single aim of further conquest, and the trade of the captured territories was carefully diverted into Assyrian hands. Nothing less than the Empire of the World was to be the eventual reward of the Great King, or of his immediate successors. With this great end in view, nothing could be safely neglected, and the favour of the highly civilized but powerless Babylonians was carefully cultivated; the holy city was raised again to the position of a second capital, and here in 729 B.C., Tiglath-Pileser the victorious was re-crowned king. The coronation of the Assyrian warrior in the holy city of Asia bears a strange resemblance to that of Charlemagne the Frankish emperor by the Pope of Rome, some fifteen hundred years later.

The reign of Tiglath-Pileser inaugurated the most glorious age that Mesopotamia as a whole had yet seen. All the known Western world was subject to her sway, and even the once proud rival of Egypt paid her tribute. The system which the Great King had devised survived him, and came within an ace of achieving his purpose; but it wore out his people and exasperated the conquered races, and in the end proved fatal to the Empire. Internal rebellions were frequent, and in 705 B.C., Babylon was razed to the ground, and the great image of Bel-Marduk removed to another site. Hezekiah of Judah also at this time headed a successful local revolt. For a while the military machine succeeded in holding the ground, but its power was running down. Rebellion in various portions of the Empire became endemic, and the situation was complicated by the unexpected irruption of hordes of wild Medes and Scythians into the north-eastern marches. Assyria, the terror of five hundred years, collapsed with surprising suddenness. Egypt and Babylon freed themselves. Calah was captured by rebels and sacked. Soon men heard that the barbaric Scythians had entered mighty Nineveh herself, and then they knew that the Assyrian captains and the Assyrian horsemen would come their way no more.

The centre of the scene shifted. Babylon, that ancient holy city, rose phœnix-like from her comparative obscurity. A new empire was carefully and slowly built up by a native ruler, Nabopolassar, a prudent king of a saving disposition, who paved the way for Nebuchadnezzar, his more famous son. Nebuchadnezzar (604-561 B.C.), was the Louis XIV of antiquity. His long and victorious reign of over forty years enriched Babylon with everything that a crowded, pleasure loving but tasteful capital could desire. Enormous

BABYLONIAN STATUE   BABYLONIAN STATUETTES

BABYLONIAN BOOKS

new walls contained a city many times larger than its predecessor ; frequent bridges and ferries conveyed the dense traffic across the ancient river ; even the late king's new palace was too humble for the luxurious taste of his son, and an elaborate inner city gradually arose in Babylon for the sole accommodation of the monarch and his army of retainers. A great main street, a hundred feet wide and paved throughout with bitumen, astonished the provincial and the traveller ; and dominating the whole city rose, tier by tier, the wonderful temple of Bel, for all the world like some gigantic pagoda perched in the heart of the metropolis. The trade of the whole East poured into this fortunate town ; money was plentiful and credit easily obtainable ; men came to Babylon for their pleasure, the cultivation of which, innocent or disreputable alike, was sedulously studied. Nothing seemed impossible for luxury to desire or for money to procure ; the city teemed with slaves, and hired labour was cheap ; the arts of construction and decoration were scientifically pursued ; and the plaintive desire of a Persian princess for the verdure of her native hills could produce the celebrated hanging gardens, a piece of engineering artistry among the most remarkable of ancient times. Well might the captive Jews, transported from a land of hard living and of simple pleasures, stand appalled before the might, the magnificence, the sheer and open wickedness of Babylon.

But the triumph of Nebuchadnezzar, like that of his French prototype, was not destined to endure. By a strange coincidence, his most distinguished successor was an archæologist, with all the intense absorption in his hobby characteristic of the type. He revelled in digging up and annotating memorials of the past, in restoring ancient temples, and classifying old histories ; to him we in modern times owe a debt of gratitude, for his researches have been our guide in many inquiries into the ages which preceded him. But he deserved less well of his contemporaries than of posterity ; for government, for war, for the daily duties of kingship he showed little aptitude or inclination. His conduct alienated the military party, and scandalized the priests and people ; and the arrival on the borders of Gobryas, the Kurdish general of Cyrus the Persian, found the country not only unable but unwilling to resist him. The king made one great effort to repel the invader by the aid of a hasty alliance with Amasis of Egypt, and Croesus, the celebrated millionaire king of Lydia; but the indifference of his own people overcame him, the unnatural alliance dissolved, and after one small battle the armies of Cyrus found Babylonia at their mercy. The citizens of the metropolis made no effort to man the powerful battlements, prepared by the careful genius of Nebuchadnezzar; and mighty Babylon fell to a Kurdish conqueror without a sword being raised in her defence. The king and his son Belshazzar were retained in captivity until their death, and Cyrus the Persian ruled as King of Babylon.

The empire of Cyrus and his successors, though Persian in name and origin, was little more than a continuation of the old Mesopotamian empire which it had supplanted. The earlier Persian rulers were careful to do everything in their power, not only to appease the Mesopotamians, but to fashion that country into a integral part of their dominions; and as time went on the latter, by virtue of its situation and its ancient inherited culture, gradually absorbed its conquerors, and itself became the principal bulwark of their rule. The old capital in Persia was abandoned for a Mesopotamian site, and the King of kings himself, in the intervals of his summer campaigns, became accustomed to pass the winter months in the mild and pleasant climate of Babylon.

The Persian was the last, as it was the greatest, of the ancient Mesopotamian empires. It is justly renowned in history for its religious toleration, the fruit of the beneficent influence of the cult of Zoroaster, the most spiritual religious conception which had so far appeared upon the earth. Encouraged by the toleration of the Government, there occurred at this time a considerable outburst of religious activity, which is best known to us by the efforts of Ezra and Nehemiah to organize the new Jerusalem. Many of the religious ideas which were born at this time can be traced in the Christianity, Islam and Judaism of the present day. Meanwhile, on the northern frontiers of the empire, the Greeks were slowly evolving a culture and a new outlook upon life which was destined not only to destroy the Persian sovereignty, but to remove the cultural supremacy of the world from Mesopotamia for ever.

The struggle between the Persians and the Greeks (499-355 B.C.) forms one of the epics of history. Its results were, as a matter of fact, neither so brilliant nor so decisive as is generally believed in European historical circles, which naturally incline to the Greek point of view. In spite of the famous disaster to the armies and navy of Xerxes, the Mesopotamian power continued to wage the war for many years with very equal success; and, ninety years after the defeat of Salamis, the word of the king of Persia was the law of the land in Greece. It was only when the Greek city states had themselves come under the sway of their northern Macedonian neighbour that the long quarrel was ended by the obliteration of both the combatants.

When Macedon rose to power, the great Persian Empire had been failing internally for many years. Greek influence and Greek ideas had achieved what Greek arms had failed to do; the Empire had lost faith in itself, and was beginning to decompose into the various national elements that went to build it up. The last Artaxerxes, an able and vigorous tyrant, only succeeded in keeping his realm intact by the prosecution of the sternest measures, which included the assassination of practically all his relations; and on the appearance of the youthful Alexander of Macedon, who came at the invitation of the half-Greek cities of Asia Minor, the great Imperial structure collapsed like a house of cards. In the course of a few months, the young general was able to conquer the whole Persian Empire; in a few years, he had consolidated it as a base for further operations in Egypt, Arabia, Turkestan and the marches of northern India. Greek culture, impersonated in a Macedonian military genius who was also a pupil of Aristotle, everywhere rode triumphant over the old corrupt Mesopotamian systems; and Alexander might hope with justice to organize, with himself as the head, a new and better Empire, in which Hellenic ideals should be combined with the political experience of the ancient centre of the world.

But the dream was not to be. The Indian campaign was

intended to be but an episode in a career of world conquest; and when Alexander returned to Mesopotamia in 323 B.C., it was merely for the purpose of enjoying a short period of rest, and of developing a navy for the circumnavigation of the coast of Arabia. The navy was due to set sail about the middle of June; the preparations for the Arabian campaign, which was part of the enterprise, were complete; and Alexander, who had been occupied for several days in the open country round Babylon in surveying the site of a new irrigation scheme, chose to spend an evening in carouse at the house of a boon companion. A slight fever, possibly due to exposure to the heat of the sun, came upon him the next day; the relaxing climate aided its rapid development; and in a few hours it became apparent that the youthful conqueror had not long to live. The efforts of his officers and camp followers, so efficacious in the hour of battle, were powerless to avert a death by sickness; his faithful northern soldiers, comrades on many a famous field, were warned to parade and pass through the room of their general, one by one; and a few minutes later the fever had completed its work, and Alexander the Great was dead. The boy who had won his first victory at the age of sixteen, and had conquered the whole Middle East before he was three and thirty, had passed away without leaving an heir. Somewhere on the banks of the Euphrates, in the vast area of rubble which constitutes Babylon to-day, lie the bones of perhaps the most remarkable military genius of all time.

The death of Alexander the Great marks the end of a definite period in the history of Mesopotamia. Hitherto the Middle East had been, in a very real sense, the world. Now the world was enlarging its borders; a purely western race, the Greeks, had evolved an indigenous civilization of their own; the cultures of the West and of the Orient, which had been united in Mesopotamia, were beginning to part for ever. Mesopotamia was the cradle of mankind; and mankind was now outgrowing the cradle. We shall follow for some centuries the efforts of both an eastern and a western power to obtain possession of the country; and when next we see Mesopotamia with a powerful native civilization of her own, it will be clear that she has become, in sentiment if not in fact, purely oriental.

CHAPTER II

THE ROMAN-PERSIAN RIVALRY

" Two dervishes may sleep under one blanket, but one country cannot contain two kings."—SA'DI.

THE sudden death of Alexander threw the affairs of his newly-won empire into confusion. He left no heir, though a posthumous son was born to him a short time after his death ; and a regency was organized which, as was practically inevitable, soon proved itself powerless to battle against the rebellious tendencies of the many conquered races and the individual ambitions of Alexander's generals. There followed a period of practically thirty years of continuous war, which desolated Mesopotamia, and threw all the neighbouring countries into confusion. Eventually there emerged a number of independent kingdoms, the largest of which, including Mesopotamia and Persia, fell to Seleucus, the founder of a dynasty which survived with varying fortunes for two hundred and fifty years. In spite of the defection of the northern provinces and of Asia Minor, Seleucus was left the ruler of a very considerable territory ; and from his two new capitals of Antioch in Syria and Seleucia on the Tigris, just below the site of the more modern Baghdad, he governed a kingdom which stretched practically from the borders of Turkestan to the Mediterranean.

His foundation of Seleucia, named after himself, was an event of outstanding importance, for the new creation was aimed directly at the age-long supremacy of Babylon. The present ruler, Greek in education and in sentiment, desired to found a capital which should act as an outpost of Hellenism in Mesopotamia, and carry on the task, commenced by Alexander, of spreading Greek civilization in the East. In addition, the more central position and the easier navigation of the Tigris were beginning to weigh in men's minds against the superior charm of the sister river; and it is significant that, from that day to this, with one very brief exception, the capital of Mesopotamia has remained on the banks of the more easterly stream. Babylon, deserted by the Government and by the trader, sank into insignificance; her wide avenues and decaying palaces became the haunt of the jackal and the brick-thief; soon she could offer shelter only to a few wandering shepherds and their flocks. Gradually, she began to assume the shape of a hopeless, interminable mass of ruins which she still retains to-day. The Biblical curse of the subject peoples, weary of exile by an alien stream, was fulfilled almost to the letter.

It soon became obvious that, in the unsettled and turbulent conditions of the time, the territory claimed by the Seleucids, or successors of Seleucus, was too diverse and widely scattered to form a single empire. On the northern border and in Asia Minor several little independent States, Pontus, Armenia, Bithynia and Pergamos, were beginning to develop strong civilizations of their own; and on the other side of the Empire, the native Persians showed less and less inclination to remain content beneath the rule of the better educated, but more effeminate, Syrian Greeks. The situation was complicated by a sudden invasion of wild Gauls from the far north, which for a short time threatened to throw the whole Middle Eastern world into confusion; but the barbarian onrush was stemmed by the determined resistance of Pergamos, whose celebrated statues of dying Gauls, designed to commemorate these victories, have been widely admired and copied in succeeding ages. The defeated barbarians were finally persuaded to settle down in a neighbouring tract of country, named after them Galatia; and their new capital of Ancyra has, under the modern style of Angora, obtained considerable notoriety in our own time.

Meanwhile in the eastern portions of the Empire the discontent of the Persians and other subject peoples eventually culminated in the rise to power of the Parthians. The home of the Parthian influence was a little semi-independent State in the mountainous country round Lake Urmia. By the year 200 B.C. the Parthians were all-powerful in Persia, and the Seleucid monarchs had been confined to Mesopotamia and Syria. The Parthians spoke the Persian language, they ruled the land in a Persian fashion, and their assumption of power was supported by the common Persian people. Their path was not altogether a smooth one, as the Turkish tribes in the far north-east were beginning to give trouble, and for a period the east of Persia was also harassed by the Yue-tshi, an obscure Mongolian people who afterwards exhausted their energy in China and the plains of northern India.

A last great effort by the Seleucid dynasty to preserve intact its crumbling dominion accidentally led to the appearance in the field of an entirely new enemy. In a series of brilliant campaigns, Antiochus III, perhaps the greatest of the Seleucid kings, defeated the Parthians, re-asserted his family position in the Middle East, and followed up his successes by invading Egypt and Asia Minor. Victorious again in these directions, he aspired to still greater triumphs; spiritual successor in his own mind to Alexander the Great, he seized the first available opportunity of crossing the Hellespont and carrying his arms into Europe. But a power had arisen in the far west who had been for some time past slowly but successfully establishing herself as the mistress of the Mediterranean; and when Antiochus attempted to secure control of the Greek islands, he found himself face to face with Rome. The Mesopotamian monarch was contemptuous of a people of whose resources he was entirely ignorant; with the result that, in the year 190 B.C., he was utterly defeated by the Romans at the battle of Magnesia, and the fortunes of the Seleucid house were crippled for ever. This battle had most important results, because it marked the beginning of Roman interference in the affairs of Asia, an interference which was in itself but a resumption of that European ambition to dominate the East which had been born in the exploits of Alexander. Henceforward for nearly eight hundred years Mesopotamia was destined to be the principal theatre of that never ending struggle between the east and the west, the issue of which is, even in our own day, still undecided.

In the first rounds of the game, all the honours went to the West. In the little independent States of Asia Minor and the Mediterranean littoral Rome found an easy prey.

Mutual jealousy and internal strife prevented the various peoples from considering any form of comprehensive plan to meet the new danger ; local Asian politics became penetrated with Roman intrigue, and it soon became only a question of time before the little States fell one by one into the lap of the great Italian empire-builder. Pergamos and Bithynia were bequeathed as heirlooms to Rome by their own kings ; and Pontus, which, under the skilful Mithridates, held out against the great enemy for many years, was finally obliged to yield before the military talent and resources of the proconsul Sulla. By the opening of the Christian era, Rome had successfully absorbed Galatia, Cappadocia, Lycia and the Syrian possessions of the Seleucids, and the Roman borders in the east marched with the western frontier of the Parthians, who had in the meanwhile established themselves as the premier power of the Middle East. Then began the long struggle between the Italian and the Mediterranean empires, which was only finally concluded by the eviction of both by yet another invader.

The Parthians had succeeded in driving the remnants of the Seleucids out of Mesopotamia by 138 B.C., in which year they captured Seleucia and commenced the building of a new capital, Ctesiphon, facing Seleucia on the opposite bank of the Tigris. In spite of faulty organization and almost continual frontier trouble in the east, the young kingdom steadily gained in strength ; and when the first direct contest with Rome was brought about by the vanity of the millionaire Crassus, who aspired to emulate the military triumphs of Pompey and Caesar, the Parthians were by no means unworthy of their celebrated opponents. Their military strength lay in their cavalry, hardy men of Turkish stock, admirably suited for manœuvre in the wide and dusty plains of Mesopotamia. Their mounted archers were accustomed to harass the opposing infantrymen, the final blow being struck at the appropriate time by the lancers, who formed the second line of their incomparable horsemen. It was unlikely that the Roman legionaries, able soldiers as they were, would wholly withstand the combined disadvantages of a strange country, an enervating climate, an amateur general, and an enemy who could continually harass their progress without himself apparently suffering any evil result.

When Crassus crossed the Euphrates in 53 B.C., there was much in the general political situation to favour him. Armenia and the Romanized provinces in the north were on his side ; and the cities of Mesopotamia, with their tradition of culture and civilization, were ready to welcome him as a deliverer from the yoke of the ignorant and barbaric Parthian. But favourable circumstances can neither excuse nor atone for bad generalship. Crassus was the leading business man of his day, but as a soldier he was negligible. The opposing armies met before the historic city of Harran (Carrhae), famous in Biblical memory as the home of the patriarch Abraham. In one great battle, the Roman forces were completely defeated ; Crassus himself was slain, and ten thousand Roman soldiers fell into the hands of their barbaric enemy. It was one of the worst reverses that Roman arms ever had to encounter.

Peculiarly enough, neither side was in a position to follow up the engagement. The bad organization of the Parthian state forbade the consideration of any campaign beyond the confines of Mesopotamia ; and, on the Roman side, the rivalry of Pompey and Caesar was straining the resources of the Republic to the utmost. The eventual victory of the latter left him free to plan the rescue of the Roman prisoners, and the avenging of the Roman name ; but his assassination caused a postponement of the project, and Mark Antony's subsequent small campaign accomplished nothing. The passing of time served to bring the two empires into a more harmonious frame of mind. Fraternization became general between educated Parthians and the Romans in Syria ; and it even became the custom for the Parthian aristocracy to send their sons to Rome for their education. Thirty years after the disaster at Harran, the Emperor Augustus received back the Roman insignia of war, and the remnant of the Roman prisoners, as a free gift from the Parthian king. History is silent as to the life of these unfortunate Roman soldiers, kept as prisoners in a corner of Persia for nearly a generation.

Soon after this, internal troubles began to make themselves felt in the Parthian realm, and the king was not sorry to court the alliance of his old enemy. A treaty was concluded with the Emperor Caligula; the Romans and the Parthians co-operated in the subjection of the troublesome mountainous country of Armenia—then, as now, a "problem"; and, a hundred years after the victory over Crassus, a Parthian monarch did not consider it beneath his dignity to repair in person to Rome, there to receive at the hands of the Emperor Nero the crown of the Armenian kingdom. After this, Parthia fell more and more into decay, but the Romans took no advantage of the situation until the year 115 A.D., when the Emperor Trajan, making the Armenian question his pretext, invaded Mesopotamia, captured the twin cities of Seleucia-Ctesiphon and even displayed the Roman eagles on the shores of the Persian Gulf. The resources of Rome at this time, however, were unequal to the strain of reorganizing and developing Mesopotamia; and the succeeding emperor, Hadrian, was content to evacuate the country and re-establish the Roman frontier on the banks of the Euphrates. Marcus Aurelius later moved the boundary forward again to the line of the upper Tigris (A.D. 165); and in 216 A.D., the Emperor Caracalla once more attacked the Parthians and extended the area of his Mesopotamian dominions. The long duel for the control of the land of the rivers might have appeared at this time to have been finally settled in favour of the Romans; the Parthian power was dissolving into hopeless confusion, and the western influence was everywhere complete and seemingly permanent.

But the people of Mesopotamia were not content to remain for ever the distant and despised appanage of an European empire; and the Parthian kingdom was on the verge of a sea-change, which resulted in the rise of yet another native power, and a worthier antagonist of the Roman arms. The natives of Persia and Mesopotamia had always viewed with some disfavour the tendency of the Parthian monarchs, themselves hailed from the far north-east, to favour Turanian ideas and the use of Turkish troops; and as the central power grew weaker and weaker, and more and more obviously unable to cope with the Roman menace, the discontent began to take an active form.

Additional opposition to the present rulers was supplied

THE GREAT ARCH AT CTESIPHON

by the Zoroastrian priesthood, the so-called Chaldeans, who viewed with alarm the growth of a policy of general religious toleration. It was an age again of religious activity. Out of the destruction of Jerusalem by the Romans (A.D. 70), and the second dispersion of the Jews, had sprung the new cult of " Judaism " ; thousands of converts had been gained in the cities of the Parthian Empire, and Mesopotamia had become the great Jewish asylum of refuge. On the heels of Judaism had come Christianity, and the activity and high level of intelligence displayed by the Christians brought them more and more believers year by year. It was obvious that the loyalty of the people to the ancient faith of Zoroaster was very gravely imperilled.

A dynasty was soon found which embodied the national hopes of the people and the religious ambitions of the priesthood in their own persons. In Persis, the ancient and historical capital of Persia proper, arose the Sassanian kings, Persians of the Persians, devoted followers of the old faith, and firm believers in the high destiny of the Iranian race. Their success was startling. In a few years they had risen from the kingship of a mere province to the position of King of kings of the still extensive Parthian realm. Their predecessors on the central throne were soon forgotten ; an united and enthusiastic people supported them ; and Mesopotamia and Persia combined to welcome a family which was ready to live in harmony with local culture, and able to restore, by the exercise of practical ability, some of the prestige of the times gone by. The Persian religion and outlook were once more sedulously cultivated ; the foreign elements in the population were kept well in hand ; and Jewish and Christian propaganda sternly suppressed. When war with Rome broke out once more, the Emperor Alexander Severus soon discovered that he was faced with an enemy worthy of his steel.

No decisive result was achieved in this war for more than ten years. At the end of that time the Persian king, collecting all his forces, boldly invaded the Roman provinces ; Antioch was invested, the country round desolated and the Persian forces only driven back to the Tigris after a severe struggle. The Emperor Gordian was compelled to compromise with the new power by ceding Armenia and

Roman Mesopotamia; but a worse disaster was in store for the Romans, for some years afterwards their main eastern armies were again utterly defeated by the Persians, and the Emperor Valerian himself was captured in battle. This last effort so exhausted the combatants that neither of them could make a further move for some years; and their temporary enfeeblement was played upon by a peculiar power, which rose and fell in the course of a few years in the unsubstantial fashion of a desert mirage.

On the edge of the Syrian desert lay the semi-independent Roman colony of Palmyra, peopled principally by Arabs, and the focus of many important local caravan routes into the interior. The local chieftain was a client of the Emperor, and natives of Palmyra had served for several generations in the Imperial legions. There exists to this day in the museum of a north-country English town an inscription, discovered locally, in the Palmyrene dialect; which undoubtedly once marked the grave of some ambitious young Arab, who, enlisting in the Roman armies under the bright sun of Tadmor, ended his life beneath the cold grey sky of Northumbria.

The chieftain of Palmyra at this time, by name Odenathus, was a man of great ambition and of decided military talent; taking advantage of the general confusion which followed upon the temporary exhaustion of Rome and Persia, he created in a short space of time a considerable dominion, and for awhile the rule of Palmyra was acknowledged from the Tigris to the Mediterranean. His work was continued after his death by his more celebrated widow Zenobia, who, however, allowed her ambition to outrun her discretion. Having provoked both Rome and Persia, she proved unable to hold her own; the Roman legions appeared before the desert capital, and razed it to the ground. The magnificence of the ruins still testifies to the wealth and ambitious taste of this strange and ill-fated city. The great accomplishment of this Arab couple gave, as it were, to the Middle Eastern world a foretaste of the might that was to come.

The long Persian-Roman duel was now resumed. In 283 A.D., the Emperor Carus invaded Mesopotamia and penetrated as far south as Seleucia-Ctesiphon; another victory was achieved by Diocletian fifteen years later, and

Armenia and several districts of the upper Tigris country became once more Roman. Under the celebrated Sapor II of Persia, who ruled nearly seventy years, the war was practically continuous, the focus of most of the campaigns being Nisibis, the modern Nisibin, which was the strongest Roman fortress in Mesopotamia. In the middle of this period came the great Christian Emperor Constantine, whose reign left a very profound effect upon the Middle Eastern world. In A.D. 325 Christianity became the official religion of the Roman Empire; the next year, the Emperor laid the foundation stone of a new capital at Byzantium on the Bosphorus, which was henceforth to be known as Constantinople. The political result of this great change was the division of the Roman Empire into two, and a regrouping of its eastern provinces. Henceforward, men in the Middle East looked to Constantinople as the metropolis, and no longer to Rome; but Constantinople, though in theory and tradition Roman, was in practice and in tongue Greek, and in inclination oriental. The foundation of Constantinople severed the intimate connection between the east and the west which had been fostered by the old Roman Empire, and struck a final blow to the hope, never again to be raised until 1914, that Mesopotamia and the adjoining countries could be brought under direct European influence and control.

The establishment of Christianity as the State religion, too, had an immediate effect on the Middle East. Hitherto the wars between Persia and Rome had been purely political; henceforward they could not escape a religious tinge. It was not alone the might of the King of kings and the Roman Emperor that met in battle now, but the spiritual rivalry of the adherents of Zoroaster and of Jesus. Both religious groups claimed the world for their faith, and both were forced, from the very necessity of that claim, to be in constant conflict. The conflict ended, so far as the Middle East was concerned, by the practical obliteration of both of them in the dawn of a newer faith.

Although not always waged with equal intensity, the struggle was practically continuous. Ctesiphon was again besieged by the Emperor Julian, "the apostate," the last Roman ruler who was content to serve the ancient gods of the Republic; but Julian was mortally wounded at Samarra, on the Tigris, and his successor Jovian compelled to accept humiliating terms. The collapse of the western half of the Roman Empire, and the invasion of the Eternal City by the northern barbarians (410 A.D.), left Constantinople alone in the field as the representative of the Roman name; and the Persian war was renewed under Justinian with results on the whole favourable to the Romans. But internal troubles at this time were weakening the resources of both Persia and Constantinople, and it was sixty years before the fight could be resumed with any vigour.

This resumption proved literally to be the last round. In a long campaign of exceptional brilliance and interest both empires fought their final duel; and the unexpected interference of a third and novel combatant resulted in the final disappearance of the one, and the permanent crippling of the other. The rulers of both in this last round were able men, and active ambitious monarchs. There are surely few more notable examples in history of the cynicism of Fate than the career of the Emperor Heraclius, who came to the throne at a time of utter disaster, who retrieved that disaster by the sheer force of his own daring and skill, but who was compelled, before the end of his reign, to relinquish practically all that he had gained to an entirely new antagonist, who had never previously entered into his calculations.

On the other side, the Persian Empire just before its final collapse presented a picture of unexampled splendour. The youthful and brilliant king Chroses II, in a series of able campaigns, conquered Roman Mesopotamia, Syria and Palestine; invaded Egypt; harassed the Roman provinces of Asia Minor; and at length actually led his armies to the southern shore of the Bosphorus, within the very sight of Constantinople itself. Heraclius, who had just ascended the Imperial throne, found himself faced across the water by the hated Persians just at the moment that he was besieged on the north by the barbarians of Europe. But his resource proved equal to the emergency. In a daringly conceived campaign, relying on the integrity of his sea power, he attacked and harassed the long lines of communication of the Persian king; the rich but defenceless Mesopotamians could do nothing to stop his progress; and Chroses, still dreaming by the Bosphorus of the fall of Constantinople, heard with horror of the destruction of his own summer palace on the Tigris, and the investment of his own capital. The subsequent fighting went in favour of Heraclius. Eventually the Persian king was glad to come to terms, and the ancient boundary of the Euphrates was once more set up as the line of demarcation between the two powers. Heraclius might congratulate himself that he had, by his own energy and daring, warded off a danger of the first magnitude, and assured peace and prosperity to his subjects for many years to come.

At this time there suddenly arrived at the court of each monarch a mission quite unlike any that had been seen there before. The delegates were Arabs, of the pure bedouin race of the south, justly admired for their bravery and physical beauty, but equally despised for their ignorance and neglect of the arts of civilization. The mission came in the name of Muhammad, a prophet who had arisen in the obscure trading city of Mecca, and who challenged in the name of one God both the polytheistic practices of the Persians and the trinitarianism of the Christians. The prophet called upon both the great monarchs to renounce their worship of three or of many gods, and to acknowledge the one true God; if they did so, no harm would come to them; but if they did not, they would surely both be swept away. This strange message, couched in the sonorous dialect of an obscure people, was received by Chroses with derision, by Heraclius with polite interest; and there is even an Arab tradition to the effect that the Emperor was secretly converted to the new faith, but was prevented from open acknowledgment of it by the threatening attitude of his own Christian people. There is not, and indeed could not be, any historical foundation for this report; and in the wars that followed the admonition of the prophet, Heraclius was almost as great a sufferer as his Persian rival. Neither of the two monarchs, as they rested after their great campaign and reorganized their armies and their public services, could have dreamt that in the short space of a few years the prophet's warning would have been fulfilled, and that their dominion would have disappeared before the onslaught of the wild and nearly naked desert men.

CHAPTER III

THE COMING OF THE ARAB

" The slender courser in the battle day
Will the fat stall-fed ox outvalue far."—SA'DI.

THE complete collapse of both Persia and Constantinople before the onset of the Arabs, though dramatic in itself, was hardly so remarkable as the casual observer might suppose. The Arabs had been generally despised by the citizens of both Empires for many years, partly owing to the general ignorance of their real condition, partly because they had as yet given but few signs of any capacity for political initiative on a grand scale. The ancient kingdom of Saba (the " Sheba " of the Bible) had, it is true, gained a local reputation for wealth and power, developed chiefly by its situation on the main trade route from India to the West ; and several great Roman generals of an earlier era, Julius Caesar included, had been credited with designs upon the indigenous sovereignty of Arabia proper. It was, no doubt, the reputed wealth of the country that induced the Emperor Augustus to sanction the disastrous expedition undertaken against the Arabs by the prefect Ælius Gallus ; and the tradition of the spices and perfumes of Araby has even come down to our own day, as a symbol and a memory of the undoubted resources of earlier Arabian civilizations. But the discovery of the possibility of rounding the straits of Bab al-Mendab by sea, and the consequent possibility of conveying goods direct from the Egyptian ports to the Persian Gulf or India ruined the trade routes of inner Arabia ; and the enterprise of the cities of Mesopotamia was responsible, in addition, for the diversion of a portion of the trade via the valley of the Euphrates and Tigris. Thus Arabia had, before this time, been shut out of the profitable direct Eastern and Western commerce on both her flanks ; and the old civilization of the country had utterly fallen into decay. Indeed, during the first six hundred years of the Christian era, Arabia, her country perpetually scourged by inter-tribal warfare, her cities but rude erections of mud and sun-dried brick, presented a picture little different from that of a country in the very earliest stages of civilization.

But while the motherland had sunk into insignificance, there were a number of very active Arab colonies which served to show that, given the opportunity, the Arab race was capable of very much greater things. Hira, on the Euphrates, just below the ancient Babylon, had held its own as a practically independent principality and centre of local trade for some centuries ; as had Nabataea, in Trans-Jordania, justly celebrated for its unique rock capital. The astonishing rise, and equally astonishing fall, of Palmyra gave evidence of the existence of political talent in the Arab character ; and the general unrest in the Peninsula just previous to the time of the prophet Muhammad might have acted as a warning to the rulers both of Persia and Constantinople, that something not altogether normal was preparing in the desolate and little-known land that lay on the flank of both of them.

To understand completely the sudden rise of the Arabs, and the subsequent influence which they exercised on Mesopotamia, an influence which has remained intact to the present day, it is necessary to consider in some detail the character of this talented but wayward people. The Arab mind is distinguished by two outstanding characteristics ; a love of personal freedom which amounts almost to a ruling passion ; and an inclination towards the exact and the matter of fact which, though in itself a talent of the highest possibilities, carries with it serious intellectual limitations. " The Arab's sense is in his eyes " ; that is to say, he can only understand or appreciate a thing which he actually sees. Like a horse in blinkers, his vision is limited, but intense ; what he does see, he sees with remarkable clearness. He is free from sentimentality, and undisturbed by romance ; his mind is mathematical, without the redeeming quality, on the idealistic side, of any desire for speculation. His language is the most mathematical in the world, controlled by a syntax at once rigid, logical and exact ; and the standard of the language is scrupulously maintained by educated Arabs, not only in their writing, but even in their everyday speech. To the Arabs we owe the foundation of modern mathematical study, and of the modern practical application of the discoveries of pure science ; and it is characteristic of the race that they were able to absorb the scientific and philosophic knowledge of the ancient Greeks, and adapt it to practical ends, but were prevented by their lack of imagination from probing further. The spirit of scientific inquiry, of the search after truth for its own sake, is quite foreign to their genius ; even the new religion propounded by Muhammad, at once the greatest and most characteristic of the Arabs, offered no truth that had not been propounded on earth many times before ; on the other hand, as an exact and mathematical way of making the ordinary man well-behaved and God-fearing, it has no equal in any other faith.

The Arab's insistent desire for personal liberty is rightly hailed as his finest quality. The Arab comes upon the scene as the first true democrat of history ; any but the most nominal control is intolerable to the true son of the desert, and it is hardly possible for the most powerful sheikh to assert his authority against the will of his fellow tribesmen and nominal subjects. The Arab people thus share this characteristic with the great modern democracies of the West, that it is only possible to control them effectually through the medium of some dominant idea ; and it was the supreme achievement of the prophet Muhammad that he was able to conceive an idea which would touch some common chord of feeling in all his turbulent and quarrelsome fellow-countrymen, and thus instil into them something of unity and a common aim. But Muhammad was well aware that the Arabs would tolerate nothing in the way of an affected superiority in their leaders, however great their political success ; and his own life and those of the first Caliphs who followed him, remained, at a time when Arab armies were conquering half the civilized world, studiously simple and even penurious.

Every race suffers from the drawbacks of its own virtues ; and the passionate love of freedom in the Arabs, and their talent for the mathematical and the matter of fact, have too often led them, on the one hand towards

THE COMING OF THE ARAB

anarchy, on the other towards the splitting of hairs. Their disinclination to yield an inch in a personal controversy, to attempt to visualize the other man's point of view, will turn them from the most practical to the most unpractical of men. Trained in the hardest school in the world, accustomed for generations to treat hardship with indifference and luxury with disdain, they are capable of making great efforts, only to throw away the results for some merely trivial end. An exact mentality unrelieved by an imaginative faculty appears to result in a lack of proportion, which allows the Arabs, having laboured for a great end, to turn away from the fruits of their labour with indifference. Thus they conquered a great empire and held it for centuries; but they failed absolutely to use it for any definite end. The influence of Athens and Rome can still be traced as an active force in the world of to-day; but the influence of the far more modern Baghdad is now only a curious memory. The descendants of the grave philosophers and teachers who flourished under Harun ar-Raschid are to-day but nomads of the desert, as were the forebears from whom they sprung. In the intellectual tittle-tattle, in the religious splitting of hairs, which to-day distinguish the conversation of the Arab *intelligentsia*, one might search in vain for any of the elements of simple greatness that once, in the course of only twenty years, changed the destiny of half the civilized world.

The Arab thus remains ever a riddle, ever the despair of his friends. Attractive, clever, capable of great personal affection, by no means indolent if he has a definite object in view, he yet seems to lack that deep and fundamental power of constructive thinking which is the foundation of all successful action. Swayed always by the need to find an exact formula for his loyalties and his beliefs, ready to quarrel over the slightest divagation, he remains the prototype of the talented man who is ruined by the lack of one quality, namely, the recognition that there are other types of people in the world beside his own. Thus in adversity he remains dignified but isolated, in prosperity hard and unrelenting; he is the great individualist, pushed, so to speak, back to his logical conclusion. From time immemorial the great world has been nothing to him but a background for his own local bickerings and personal animosities, and apparently so it will be till the end. Such a people will produce great individuals and perhaps distinguished ideas, but can never, it would seem, achieve permanent political success.

It is important to recall in this respect that the so-called Arab of Mesopotamia or Iraq is by no means purely Arab or wholly true to type. When the Arabs invaded Mesopotamia, they found, as we have seen, a complicated civilization with a long history actually in existence; and they did not so much absorb it as become absorbed by it. Thus it is not strictly accurate to regard the Iraqi as actually typical of the Arab character; Arab blood is predominant in Iraq, but it is very considerably mixed with Persian, Kurdish, Turkish and ancient Mesopotamian strains. The problem of modern Mesopotamia, as we shall see, is less an Arab problem than a question of fitting the various types of resident Iraqi with something approaching a general national consciousness.

The main features of the life and teaching of the prophet Muhammad are too well known to need more than a brief recapitulation. The Prophet was born in Mecca, the principal trading centre and holy city of Arabia, on or about April 20th, 570 A.D. He came of good family, and of the tribe of Quraish, considered to represent the best blood of Arabia. No nation places so high an estimate upon family connections as the Arab, and Muhammad was thus, in this most essential connection, most fortunately situated. His early childhood was spent with a foster-mother in the tents of the Beni Sa'd, famous for the purity of their speech; and he thus, in an early familiarity with the classical tongue, gained another important qualification for his future public career. His later boyhood was passed in the household of his uncle, who, though aristocratic, was poor; and the lad had early to earn his own living, working first in several menial occupations, including that of a shepherd, a trade singularly in keeping with the prophetic tradition. He afterwards improved his worldly position by becoming an agent for privately owned merchant caravans; and while engaged on this work, he was fortunate enough, at the age of twenty-five, to win the favour of a rich and noble widow, who, though some years his senior, insisted upon marrying him, much to the indignation of her relations. Muhammad henceforth had no need to worry about money, and he appears for some time to have led the life of a Meccan gentleman of means.

Always of a contemplative and religious disposition, he seems to have spent a considerable portion of his time in solitude and silent meditation ; and the low moral condition of his people, their idolatry, their blood feuds, and their open sensuality began to weigh increasingly upon his mind. Finally he became convinced that only a complete spiritual regeneration would avail to raise his countrymen from the depths of their degradation ; and, confirmed himself in the faith of the one true God, he set himself the task of leading the Meccans away from the worship of the many tribal gods, and, at the same time, of cleansing and purifying their moral outlook. For some time an almost morbid shyness prevented his pleading his mission in public ; and his first converts were made in the privacy of his own home. They included his wife and his youthful cousin Ali, destined to become one of the most important figures in the immediate history of Mesopotamia ; as well as two men in middle life, Abu Bekr and Omar, afterwards famous as the first two Caliphs of the Muhammadan era.

But the time came when the existence of the new cult could no longer be concealed, and the founder and his disciples were compelled to take the field openly. Muhammad's mission was received both by the Quraish and by the general population at first with derision and disdain, afterwards with annoyance and alarm. It was gradually discovered that the Prophet's influence in the city was already considerable, and the " vested interests " in the old idolatrous faiths were forced to take active steps to uproot the new heresy. The customs governing tribal feuds forbade them to touch Muhammad, because of his influential family connections ; but a persecution of the humbler members of the new body was instituted, and the Prophet was forced to arrange an asylum for his followers in the territory of the Christian king of Abyssinia. Meanwhile on his side, he did not remain inactive ; he attempted unsuccessfully to secure a safe place for himself and his followers in the neighbouring city of Taif, and, repulsed in that direction, he opened overtures with the northern town of Yathrib, the inhabitants of which, strongly tinged with Jewish influence, regarded with favour his monotheistic crusade.

Yathrib was a trade rival, and a dangerous one, of Mecca; and the discovery that Muhammad had actually been invited to proceed to the northern town stung the Meccans to fury. His assassination was finally decided upon, an arrangement having been reached that, in order to escape the operation of the custom of tribal vengeance, blood-guiltiness should be shared by a number of influential people. But the Prophet had been warned in time, and when the conspirators, after surrounding the house, forced their way into his room, they found the bed occupied only by the youthful Ali. This secret flight of Muhammad is the " Hijrah," usually anglicized as " Hegira," which marks the opening of the era of the Moslem calendar.

Yathrib lay athwart the caravan route from Mecca to the north, and Muhammad, after several ups and downs, was eventually in a position to threaten the trade of the sacred city. His success in Yathrib, where he had accomplished the union of the local tribes and effected a noticeable improvement in the morals and behaviour of the people, did not fail to strike the shrewd minds of his old fellow-townsmen; and they began to realize that, religious questions apart, his political doctrine of an united nation with a single faith and a single outlook, was not only practicable but desirable. Seven years after the Flight, the disciples of Islam were given formal permission to come on pilgrimage to the sacred city on the same terms as the followers of the older creeds; and after this the resistance of the Meccans practically collapsed. Next year the faithful entered the city as conquerors with the Prophet at their head, and the idols that surrounded the black stone Kaaba and the sacred well Zemzem were thrown down. The Kaaba alone was left, by a happy inspiration, to mark the one stable spot towards which, in the shifting sands of this world's cares and changes, the hearts of the faithful might always be directed; an outward and visible sign of the permanence of God.

The Prophet's triumph was complete. The capitulation of Mecca brought practically the whole of Arabia to his feet. He had found the Arabs but a collection of tribes, and in nine years he had welded them into a nation. But his work was now nearly at an end. The damp and malarious atmosphere of Yathrib was injurious to a constitution bred in the dry climate of the south; and on the great pilgrimage of 642 A.D., just ten years after the Flight, instinct warned him that the end could not be far off. From the mount of Arafat he delivered a farewell sermon to the multitude of his fellow-countrymen assembled round him.

"Ye people, listen to my words, for I know not whether another year will be vouchsafed to me after this year to find myself among you. . . .

"Know that all Moslems are brothers one unto another. Ye are one brotherhood . . . remember that ye shall have to appear before the Lord, who shall demand from you an account of all your actions. . . .

"Let him that is present tell it unto him that is absent. . . ."

From the mount of Arafat were announced the customs, the manners and the way of living which have been observed by all good Moslems from that day to this. The premonition of the Prophet proved correct. A short time after his return to Yathrib he fell ill of a fever; his attenuated frame, worn out with the struggles and excitements of the last fifteen years, was unable to cope with the disease; and one day, after rising, perhaps unwisely, to attend the morning prayer, he passed away quietly in the house of his young wife Ayesha, the daughter of his friend Abu Bekr.

There had latterly arisen a certain party among the faithful who assumed immortality for the Prophet, and his sudden death caused immediate consternation. But the situation was saved by the firmness of the aged Abu Bekr, who, on being elected to succeed Muhammad with the title of Caliph or Vice-Regent, immediately set to work to consolidate the little State. No child of the Prophet survived him except his daughter Fatima, who had previously married Ali; thus Ali's sons, Hassan and Hosein, were the only male descendants of the Prophet. Ali's position, though he does not appear to have done anything at the time to trade upon it for his own ends, was regarded with jealousy by Ayesha ; and the rivalry between the two was destined to have evil consequences for the whole of Islam, and particularly for Mesopotamia.

Abu Bekr ruled two years only, but to him more than any other man was due the firm establishment of the new religion and State. The national vice of the Arabs began to assert itself the moment that the firm hand of Muhammad had been removed by death ; new prophets and pseudo-prophets of all kinds, including one lady, sprang up on every hand ; and Arabia threatened once more to fall back into a condition of anarchy. But the coolness and determination of the gentle Abu Bekr, strengthened by his never-wavering faith in his dead friend and master, proved equal to the emergency ; Yathrib, now named Medinat al-Nebi, " The City of the Prophet," or, for short, Medina, was preserved from the threatened invasion of the tribes ; eleven military expeditions were despatched to different parts of the country ; and the nation was united once more, in name at least, under a single ruler. But the union could not, in the nature of things, be expected to be either permanent or popular ; and it is possible that both the religion and the political organization of Muhammad and Abu Bekr would have succumbed to internal pressure, had not circumstances arisen which served to turn the attention of the nation in a new direction.

It was almost inevitable that, in the effort to reduce the rebellious tribes to submission, the armies of Abu Bekr should come into collision with the people of the Mesopotamian and Syrian borders. These frontier tribes, though partly heathen and partly Christian in religion, were wholly Arab in blood ; and it was natural that they should have followed with a keen interest all the untoward events which had been taking place in the motherland during the preceding ten years. Some of the tribes were inclined favourably towards the Moslems, some were not ; and, in the border struggles that ensued, the Medina government suddenly found itself embroiled in quarrels with the empires of Persia and Constantinople, whose clients and nominal subjects the frontier tribes were. Thus the horizon of war imperceptibly widened, and Islam, a faith originally designed by an Arab for Arabs, and revealed " in simple Arabic " for the understanding of the people, entered the lists of militant religions whose aim is world-wide.

It is unquestionable that this enlargement made all the difference to the loyalty of the ordinary Arab tribesman. His restless nature was now offered an opening after its own heart ; the greed of the tribal brigand could be satisfied in the rich foreign fields of Mesopotamia and Syria to an extent impossible within the barren confines of Arabia ; and, if the soldier died in battle, he fell in the odour of sanctity and with every assurance of the blessings of Paradise. It was hardly to be wondered at that after the first foreign successes the carping criticism of the bedouin was silenced for ever, and tribe after tribe reported themselves at Medina for reorganization and despatch to the northern battle-fields.

The first actual invasion of Mesopotamia came about by accident. Abu Bekr had sent a force to Bahrein on the Persian Gulf to subdue certain local disorders ; the force, having accomplished its object, commenced to move northwards, and had soon carried its victorious arms along the coast into the delta of the Euphrates. The tidings of success reached Medina too late for Abu Bekr to do anything but give the enterprise his pious blessing ; and eventually he was persuaded to send a larger force to Mesopotamia in support, under the command of Khalid, who was destined later to become a general of more than passing fame. Lower Mesopotamia was peopled at this time by Arab peasantry, tilling the fields under Persian overseers ; the invading force was welcomed by them with enthusiasm, and the overlords were forced to flee. The satrap of the delta with his troops met the invading force at Hafir, due west of the head of the Persian Gulf ; challenged to single combat by Khalid, he was slain ; the Persian soldiers broke and fled, and the victorious Arabs pursued them to the banks of the Euphrates. One party of them crossed the river and were soon in danger of being cut off by another Persian army. Khalid hastened to their aid ; the new army was completely defeated ; and all the men fit for war in the neighbourhood were put to death and their women taken captive. In a short campaign the Arabs had twice defeated the troops of the Persian government, and had sent back to Medina booty and captives innumerable.

Previously the Persian government had regarded this foray with a certain amount of indifference; but now it was thoroughly alarmed. A large force of Arabs whose loyalty to the Government was assured was hastily assembled and placed under the command of a trusted general. The two armies met near the junction of the two great rivers, and again the discomfiture of the Government troops was complete. Many of the King's Arabs were taken prisoners by their fellow-countrymen, and the cruel treatment meted out to them roused the fury of the other local Arab tribes. A new army was quickly got together, from among the Christians of both banks of the Euphrates, supported by Persian regular troops. Khalid was compelled to retire across the river, on the other side of which he met the opposing army. The Christian Arabs first sprang to the attack, followed by the Persian soldiers. The Moslems were pressed as never before. In the midst of the battle Khalid swore aloud a great oath that, if the Moslems were victorious, the blood of their enemies should flow as if in a stream. The battle was won and the oath literally fulfilled. The prisoners were all preserved for one gigantic slaughter, and the blood of the slain poured into the running stream of a canal. Thereafter the spot was known as "The river of blood."

But Khalid's work was by no means over. The Arab city of Hira was most active in its opposition to the newcomers, and it had found powerful allies in several of the tribes to the rear of the Moslems. Khalid was finally compelled to consider the subjugation of the whole area west of the Euphrates. Quickly moving up the bank of the river, he arrived before the gates of Hira; the Persian satrap fled, but the city, well defended by citadel and ramparts, refused to capitulate. Finally, however, the siege began to tell; the city contained a wealthy Christian monastery, and the monks, fearful of their possible fate, urged capitulation. Easy terms were secured from Khalid, and ratified by Abu Bekr. The men of Hira agreed to pay a yearly tribute, assessable upon all but religious mendicants; and the Moslems bound themselves to protect the city.

Public prayer was established; and the voice of the muezzin could be heard in the streets. Thus the Moslems successfully concluded their first political agreement with a power lying outside the borders of Arabia. Nevertheless the local Arab Christians showed no great eagerness to forsake the faith of their forefathers; and many years afterwards there were still large numbers of Christians to be found in the neighbourhood.

Meanwhile the government of Persia was sinking into a condition of absolute chaos. No clear heir could be found for the throne, and a number of rival claimants spent the time in quarrelling among themselves, with the support of various provincial factions. No effort was made to turn the Moslems out of their newly-won territory. Khalid, however, took no advantage of this inaction except to push on farther up the right bank of the Euphrates, extending the Moslem border as far north as Hit. His temporary absence in Palestine, where an additional campaign was now in progress, was the signal for a general rising of the newly conquered tribes; but it was completely crushed on his return. The Persian troops who had arrived to assist the rebels were defeated; and the Moslems rested for the holy month of Ramadhan in Anah. The Roman garrison to the north of the town soon afterwards took alarm and organized a joint attack with the Persians; but once more the non-Moslem forces were completely defeated. For a time the position of the invaders seemed so secure that the Caliph did not hesitate to order Khalid once more to Palestine.

But though the Moslems could win victories, they could not consolidate their conquests; and the Mesopotamian general was soon compelled to plead for reinforcements in person at Medina. He found the aged Abu Bekr dying, completely worn out with the fatigues of his two-years' rule. He had found Islam disunited and its future precarious; he left it triumphant and already in possession of a considerable empire. His personal life was simple, and he devoted the whole of his energy and time to the interests of the youthful State. In the midst of the temptations of an Oriental court rapidly growing in power and influence, he maintained to the end a puritanical

D

simplicity. There are few characters in history more striking than that of Abu Bekr, called upon at an advanced age to rule a turbulent people and to organize a growing State; and responding to the call with such distinction.

Abu Bekr was succeeded by Omar, during whose short caliphate the Arab dominions attained to almost their greatest extent. His reign was one long triumph; Ctesiphon, Jerusalem, Damascus, the whole of Mesopotamia, western Persia and Syria, as well as Egypt and northern Africa, yielded to the efforts of his victorious troops; and for a brief space of time the little desert city of Medina ruled the whole of the Near and Middle East.

But for the moment the situation of the Moslems in Mesopotamia was anything but a safe one. The Persians had at last been roused to a full recognition of their extreme danger. Two strong columns were organized and despatched against the Arabs, and the latter were obliged to evacuate Hira and retire to the borderland of the desert. Some months later, reinforced from Medina, the Arabs re-advanced, drove in the Persian outposts, and occupied the delta country; the main army of the Persians, in the meanwhile, preparing to meet them near the ruins of Babylon. In the battle that followed, the Moslems suffered a severe defeat; many Arabs were slain, and had the Persian leader been able to follow up his victory, the tide of invasion might have been permanently stayed. But a new revolution in the Persian capital distracted his attention; reinforcements were hurried forward to the Arab armies from Medina; and when the two armies met again, not far from the future site of Kufa, the result was a victory for the Moslems. This battle, known as the "Field of Tens" because every warrior claimed to have killed ten of the enemy, was remarkable in that it was won only with the active aid of the Christian Arabs, who suddenly entered the fray at a critical moment; and it was even a Christian youth who slew the Persian general, riding back to the Arab lines with the proud cry: "I am of the Beni Taghlib. I am he that hath slain the chief!"

This victory, though not decisive, had a far-reaching effect. The Moslems were now free to pillage the country right to the very walls of Ctesiphon, and even as far north along the Tigris as the little market towns of Baghdad and Tekrit.

A supreme effort was now undertaken by the Persian government. A youth of Royal blood was found, ready to undertake the responsibility of leadership; and Yesdigerd "the hapless" commenced his fateful reign. At first fortune favoured the Persians. Nobles and people rallied round the young monarch. New armies were raised and sent into battle, and the Moslems were compelled once more to retreat nearly to the edge of the desert. But the Caliph Omar had now realized that Mesopotamia could never be held unless the Persians were completely driven out of it; and he set himself to assemble the largest army yet sent out from Medina, headed by the chivalry of the whole Arab nation. Additional reinforcements were sent from the Syrian front; and the Moslem army possibly numbered more than 30,000 men, including over a thousand of the Companions of the Prophet.

For some weeks the two armies faced each other at a distance, along the banks of the Euphrates; but the continual foraging raids of the Arabs finally infuriated the Persian landowners, and pressure was brought to bear upon the young King to order the attack. Against the advice of his general, the advance was ordered; for four whole days the two armies fought for mastery on the plain of Kadisiyah; then at last the Persian forces broke, their leader was killed and thousands of their soldiers were put to death. The results of this battle were permanent. The Persian government was never able again to put a large force in the field; the loyalty of the Christian Arabs was now finally secured, and many of the tribes adopted Islam. In a few weeks Ctesiphon itself had fallen, and the famous palace of the Chroses consecrated to the use of a cathedral mosque.

Similar victories had favoured the Arab arms in Palestine and Syria; and, only seventeen years after the flight of the Prophet from Mecca to Medina, his followers occupied a territory reaching from the Indian Ocean to the mountains of Armenia. Mesopotamia, the land of many civilizations, near neighbour to the Arab homeland, had become at last an Arab country; and an Arab country, in the main, it still is to-day.

CHAPTER IV

THE DIVISION OF ISLAM

" Man will wrangle for religion ; write for it, fight for it, die for it ; anything but—live for it."—CHARLES COLTON.

IT is notoriously impossible to govern a great empire from a backwater, and it was inevitable that the isolated and sparsely populated land of Arabia, however dear to its victorious sons on sentimental grounds, should quite early in the new era find itself compelled to abdicate in favour of the rich and previously powerful countries which lay to the north of it. The new State, victorious on its frontiers and secure in its administration, was now, in typical Arab fashion, given over to internal feud. The old local rivalries of the tribes became involved with the national aspirations, by no means dead, of the conquered subject peoples ; and, in conformity with the spirit of the times, these were given a religious background. In the struggles that ensued, most of them fought out on the soil of Mesopotamia, Islam was rent permanently in twain, and the cause of the new faith in the outside world irretrievably damaged.

One of the first administrative acts of the Arabs in Mesopotamia was the foundation of two new cities, to act as garrison colonies in the conquered territory. The first of these was Basrah, the second Kufa ; the former being occupied largely by men from the north of Arabia, the latter by men of the south. Both cities grew with astonishing rapidity, in the manner of towns in semi-tropical countries, and the population of each soon amounted to nearly a quarter of a million. To them flocked all the restless spirits of these restless days, and in them the great Arab generals and their followers took their leisure in the intervals of fighting. This mixture of penniless adventurers and idle military men gave rise to frequent disorder ; and many of the countless plots and disturbances which occurred within the confines of the Empire, could be directly traced to the clubs and coffee shops of Kufa.

Probably the main feature in determining Mesopotamia as the scene of the great schism which rent Islam was the inevitable clash between the two dominant racial strains of Arab and Persian. The matter-of-fact Arab genius was intolerable to the visionary and imaginative Persian; and the latter had no sooner accepted Islam than he began to search out for himself some means of adapting the new religion to his own mentality and aspirations. Thus the Islamic world became insensibly divided into the two great bodies of the "Sunni" or orthodox, and the "Shiah" or schismatic; and these divisions have continued, in their main outlines, until the present day. The Shiahs, by reading a hidden significance into every revelation of the Prophet, were able comfortably to transform his religion into something more congenial to the Persian racial outlook; and many of the Persian doctrines, though doubtless respectable in their way, would hardly have been recognized by the Prophet as the fruit of his own teaching.

The rise of the Shiah schism centres round the personality of Ali; and, so obscured has history become by tradition and pious fraud, that it is almost impossible to place a just estimate on the character of this undoubtedly great figure. By his close personal connection with the Prophet, Ali was in any case bound to become an outstanding personage in the early days of Islam. It was Ali who, little more than a boy, had been one of the Prophet's earliest disciples; it was Ali who had risked the fury of the Prophet's enemies, at the time of the Flight, by remaining in his bed when he himself had gone; it was Ali who had married Fatima, and thus become the father of the Prophet's only grandsons; and when the time came for death to part the Prophet and his Companions, it was Ali who was chosen, by universal consent, to perform the last rites of a friend by preparing the body for burial. It was now to be Ali's unfortunate fate to be forced to exchange the rôle of the Prophet's dearest friend for that of a focus of political and spiritual upheaval.

The Prophet had left no indication as to how the succession to the headship of the State was to be determined after his death; and, indeed, it was probably only the extreme urgency of the situation which enabled Abu Bekr to claim the responsibility over the heads of his equals and fellow Companions. The military successes which marked his reign and that of his successor Omar, turned men's minds in other directions; but at the same time the rapid expansion of the Empire led to the employment in responsible offices of many scions of the Meccan nobility who had been, even to the last, bitter opponents of the Prophet and his followers. In the reign of Omar practically all distinction between the original Companions and the later disciples had been wiped out; and under these changed circumstances the power of the wealthy and well-organized Meccan noble families inevitably began again to make itself felt. Consequently, there arose almost imperceptibly two parties in the State; one which aimed at keeping the influence of the Companions intact and the memory of the Prophet green, by retaining the head office of the State in the Prophet's family; and a second one which supported the Meccan nobles, as the natural guardians and protectors of the rising Arab power. The first party tended more and more to centre round Ali; the second round the family of Ummeya, the ablest of the old aristocratic families of the Quraish. Even under Abu Bekr members of the Ummeyad family, although almost the last of the Meccan nobility to accept Islam, had been appointed to high posts in the conquered provinces; and this policy became more noticeable under Omar, as the increase in the size and responsibilities of the Empire made apparent the dearth of administrative ability among the Companions and their entourage. It was Omar, for example, who was responsible for appointing Moawiyah, one of the Ummeyad clan, to the governorship of Syria, a step which, though justified by the latter's ability and success, had eventually serious consequences for Islam.

The first open breach between the Companions and the aristocracy occurred on the death of Omar. Had the latter been spared to make suitable arrangements for the choice of his successor, the rupture might possibly have been avoided, and the history of Islam materially altered. But Omar was assassinated by a Kufan artisan on the score of a private grievance, and, in the few minutes of life left to him after the attack, he delegated the choosing of the new

THE DIVISION OF ISLAM

Caliph to a committee of six. The step proved fatal. At the end of three days' discussion Ali tied in the voting with the Ummeyad Othman, a personal friend of the late ruler; and when Othman was finally chosen by a narrow majority, it had already become clear that the supporters of Ali were not prepared to accept the decision with absolute complacence. Had Othman been a man of energy and resource, the situation need not have become dangerous; but he was already an elderly man, of a weak and gentle nature, and quite incapable of controlling the factions into which the State was drifting. For twelve years he managed to keep the reins in his wavering hands, years which included another period of great military glory abroad; but the Caliph whose renown was being spread by his armies throughout the civilized world, had to submit in his own capital to constant humiliation. The very fact that so many of the high offices in the armies or the provinces were in the hands of his own family, the Ummeyads, served to go against him in Medina; and the time came at last when the aged ruler was besieged by his political enemies in his own house. He held out with dignity until the last possible moment, hoping against hope that a message which he had smuggled out to his kinsman Moawiyah, in Syria, would reach him in time to procure his own rescue; but at length a band of ruffians succeeded in gaining entrance to his room, and he was unceremoniously put to death. Ali was immediately saluted as Caliph; his claim to the succession was unquestionable, but it was gravely soiled by the fact that some of his supporters were compromised in his predecessor's sudden end, which he himself had done nothing whatever to prevent. A number of malcontents and Ummeyad supporters, including the energetic Ayesha, the widow of the Prophet, immediately took the field against him. He defeated them, however, at the so-called "Battle of the Camel," fought on the outskirts of Basrah, and Ayesha, who was present in person to supervise the efforts of her troops, had to suffer the indignity of being captured on the field. For the time being Ali was left as undisputed Caliph, so far as Arabia proper and Mesopotamia were concerned.

But in Syria a more serious situation had arisen.

Moawiyah, as the kinsman of the murdered Othman, was justified in pressing for some satisfaction for that ignoble act ; and Ali's failure to bring the murderers to justice (a failure explained, but not excused, by their support of his own cause), determined him to seek consolation for the insult to his own family in the pressing of a personal ambition. He demanded as a condition of his submission to Ali as Caliph that those responsible for the assassination of Othman should be brought to justice ; Ali was not in a position to accede to his request ; and Moawiyah, having refused his allegiance, was saluted by his family and supporters in Damascus as Commander of the Faithful.

Ali had in Moawiyah an antagonist, not only far more dangerous than Ayesha and the Arabian rebels, but also more able and active than himself. Ali was a man of high intellect, and his devotion to the scholastic development of early Islam, in the promotion of schools and the encouragement of learning, does him every credit ; but on the political side he suffered from a peculiar indolence not uncommon in intellectual men, and he was no match at all for his energetic and determined opponent. Moawiyah had governed Syria for some years, and had governed it justly and well ; the people of that country, who were more highly civilized at this period than either the Arabs or Mesopotamians, had prospered under his rule, and, as they watched the tumults continually disturbing other parts of the Empire, they were grateful for the wise and strong hand which had enabled them to avoid similar occurrences. The issue which was now joined was soon decided. The result of the civil war went against Ali ; his authority was soon reduced to the sovereignty of Mesopotamia alone ; and he in turn had to meet assassination at the hands of a fanatic, in the cathedral mosque at Kufa, A.D. 661. Neither of his two sons, Hassan and Hosein, was able to shake the political power of the Ummeyad Caliph. Hassan possessed his father's indolence without his intellectual gifts ; and he was content to resign all claim to the Caliphate in return for a very considerable monetary consolation, drawn from the treasury of the unwilling inhabitants of Basrah. Hosein was made of sterner stuff. Persuaded that all Mesopotamia was ready to rise in his cause, he left Arabia in the company of a few faithful followers, and encamped at Kerbela, a village in the environs of Kufa. The fickle Kufans made no effort to rally to his standard; his little band was soon surrounded by the Government forces; he was slain, and his head exposed to the derision of the Kufan mob. Yezid, the son of Moawiyah, remained the master of the situation, and the political control of the Empire remained in the hands of the Ummeyad Caliphs for the next seventy years.

Neither Ali nor Hosein had in their lifetime given any great promise of political ability, or even of high ambition; but the manner of their death, no less than their close relationship to the Prophet, was destined to bring them immortality, and such high influence as they never could have hoped to enjoy when living. Their end was looked upon as martyrdom, the places of their passing, holy shrines. Henceforth Mesopotamia was destined to occupy in the polity of Islam almost as holy a position as Arabia itself. Najaf, the reputed burial place of Ali, and Kerbela, the scene of Hosein's defeat and death, were raised, by the devotion of later ages, to the position of holy cities; and to this day every Shiah regards a pilgrimage to Mesopotamia as hardly less worthy than a pilgrimage to Mecca itself. To these events is due the great spiritual and political influence of the holy cities, to which we shall have occasion to refer again.

The Shiah-Alid schism had one immediate political consequence of the first importance. The Shiahs, holding more and more to the doctrine of the divine right of the descendants of Ali to the Caliphate (a doctrine which can be traced directly to the ancient Persian doctrine of the divine right of kings), refused to acknowledge the authority of the reigning Pontiff in spiritual affairs, a refusal which has always ever since been maintained. The hopelessness of the political future of the Alid house caused their supporters to be driven more and more into the field of spiritual consolation; and thus arose the important Shiah belief in the "divinely appointed Imams." Briefly, this creed maintains that an Imam, or leader, of the house of Ali, must always be the ruler of the faithful; this is God's ordinance, and an article of faith. Twelve Imams (including Ali, Hassan and Hosein), are followed in the direct line to Muhammad al-Mahdi (A.D. 890), who is reputed to have disappeared mysteriously in a cave at Samarra. Since his disappearance no living Imam has been acknowledged, the Shiah community awaiting his return to the world in a state of spiritual expectancy, a state which renders them peculiarly liable to influence by self-styled " Mahdis," " incarnations " or " doors " of the hidden Imam, of whom there have arisen a great number even in comparatively recent times. The close connection of Mesopotamia with the line of the twelve has been responsible for giving the country two more notable places of Shiah pilgrimage ; Samarra, where the last of the line was translated, and Khadhimain (a suburb of Baghdad), where two of his predecessors are buried.

In considering both the history and the present condition of Mesopotamia, the importance of the Shiah schism can hardly be overestimated. In the political sphere, it is the old quarrel of racial temperament ; the mystic Persian craving for a divinely appointed king, against the common-sense Arab's leaning towards democracy. Mesopotamia was, and has always since remained, the battle-ground of the two antagonists ; and she bears to-day the inevitable marks of the conflict. Though Arab in speech, the country is largely Shiah in faith ; with the result that both the Arab and the Persian elements are to some extent denationalized. Predominantly an Arab land, half its inhabitants are out of religious communion with their fellow Arabs of the motherland, and even with their own king. It is considerations of this sort which make the task awaiting the founders of the new Iraq State so peculiarly complicated and difficult.

It was hardly to be expected that the Alids would content themselves wholly with spiritual consolation, allowing the hated Ummeyad family to enjoy the sweets of temporal power undisturbed. The odd-hundred years' rule of the Damascus dynasty, though outwardly prosperous and successful, was interrupted by frequent internal revolts and disturbances. There was a good deal of intellectual activity at this time, which, combined with the general contempt of death so common in the East, brought about

NAJAF: THE SHRINE OF ALI IN THE CENTRE

the rise of small sects and bodies, some of them difficult to suppress. There was a strong party of Moslem communists, who based their case on the various passages in the Koran dealing with the essential equality of man; there was a strong party of freethinkers, always a prominent group in any advanced Moslem country; and there was a select but influential group that carried on the tradition of the Companions of the Prophet. The revolutionary activities of the latter were so pronounced at one period as to compel the investment of Mecca and Medina by the troops of the Government. In the midst of this strange confusion of political and religious issues wandered, as close companions of the Alids and Shiahs, the sinister emissaries of one of the most brilliant families that Islam has ever produced.

The Prophet had a number of uncles, of whom the eldest, Abbas by name, was destined through his descendants to exercise a considerable influence upon later political history. Abbas and his immediate progeny seem to have attained to a position of some power in Mecca, as hereditary custodians of the Holy Places; and they appear also to have been endowed with their full share of the virtues which were afterwards so marked in their descendants, high ambition, a distinct talent for affairs and an absolute disregard for ordinary scruples. It had been an old-established custom among the Arabs that the first heir in succession might be the eldest paternal uncle; the origin of the idea is obscure, but it enjoyed sufficient prestige among the people to allow of the descendants of Abbas utilizing it as a lever for their own ambitions. The Caliphate, according to the doctrine of the Shiahs, ought to be the prerogative of the Prophet's family; there was an old Arab custom that the eldest paternal uncle might inherit; Abbas, their progenitor, had been the eldest paternal uncle of the Prophet; the connection and deduction were obvious.

It is not known to which member of this talented family the inception of this remarkable theory was due; but once launched, it was followed up from father to son with notable persistence for nearly a century, being afterwards reinforced by another equally indefinite, but rather stronger claim. In addition to Hassan and Hosein, Ali had been the father of another son, though not by Fatima. This man, by name Muhammad ibn al-Hanafiyah ("The son of the Hanafite woman," his mother having been of that tribe), was accepted by a sub-sect of the Shiahs as their Imam after the death of Hosein, and the dignity was eventually handed on to his son. The latter became very intimate with the then head of the Abbassid family, and even confided to him various secret rites of his sect, and their political ambition. On the Imam dying without issue, the Abbassid was able without difficulty to gather the strings of the organization into his own hands; and thus from this time onwards the family exercised a shadowy claim to the Imamate of a Shiah sect. But the advantage was early realized of concealing their real intentions, and of joining forces with the popular Alid cause; and so, behind the various Alid and Shiah movements of this unsettled time stood always the Abbassids, never too prominent, and but rarely suspected of complicity, ready at the appropriate moment to procure the overthrow of their friends and their enemies alike.

Meanwhile to outward seeming there appeared no limit to the prowess and good fortune of the Arab arms abroad. Egypt and northern Africa had long been Arab provinces; Sicily was now invaded, several of the Mediterranean islands captured, and Spain and Portugal added to the Empire. The triumphant Moslems crossed the Pyrenees and for some time held southern France; at the same moment that, farther east, Constantinople itself was invested, and the eastern Roman Empire appeared at last to be tottering to its fall. Nor were the Arab successes confined to Europe. The boundaries of Persia were pushed forward through Balkh and Samarkand to the banks of the Oxus; Afghanistan was conquered, and the foundations laid of the Moslem power in India. For a brief space the marshes of the Punjab, the steppes of Turkestan, the cities of Asia Minor, the Moroccan shore and the fair plains of southern France alike acknowledged the authority of the Caliph of Damascus. Rome herself had never ruled such an empire; the Arab was the greatest, as it was the last, effort to hold all civilized mankind in one

THE DIVISION OF ISLAM

comprehensive administrative whole. That the attempt was doomed to failure was soon to be proved. The influence of Damascus fell a victim to internal troubles; and the new capital of Baghdad was never able to acquire the predominant and undisputed position of her Syrian sister. When the secret and laborious efforts of the house of Abbas had been at last rewarded, it was over a truncated and dismembered empire that they came to rule.

The Ummeyad Caliphs were, on the whole, wise and able men, but they became involved before long in that bugbear of autocratic rule, disagreement over the succession. The Arabs had never succeeded in overcoming their passion for tribal feuds, and dynastic troubles offered a tempting opportunity for the revival of old hatreds and old rivalries. The decline of the Ummeyad family became apparent during the reign of Hisham, who died in A.D. 743. He was a capable man, but not a popular monarch. He preferred the country to the town, and, in his palace on the edge of the desert, kept himself aloof from his subjects. His large schemes for the material improvement of the Empire necessitated increases in the revenue; with the result that his subjects accused him, perhaps not unjustly, of overburdening them for the benefit of future ages. There was a growing feeling of discontent, carefully fanned by the revolutionary elements, throughout the Empire; and as soon as the strong hand of Hisham was removed, the trouble rose to the surface. His successor was almost immediately assassinated; the next ruler lived only five months; and the next, after an ignominious reign of two months, was forced to yield the throne to a distant relative, who invaded the heart of the Empire at the head of a large army. This man, Merwan, was the last of the Ummeyad Caliphs. He was an able and energetic man, and might have saved the fortunes of his house had the disorder been less widespread. He is important in Mesopotamian history because of his removal of the capital from Damascus to the land of the rivers, where henceforth it was destined to remain. For his seat of government he chose Harran, of Biblical memory, and the site of the great defeat of the Roman Crassus by the Parthians eight hundred years earlier.

Merwan's cause was rendered almost hopeless from the

first by bitter disagreement among the Ummeyad family. He came of a junior branch, and his mother was a slave girl; and his aristocratic relations flatly refused to submit loyally to his rule. In addition, the Syrians were alienated by the removal of the capital, and the leading Arab families were too preoccupied with their tribal quarrels to make any organized effort to rally round the throne. In the midst of the general confusion, an insurrection in Khorassan, on the eastern borders of the Empire, heralded the rise of another Caliph and the final triumph of the Abbassids.

The latter family at this time enjoyed the services of a Persian client named Abu Muslim, a man of very exceptional political ability, who, though secretly in the service of the Abbassids, had early given outward proof of his devotion to the Alid cause. He had been for some time past resident in Khorassan, always a stronghold of Shiah intrigue, where he had been busily engaged in co-ordinating the rapidly growing forces of discontented Shiahs, Alids and Abbassids. With these he was careful to join the large number of non-Arab peoples, Persians, Kurds, Turks and Tartars, who, having embraced Islam, only awaited an opportunity to try conclusions with their haughty Arab masters. The Arab nobles in Khorassan, loyal to the Caliph but, as usual, hopelessly disunited among themselves, were deaf to the entreaties of the governor, who alone had grasped the real significance of Abu Muslim's crafty work; and Merwan, in spite of his realization of the danger, was unable to spare Imperial troops for distant Khorassan. Meanwhile the Alids openly raised the standard of revolt at Kufa, and Abu Muslim eventually followed by throwing off all disguise and unfurling the black flag of the " coming Imam " on the eastern border. The actual identity of the Imam was not revealed, and the Alids were persuaded to join forces with Abu Muslim; Khorassan and Persia were rapidly overrun, and Mesopotamia secured for the cause. Then it was that Abu Muslim played his master card. Having secured control of the whole joint organization, he produced the hidden Imam in the person of the head of the Abbassid house; the disconcerted Alids discovered too late that they had been tricked; and the soldiers and people of Kufa saluted as Caliph the descendant of the uncle of the Prophet. Having made use of the Shiahs as long as they needed them, the Abbassids now turned to the orthodox party, and all talk of the Alid cause was dropped. Orthodox Islam was now reminded of the legitimacy of the new Caliph's claim to the throne owing to the special position of his ancestor, Abbas, and of the many evils wrought by the Ummeyad house. The revolution continued its course. In a great battle by the banks of the Zab in upper Mesopotamia the Abbassid forces completely defeated the army of Merwan; the Ummeyads and their more important supporters were put to the sword; and the Abbassids, conquerors alike of their friends and their enemies, proceeded to the task of consolidating their newly-won position.

The triumph of this family meant the return to Mesopotamia of a prosperity such as she had not known for many centuries. She was now to be the centre of the Empire. Syria had been too deeply involved in the Ummeyad connection to be possible as a residence for their successors; and a return to one or other of the primitive capitals of Arabia proper would have been impracticable. In addition, the balance of power in the Moslem world was tending to shift eastward. The authority of the Abbassids rested, not upon an Arab, but upon a Persian foundation; they had been raised to the throne by the armies of Khorassan, and they ruled, not in the manner of the simple Arab Caliphs, but as typical Persian monarchs of the old school, with all the pomp and magnificence of the traditional Oriental court. At the same time by the loss of Spain and Morocco, which took advantage of the general confusion to set up for themselves as independent kingdoms, western influence was largely withdrawn from the Caliphate; and the monarchs became more and more dependent as time went on upon their beloved Persians, and their faithful henchmen from Khorassan. This tendency ended by driving them into the arms of a still more virile and warlike race, the Turks, who, by undermining the edifice of the throne, were in the end able to supersede it.

The Arabs, on the other hand, cease from this time onwards to take an active part in the affairs of the Empire which their genius had built up. The etiquette of court life, the pomp and magnificence surrounding an Imperial throne, are foreign to the Arab genius and hateful to their democratic temperament. More and more the leading Arab families, disgusted at the turn which events had taken, tended to retire to the quiet interests of Mecca or Medina, or the charms of an independent bedouin existence. Armed with the strength of a simple faith, supported by a healthy and natural life, they had overcome for a time the effete and subtle peoples of the Mesopotamian plain ; but eventually they had again been conquered. The virtues of strong and simple men are needed less and less in the growing complexity of an expanding civilization ; and the Arabs as a race have ever been incapable of compromise. True to their destiny, they preferred to retire with dignity to the desert that had reared them, rather than risk being compelled to bend the knee before a polished and effeminate court of Persians, Jews and Christian Syrians. " The Yemen," runs an Arab proverb, "is the cradle of our race ; the Iraq is its grave." The life of the black tent and the wide plain is the proper existence for the proud and lusty sons of Ishmael ; let civilization be the work of those who will accept its conventions and who enjoy its advantages.

Nevertheless, the withdrawal of the Arab element from public life had a seriously weakening effect upon the Caliphate. The Arabs, with all their faults, had supplied the one virile element in the hotch-potch of races that now formed the Empire ; the Persians, Syrians and Mesopotamians, subtle, witty and intellectual, were lacking entirely in that quality of hardness and determination without which an imperial system cannot, in the last event, be carried on. They were bound to succumb, as soon as Arab loyalty and Arab support were withdrawn, before the attack of any strong outside race who happened to present themselves. Meanwhile, Mesopotamia, that land of innumerable civilizations, burst forth once more into another blaze of glory ; the pride of Kish, the magnificence of Babylon, were combined in the new foundation of Baghdad ; for a short period the land of the rivers became once more the centre of the cultivated world. The last great Mesopotamian civilization may perhaps claim with some degree of truth that it was not unworthy of its famous predecessors.

CHAPTER V

THE GOLDEN AGE

" Know that wherever there is a rose there is a thorn, and with wine there is intoxication, and over a treasure is coiled a serpent, and where there are royal pearls there are also devouring monsters."—SA'DI.

THE triumph of the Abbassids marks the inauguration of what has been justly termed the Golden Age of the Caliphate, an age which has always, in the minds of Western readers, been associated with the new foundation of Baghdad, and the unscrupulous but brilliant personality of Harun ar-Rashid. The impartial historian is compelled to admit that Harun must yield in administrative ability to his grandfather Mansur, and in intellectual gifts to his son Mamun; but it was perhaps in his reign that the Golden Age reached its zenith, and his romantic figure will remain to the end of time as peculiarly characteristic of the splendour, the intellectual eminence, the cruelty and the shameless demoralization of the last of the Mesopotamian civilizations.

The Golden Age is roughly covered by the reigns of the first seven sovereigns of the Abbassid dynasty. The determination of the new rulers to regard Mesopotamia as the centre of the Empire was sounded by the inaugural address of the first of the line. " O men of Kufa," said he, on being saluted as Caliph by Abu Muslim's troops, " Ye are those whose affections towards us have ever been constant and true; ye have never changed your mind, nor swerved from it, notwithstanding all the pressure of the unjust upon you. At last our time has come, and the Lord has brought you the new era. Through us ye are the happiest of men, and the dearest to us."

Notwithstanding this oratorical compliment, the new Caliph was fully conscious of the treacherous reputation of the Mesopotamians, and he was careful never to remain among them for very long at a time. The real sympathy of the country, as he probably knew, was with the Alids who had been cheated of their destiny at the moment of triumph by the superior political sagacity of the Abbassids; and it was already a saying among the common people that "Khorassan was with the Abbassids, Iraq with the Alids, while Syria would follow any rebel." Indeed, the numerous rebellions which occurred throughout his reign and that of his successor showed the strength and vitality of the opposition. Several independent Caliphs, and an almost endless number of pseudo-prophets and "mahdis," had to be put down by force of arms; and the celebrated al-Moqanna, the "veiled prophet of Khorassan," immortalized in modern song, held out against all the force which the Government could bring against him for nearly three years.

But the intelligence, the resources and the lack of scruple of the Abbassid monarchs enabled them eventually to triumph over all opposition, whether of enemies or of too powerful friends. The remnants of the Ummeyad house were exterminated, root and branch. The wretched Syrian populace, who had complained of the cruelties of the old regime, had now to witness such wholesale butchery as Damascus at its worst had never offered. Where force alone was insufficient to procure its object, treachery was freely added. Even the members of the Ummeyad family who had taken refuge in the sanctuaries of Mecca and Medina were sought out and slain; the tombs of the dead Caliphs of Damascus were opened and their ashes scattered to the winds; and the townspeople of Mosul, who had rebelled at an unfortunate moment against the new dispensation, were slaughtered to a man in the courtyard of their principal mosque, their womenfolk being surrendered to the embraces of the soldiery. One youthful member of the house of Ali, suspected of revolutionary tendencies, was built alive into the wall of his prison; and the Caliph's own uncle, who had rebelled but who had afterwards been given reason to expect clemency, was granted a residence in a house constructed on salt foundations, which, the first night of the ensuing rainy season, collapsed on top of him and killed him. With such humorous diversions did the early Abbassids lighten the monotony of their cruel progress.

The victim of what was perhaps the new family's

meanest and most reprehensible act was the man to whom, of all men, they owed most gratitude. Their rapid rise was due, as we have seen, in no small measure to the great ability and untiring energy of the Persian freedman, Abu Muslim. He had not only planned the events which led to the final overthrow of the Ummeyads, but he had known how to conquer the perplexed and divided Empire on behalf of his masters ; and it was his subterfuge that had procured the proclamation of an Abbassid Caliph before the followers of the Alid cause had grasped the situation. It would hardly be too much to say that to Abu Muslim the Abbassids owed the throne ; but neither his past services nor his present loyalty availed to save him now. No suspicion had reached the Caliph as yet reflecting in any way upon the loyalty of his great client ; but he was known to be feared by the people and worshipped by the soldiers, and, in political situations, prevention is notoriously better than cure. Abu Muslim, even then engaged in consolidating a recent victory, was sent for by his Royal master ; he was cordially received ; some slight annoyance was expressed by the monarch concerning a recent incident, and hot words passed ; at a given signal five assassins stepped from behind the curtains of the audience chamber, and the man who had been the principal instrument in raising the Caliph to power was murdered before his eyes. No public excuse whatever was made for this dastardly act ; and, indeed, the only possible one would seem to be that adopted by a well-known wit of the time, who, on being asked his opinion of the event, remarked, in the words of a celebrated passage from the Koran, that " If there were two Gods, the universe would be ruined."

The Caliph responsible for this treacherous action was Jafar, surnamed al-Mansur or " The Glorious," and the second of the Abbassid line ; a man who, cruel and unscrupulous in matters where his own interests were concerned, was nevertheless an energetic and far-sighted ruler. Ruthless in his determination to retain his position, he was just and tolerant in public affairs ; and even those of his subjects who possessed an intimate record of his private life, could not but admire his public spirit, and his ceaseless efforts to further the interests of the millions over whom he ruled. It must not be forgotten that Mansur's position, as the head of a new and still untried dynasty, attempting to govern a mixed and fickle population, was one of singular difficulty ; and many western monarchs, far more modern in point of time, have not scrupled, when faced with similar situations, to make use of similar weapons.

The constant feeling of insecurity which brought into such strong relief the unpleasant sides of his character, was also responsible for the conception of a plan destined to bring him more than passing fame. Beset with constant wars or rumours of wars, compelled to maintain a large standing army for the preservation of his position, he was soon obliged to recognize the necessity, in view of the fickle and uncertain nature of his subjects, of isolating the army to some extent from the general population. This recognition led him to the decision that the army, together with the leading officials of the Government, should be housed in some central place, away from the large cities, but accessible to all parts of the Empire. He finally determined upon the construction of a new capital, of a novel design, large enough to accommodate his person, his officials and his troops, but small enough to prevent the growth of an overwhelming civilian element. From this handy citadel he would be able, by a system of good roads, to make his influence felt in any portion of his dominions with the expenditure of a minimum of time and trouble ; and he could safely rely, through the vigilance of the police, upon the exclusion from Government circles of all subversive and revolutionary elements. Freed from the distractions of a great city, secure in the swords of a prætorian guard, the monarch and his officials would be at liberty to deal with each and every danger, as and when they might arise.

For some months the Caliph searched the central portions of his realm for a suitable site for the new foundation until his attention was drawn to the favourable qualities of the little market town of Baghdad, nestling amid the palm trees on a wide bend of the Tigris. The origin of the little settlement was, and is, unknown ; but the name has been discovered in the records of at least one Assyrian king, and at the time of the Arab invasion it had developed into a prosperous country town, from which considerable loot was obtained in one of the marauding expeditions of Khalid. The site was central, the district was liberally provided with canals, and river communication was assured. The climate was equable and free from malaria; the heat of the summer days was tempered by the soft breeze of the plain; and the ruins of the adjacent summer palace of the Persian kings testified to the favour with which the locality had been regarded in former times. Tradition avers that the Caliph's final choice was determined by the advice of some Christian monks, the inhabitants of a monastery in the vicinity, who entertained the monarch to luncheon on one of his tours of inspection; but it is more probable that he was influenced by the obvious recommendations of the site, and by the memory of Seleucia-Ctesiphon, but fifteen miles away, from which for so many centuries Mesopotamia and Persia had been successfully administered. Whatever the actual reason, Baghdad was finally decided upon as the Caliph's future home and capital, and preparations were undertaken for the erection of a camp city which should satisfy the monarch's desire for isolation, and his need for security.

The foundation of the new city took place in A.D. 762, the Caliph himself laying the first brick, with a short oration appropriate to the occasion. The building was soon interrupted by the outbreak of the most serious rebellion which Mansur had so far been called upon to meet, and the danger to which he was subjected on this occasion made him all the more anxious, once his final victory had been assured, to complete the erection of his new capital. The cities of the Empire were ransacked for artificers and for treasures to adorn the young metropolis; their monuments and public buildings were stripped of their ornaments; and even the ruins of past majesty forfeited the respect due to age in the face of the urgent necessity of the present. Ctesiphon proved a veritable mine to the Royal builder; Kufa, Wasit and Damascus had each to yield their handsome iron gates; and many of the houses in the new Baghdad were built of Babylonian brick. The youthful foundation might be termed in literal truth the child of all the great Mesopotamian cities that had preceded her.

The Baghdad of Mansur (called after him, for many years, "Mansurieh") was situated on the right or western bank of the Tigris, somewhere in the neighbourhood of the present West railway station. It was built in the form of a circle, and consisted of three parallel walls, the two outer serving the purposes of defence, the inner one containing the reserved Royal and Governmental quarter. Four gates, each with a bridge crossing the intervening space between the first and second walls, and each duplicated in the latter, gave admittance to the city. In the innermost circle, and adjoining the Palace of the Caliph, lay the Government offices, the Cathedral Mosque, and an open maidan, or space, for military parades, spectacles and races. The streets and houses of the city proper lay entirely between the second and inner walls. Once within the latter, no man might ride a horse or travel in a carriage without the permission of the Caliph; a precaution probably designed to prevent possible attacks upon the monarch's person by individual assassins. Barracks for the soldiers were constructed on the other bank of the river, separate blocks being provided for the Arabs, the Persians and the Khorassanians; they were connected with the "Round City," as the creation of Mansur came to be called, by a bridge across the Tigris, which led directly into the east or Khorassan gate.

With the exception of small bazaars for the sale of foodstuffs and other ordinary necessities, which were under the strict supervision of the police, shops and places of business were rigidly excluded from the new city; on the advice, so tradition asserts, of the Roman ambassador. Merchants were afterwards accommodated in Karkh, a large suburb which sprang up outside the western gate, and whose name survives in the official designation of west Baghdad to-day.

Karkh was not the only suburb which sprang up outside the gates as a protest against the artificial limitations of the new capital. The presence of the barracks across the river soon brought into being another city, in spite of the efforts made by Mansur to preserve the integrity of his original design. Royal favour was conferred upon the new settlement by the Crown Prince, Muhammad al-Mahdi, who built himself a palace on the eastern bank of the river, and allowed the rising city to be named Mahdieh after himself. In the years that followed Mahdieh outstripped Mansurieh and Karkh both in population and wealth; and a new wall had to be constructed to include it and a twin settlement named Rusafah. In the disturbances which followed the death of Harun ar-Rashid the round city was destroyed, and the official buildings removed across the river. Henceforward east Baghdad, still known even to-day as Rusafah, was destined to remain the larger and more important portion of the city. So completely did the original creation of Mansur sink into oblivion that even its location is not now known with any exactness.

 The erection of the new Baghdad took, including the period of the rebellion, five years, and it was not until A.D. 767 that the city was ready to take its place as the metropolis of the Empire. Once, so to speak, officially "opened," the new capital grew with astonishing rapidity. Her population in the time of Harun has been estimated at two millions, so that, if this figure is accepted, she must have risen from a small country town into the second greatest city in the world in the short space of thirty years. She continued to maintain her predominant position for five hundred years; and, throughout the Middle Ages, Baghdad, in population, in wealth, in influence or intellectual achievement, yielded only to Constantinople. The fame of her beauty and her power, and of the riches, erudition and gaiety of her citizens, spread to the ends of the earth; and Charlemagne, the Emperor of all Europe, did not disdain to accept gifts from the Caliph of Baghdad. Baghdad, the "House of Peace," the "Eye of Islam," became the home of the Thousand and One Nights, the embodiment of Oriental luxury and magnificence; and the glories even of Damascus, that earthly Paradise, paled before the proud city on the Tigris, to which the restless traveller, the ambitious politician, the philosophic inquirer and the religious mendicant alike bent their steps. Seat of both temporal and spiritual power, the great city reflected the dignity of her dual position; and, surrounded with all the luxurious appointments that a great industrial people could provide, her fortunate inhabitants gave themselves up to the delights of social intercourse, of the study of philosophy and the arts, or of the myriad less reputable pleasures which the low morality of the times allowed.

The reigns of Mansur's immediate successors were distinguished only by the continued progress and consolidation of the Empire; a process which reached its highest point in the reigns of Harun and his son Mamun. Harun was a monarch of the old Persian type, and the traditions and tales which centre round his person (many of them Persian in origin) might, with a change of background, be applied with equal facility to the kings of the lines of Cyrus or of Chroses. He was fortunate in his servants, particularly in the great family of the Barmecides (of " Barmecide feast " fame), whom, with typical Abbassid perfidy, he eventually disgraced. The story of this celebrated Persian family is significant both of the opportunities and of the morality of the time. Of humble origin, the family advanced in status under Mansur, and one of them, Yahya, was Harun's tutor in his early years. It was largely through Yahya's firmness that Harun secured the throne at all, for his elder brother, who preceded him as Caliph, had planned to supersede him in favour of his own son. Indeed, tradition asserts that Harun himself had no desire for public life and would have assented to his brother's design, but for the importuning of Yahya and of his own mother, who finally settled the matter herself by having her elder son assassinated. Harun rewarded Yahya by making him his sole Minister, with practically autocratic powers; and he also promoted to high office Yahya's two sons, Fadl and Jafar, the latter the companion of the Caliph in several romantic legends. For nearly twenty years this talented family served the State faithfully and well; but they were not without their detractors at court, and Harun had his full share of Abbassid jealousy and suspicion. When the blow fell, it fell quickly. In one day all the Barmecides were arrested and thrown into prison; and Jafar, who only the day before had been hunting with the Caliph, was secretly beheaded in a castle on the monarch's estate. The Barmecides never recovered from this disgrace, though their liberties and properties were afterwards restored to them by Mamun.

THE GOLDEN AGE 73

The special punishment of death meted out to Jafar gave rise to a remarkable story, which is celebrated in Arab romantic tradition. The Caliph delighted, so the story runs, in the company of Jafar and of his own sister Abbassa, and spent much of his leisure time in their society. Moslem custom might point to a breach of propriety in so mixed a company, and so Harun suggested a marriage between Jafar and Abbassa, stipulating only (probably with the thought of Barmecide ambition centring upon a possible child) that the marriage should be one in form only. The condition was disregarded, the story continues, owing to the importunity of Abbassa, who had fallen in love with her husband, and took advantage of him when in a drunken state; and when, in due course, a baby was born, its birth was carefully concealed and it was hurried away to Mecca. An angry retainer, who had been unjustly dismissed from the Princess's household, later revealed the circumstance to the Caliph; and the latter, on the occasion of his next pilgrimage to the holy city, was careful to verify the accuracy of the information. It was as a punishment for this, the tale concludes, that Jafar was hastily assassinated. The candid historian must admit, however, that it is far more probable that his death was due to his failure as a warder; for a member of the Alid family, suspected by Harun of revolutionary tendencies, had been committed to his care, and he had allowed him to escape.

Although his name is so strongly associated with Baghdad in romantic tradition, Harun ar-Rashid had in fact very little love for his capital; and much of his time, when not in camp directing the frequent campaigns which were a feature of his reign, was spent in country places, particularly Rakka on the upper Euphrates. He was several times in the field against the treacherous Roman Emperor Nicephorus; and the feats of his armies in these campaigns have aroused the admiration of Gibbon. The Empress Irene, who preceded Nicephorus on the throne of Constantinople, had been forced to pay a heavy tribute to the Baghdad Government; and Nicephorus reopened hostilities with a diplomatic note characteristic of the official correspondence of the period. "From Nicephorus, the Roman Emperor," the letter ran, "to Harun, sovereign of the Arabs. Verily, the Empress who preceded me gave thee the rank of a rook and herself that of a pawn,* and conveyed to thee many loads of her wealth, and this through the weakness of women and their folly. Now, when thou hast read this letter of mine, return what thou hast received of her substance, otherwise the sword shall decide between me and thee." Harun's answer, written on the back of the Emperor's letter, was short and to the point. "From Harun, the Commander of the Faithful," it ran, "to Nicephorus, the dog of a Roman; verily, I have read thy letter. Thou shalt not hear, but see my answer." Harun was as good as his word. In the subsequent fighting the Romans sustained a severe defeat, and the Emperor himself three wounds; and though they continued treacherously to break their treaty obligations whenever Harun's armies were otherwise engaged, they were invariably heavily defeated in the field. Eventually the position of the Romans became so precarious that it seemed that Constantinople itself would hardly hold out against the Arab pressure; but possibly Harun realized the limitations of his own strength, for he never attempted to press his advantage to its logical conclusion.

The material splendour of Harun's reign was capped by the intellectual brilliance of that of his son Mamun. In person Abdullah surnamed Mamun ("He in whom men trust") offered that strange but not uncommon combination of an autocrat of domineering character, but radical, almost revolutionary, ideas. His reign coincided with a period of great intellectual brilliance, and he was in many ways eminently suited to lead the fashion of the time. He was himself a poet of distinction; and an eminent bard of the period, who had come to Court to recite a topical composition of some intricacy, was astonished to hear the Caliph "cap" all his lines, wittily and correctly, as he went along.

But Mamun's interests were by no means confined to poetry. He was devoted to scientific studies, especially mathematics and astronomy; and he ordered a systematic translation of the works of all the ancient Greek, Persian

---

* The allusion is to chess, a very popular game of the period, introduced, so it is said, from Persia by Harun ar-Rashid.

THE GOLDEN AGE

and Coptic mathematicians, philosophers and men of science, for the purpose of accurate comparison. The first Arabic translation of Euclid was dedicated to him. An academy for advanced studies was founded in Baghdad, fully equipped with a library and observatory; and two eminent professors were engaged for some time in a special undertaking to measure the circumference of the earth. It was at this time also that the principal Arab historians and annalists flourished, as well as the authors and editors of the vast Arabic literature of belles-lettres and stories; and there commenced that enormous collection of books dealing with religious disputation, in which the Arabic language is so rich. The masters of the four great Sunni, or orthodox, schools of Islam all flourished about this period; one of them had to endure persecution at the hands of Mamun. Such decorative arts, too, as the teaching of Islam allows, were assiduously cultivated. Europe had relapsed into barbarism, and Constantinople, intellectually speaking, was living on the past; almost all creative intellectual life was confined to the two Moslem courts of Cordova and Baghdad, and of these Baghdad's legacy to the world was incomparably the finer. Indeed, if ancient Athens be excepted, it may be said that possibly no other city has ever produced within the space of a few decades such an imposing array of men of distinction, excelling in such a variety of activities and pursuits.

It was perhaps in the religious sphere that Mamun's restless and versatile mentality found its greatest scope. Reared by a Persian mother, and trained under Persian tutors, he was naturally inclined more towards the Shiah than the Sunni faith; and quite early in his reign he astonished his friends and outraged his supporters by adopting as his heir the then head of the Alid party. But on this occasion Mamun was quick to realize that he had committed a political error, which led, indeed, to a very serious outbreak in Baghdad; and the convenient death shortly afterwards of the Alid heir was ascribed, and possibly with truth, to the intervention of the Caliph, although he was in public careful to demonstrate his grief. If this selection had been better received by the people, the history of Islam might have been very materially altered.

Mamun's unorthodox predilections led him shortly afterwards into attachment to an even more rebellious sect, that of the Mu'tazilites, or rationalists. One of the principal points in their doctrine turned on the question of the creation of the Koran. In the eyes of orthodox Islam, the Koran is uncreated, being the word of God; the rationalists, on the other hand, asserted that, though remaining the word of God, it must, being a thing of this world and a physical entity, have been created. A heavy dispute arose over this obscure point, which distracted Baghdad for many months; until the Caliph once again astonished the faithful by acknowledging the Mu'tazilite doctrine in public, and formally recognizing it as the official belief of the State. He introduced at the same time several minor articles of faith, such as predestination and the worship of Ali as the "Wali" or "Confidant" of God; and these doctrines are still professed by the Shiah community to-day. The Mu'tazilites afterwards sank into insignificance, but they are still represented at the present day by various small sects, the most important of which is possibly the body presided over by the Aga Khan.

But if Mamun was liberal in his intellectual outlook, and almost heretical in his religion, he was grossly intolerant in his methods of carrying his radical ideas into execution. A religious inquisition was established in Baghdad, and all who refused to acknowledge the tenets of the new State religion were thrown into prison. Many well-known orthodox doctors suffered in this way for their faith. None the less, Mamun was generous towards the followers of other creeds; Christians and Jews were free to come and go as they pleased; and many non-Moslems held high office in the State. The celebrated "Apology of al-Kindi," published in this reign, which represents an argument between a Moslem and a Christian on the merits and demerits of the two religions, is in itself a remarkable memorial to the liberality of the times. It is but fair to remember that, in spite of certain lapses from tolerance, the dominant attitude of Mamun was that of a demand for greater freedom; and had his work been carried on and developed by his successors, the intellectual cloud which was about to descend upon orthodox Islam, stifling it in inflexible dogma and irrevisable belief, effectually preventing all spiritual and social development, might have been averted. There is nothing in the teaching of the Prophet himself to encourage the swathing of men's minds in intellectual bandages, or the prevention of the recognition of the new needs of new times. Rightly directed, the faith of Islam might have shown itself as progressive and as sensitive to the varying necessities of succeeding ages as Christianity; and the Near and Middle East might yet be rivalling Europe in spreading the cause of civilization and enlightenment. But the seeds of freedom and unfettered inquiry which were sown by Mamun were not allowed to bear fruit; the orthodox doctors of law were soon engaged in building up doctrines and laws of life which should, contrary to all the teachings of Nature, be absolutely rigid and unchanging; and the results of their fatal success can be seen to-day in any Moslem land. The work of Mamun was undone; the Golden Age was over; the orthodox returned in triumph; the Turkish influence, strong, stupid and unimaginative, began to gain paramountcy in the State; and the intellect of the Arab, the subtlety of the Persian, became more and more lost to the world. Islam began to assume the fettered, hopeless shape that has distinguished it ever since until very recent times.

CHAPTER VI

LIFE IN THE GOLDEN AGE

"Much done, and much designed, and more desired."—WORDSWORTH.

THE Golden Age, from the acclamation of the first Abbassid Caliph in the cathedral mosque at Kufa to the death of Mamun (A.D. 833), lasted just over eighty years. It was a time of wonderful brilliance, and of very solid progress. The organization of the empire was laid down on definite lines ; the boundaries of the provinces were carefully marked out ; and a complicated system of roads connected the capital alike with the Mediterranean, the heart of Arabia, the mountains of Asia Minor, and the borders of China. All executive power remained theoretically in the hands of the Caliph, though the tendency to appoint a wazir (vizier) or minister of state, to relieve the monarch of his executive duties became more and more marked as time went on. Mamun in addition created a kind of Cabinet or Council of State, and appeared to cherish political ideals as liberal as his spiritual tendencies. In practice, the ruler retained a firm hand over the provincial Governors, who were, however, possessed of autocratic power within their respective administrative spheres ; and an elaborate system of secret police kept him directly informed of provincial events. One of his confidential spies was invariably placed in the post offices of the great cities, where he had unequalled opportunities of hearing local gossip and watching local people ; and, indeed, this spy was not infrequently the postmaster himself. The Caliph also employed many unofficial secret agents, especially among the merchant class, and he possessed his own spies in foreign capitals. These spies had a curious subsequent history, for, as the political power of the Caliph declined and he tended to become merely the spiritual father of his people, his former confidential agents became practically " Papal " legates at the various small courts which had grown out of the dismemberment of the empire. These legates frequently procured enormous influence, for it was the essential policy of each local ruler to obtain as strong a position at the Papal court as possible, and the resident legate could make himself a very useful friend.

One point which distinguished the administration of the early Abbassids from that of the Moslem states which followed them, and even from that of many modern Christian states, was their entire disregard of racial and religious differences. The highest posts in the empire were open to Christians and Jews as well as to Moslems ; to Persians, Turks and Indians as well as to Arabs. The cosmopolitan character of the population was reflected even in the most exalted offices of state ; and the rise from obscurity of several great families, such as the Barmecides, who served the empire well, would have been practically impossible in most European states until modern times. Indeed it might be said with truth that nowhere in the twentieth century, except in London, and, possibly, Washington, is a great career open to talent alone in as free and unfettered a manner as it was in the Baghdad of the Abbassids. In not a few respects these eminent rulers were more modern than the moderns. The control of so vast an empire, stretching from Egypt and Cyprus to the borders of China, and from Tiflis to the Indian Ocean, naturally necessitated the employment of a large army ; and the organization of the Imperial forces is not without interest. The army consisted of regulars and volunteers ; the former were in the pay of the Caliph, the latter received rations only, while on active service ; their families at home, in the meanwhile, receiving maintenance from the State. The troops were divided into infantry, armed with lance, sword and shield, and cavalry ; there were also corps of archers and of specialized troops such as " naphtha firemen," who were experts in the use of Greek fire ; sappers and engineers ; signallers, messengers, etc. The troops wore distinctive uniforms according to their corps, and were divided for administrative purposes into sections of ten, companies of a hundred, battalions of a thousand and corps of ten thousand men. The latter, under the command of an amir, or general, formed the strategical unit of the army. The Caliph's personal guard formed a separate composite force, and was latterly always recruited from foreign peoples, usually Turks. The uniform of the guard was noticeably splendid, and the men enlisted in it received higher pay than the ordinary troops. This prætorian guard gradually obtained unlimited power in the capital, and was later the source of much mischief. Slightly inferior to the prætorians, but also highly privileged, and stationed permanently in the capital, were the household troops and the corps of aides-de-camp, from whom the Caliph drew his personal attendants. The latter were taken into the service as boys, and used as Court pages; their education was carried on at Court, and they occupied special barracks of their own, where they lived under a severe semi-monkish discipline.

Theoretically, every able-bodied Arab was liable to military service, but the rapid growth of a professional army and the employment of foreign troops in privileged positions led to the summons being generally disregarded; and as the Arab chieftains began to come less and less to Court, their tribesmen became more and more inclined to enrol themselves only under their own tribal banner. The gradual growth of these local armies led to the establishment of a military feudal system, and very materially aided the disintegration of the empire.

The army in the field was usually equipped to the standard of five divisions, the centre, the right wing, left wing, vanguard and rearguard. The amir and his staff rode with the centre, and a march through hostile country was always conducted in this formation. The vanguard, chiefly of light cavalry, acted as the scouts of the army, and with them lay the duty of preparing maps of new country for the use of the staff. Either the centre or rearguard had charge of the supply train, ambulance and artillery, the materials for all of which were transported on the backs of camels. Camp was always formed on the Roman model, and was invariably heavily entrenched. It was the great superiority of the camel train over the primitive horse and mule trains of the Greeks and Persians that was largely responsible for the Arabs' striking successes in the field. When speed of movement was particularly required, the infantry were mounted temporarily on camels, or the cavalry took each a foot soldier behind them on their horses.

The navy was a well-developed arm under the early Abbassids. It was some time before the Arabs took to the water, though from time immemorial there had been Arab sea traders and corsairs in the waters of the Persian Gulf; and the disaster which overtook an early naval expedition on the Red Sea had led the Caliph Omar to declare that never again would he permit his soldiers to embark upon an element so treacherous. But ready recruits for the navy were eventually found among the seafaring men of Basrah and Bahrein, and among the inhabitants of the Syrian and Palestinian towns on the Mediterranean shore, who for centuries had possessed the love and knowledge of the sea in their blood. The navy, though a recognized force, appears to have been always formed on a territorial basis, the various ports of the empire being liable to the " calling up " of a proportion of their vessels in time of war. The navy was responsible for many notable victories, of which the greatest was perhaps the conquest of Cyprus from the Roman Empire. The discovery of the maritime compass has been claimed by the Arabs, but the claim is not absolutely proved. The amir in command of the fleet was termed " Amir-al-Ma " (General of the sea), from which is derived the modern English word " Admiral."

The revenues of the empire were principally derived from the land tax, the tithes or income tax, the percentage tax in kind, and the head tax upon non-Moslems in lieu of military service. There were under the Abbassids a large number of minor taxes, including dues on salt, fisheries, imports, bazaar stall-holdings, and mills and factories; there was also at one time a luxury tax. The expenses of the administration were very large, and the extravagance of the Court notorious, especially under Harun and Mamun; in addition to which the taxation of the provinces was not always well supervised, and many provincial Governors made large fortunes on their own account. The sums spent on entertaining Royalty, and on the bribery of Court officials, were enormous. In the time of Harun, for instance, one of the provinces rebelled under

F

the load of taxation imposed by an unpopular Governor. The Caliph went in person with his advisers to investigate the causes of the rebellion ; but the Governor distributed such generous sums among the Government officials that when the time came for the inquiry nobody could be found ready to accuse him. The real state of affairs was carefully kept concealed from Harun ; and the unhappy province had to endure the presence of their detested Governor for yet another term.

On the occasion of the marriage of Mamun to the daughter of his principal minister of state, the celebrations were continued for seventeen days. At the ceremony itself, a thousand pearls were showered upon the Caliph and his bride, and each of the guests received a ball of musk, which, when opened, was found to contain a ticket entitling the fortunate recipient to an estate, a cultured slave, a well-bred horse or other equally generous gift. Sums equal to a million sterling are mentioned by tradition in connection with the cost of this event ; and, even if exaggerated, they throw a vivid light upon the reckless and extravagant habits of the age. The hospitality of the minister on this occasion was rewarded by the allotment of the revenues of two prosperous provinces for a year ; and to the unhappy provincials fell the eventual task of paying the cost of so fabulous an entertainment.

The luxury and extravagance of the time found their culmination, and their excuse, in the brilliant and sparkling life of the capital. Baghdad became a city of palaces ; her mansions were lavishly decorated, and the individual rooms tastefully hung with rare tapestries, and furnished with costly ornaments. The halls of the Imperial palaces were inlaid with jewels, and distinguished from each other by the various styles of their ornamentation ; thus, one was designed entirely in gold, another in precious stones, another in marble. Here were held the great receptions of the Caliphs, always on a scale of great magnificence. The public drawing-rooms were held in state, the head officials and the Imperial guard being present. In addition to these functions, there were a number of semi-public receptions, held on a more informal plan, and without the presence of the troops ; sometimes such a reception would be held for the discussion of some literary or scientific novelty, and would be attended by the best-known litterateurs and dilettanti of the day. During the fasting month of Ramadhan it was customary for the provincial officers of the Caliph to visit the capital, and a reception was usually held in their honour; and at the feast of Id-al-Fitr, which immediately follows Ramadhan, the monarch personally entertained the city notables of the metropolis.

It was the duty of the Caliph, as the spiritual head of Islam, to preside in person at the Friday service in the great cathedral mosque; and his progress through the streets was always made the occasion of an impressive ceremony. The procession was headed by the Guards, with banners flying; the princes of the Royal house followed, in the rear of whom came the Caliph himself, dressed in black, and mounted on a pure white horse; he wore a wide belt studded with jewels round his waist, a chain of gold about his neck, and a high-peaked hat, ornamented by a single diamond. The short address customary at the Friday service was invariably delivered by the more intellectual monarchs of the dynasty in person, and offered a suitable opportunity for the enunciation of political, as well as religious sentiments. Several of the less reputable monarchs scandalized the society of their time by not appearing at the Friday services in person, probably because they feared the ordeal of leading the prayers and of giving the address; and there is even an instance on record of an irreligious and scurrilous ruler who sent one of the favourite ladies of his harem to the cathedral to conduct the service, modestly disguised as a youthful doctor of law. The dress of Baghdad society was modelled upon that of the Caliph, but certain sections of the people were distinguished by minor differences of dress, as is indeed the custom in the Near and Middle East to this day. Professors and intellectuals, for example, wore a turban in place of the high-peaked hat, throwing over the turban a wide scarf which covered the shoulders, in imitation of the traditional fashion of the Prophet. This practice was imitated by the pupils of the various universities and colleges, and was the parent of the academical scarf or "hood" which is still a mark of student society in western Europe. Gentlemen of fashion affected loose pantaloons, under which were worn the wide drawers still characteristic of Near Eastern dress, the body being covered by a loose undershirt termed "kamis," a name which, in the French form "chemise," is used even to-day to designate an article of attire, though no longer of the masculine variety. Over the kamis were worn a jacket and vest, a decorated cloak, and, over all, an outer mantle, the traditional Arab "abba" which is still worn to-day. Stockings and socks were in use among the rich, as were also boots and shoes; sometimes two pair of the latter were worn simultaneously, the outer pair only being removed when entering a mosque or a private house.

Ladies of position affected elaborate head-dresses, and were plentifully adorned with jewelry. Charms against ill-fortune were much fancied, being worn usually hanging from the belt or girdle. Artificial aids to beauty, originally introduced by the Persians, were freely employed. The Arab ideal of beauty was a tall and slender type, fair in complexion, but with dark eyes and hair.

The restrictions regarding the free movement of ladies, which came into fashion at a later time with the revival of religious orthodoxy and the increase of the Turkish influence, were not generally enforced at this time, and, provided that the proprieties were observed, women were free to go about much as they pleased. Two female relations of Mansur fought in the Greek wars in performance of a religious vow, and under Harun there were cases of Arab girls serving as soldiers, and even as officers, with distinction. The mother of one of the early Abbassids, in order to save her son's valuable time, used to preside personally at the Court of Appeal, and sometimes gave audiences to foreign ambassadors. The famous Zobeida, the wife of Harun, is celebrated in tradition as a type of energetic and public-spirited womanhood. She personally supervised the reconstruction of the pilgrim road to Mecca, established hostels for the comfort of the pilgrims, and presented the holy city with a much-needed aqueduct. In private life she was a poetess of fair talent, and many of her letters to her husband were written in the form of poetical addresses.

Conversaziones and receptions at the houses of well-known society ladies were a constant feature of Baghdad life, and the universal love of the Arabs for the art of recitation made these occasions openings for youthful and promising poets and raconteurs. The general spread of education gave a great impetus to the trade in books, and the booksellers' shops in the bazaar became the general resort and gossiping place of the intellectual. Music was much cultivated, especially by women, and musical composition was successfully undertaken by them. One of the best-known tambourinists of the age was a woman ; and dancing was only relegated to an unfashionable position because of the rise of a class of professional dancing girls, whose behaviour and character were offensive to the quieter elements of society. Even the more staid professions were at this time adorned by women. One lady lecturer on history attained to great eminence in Baghdad, and there were cases of ladies being licensed to practise the law. The depressing world of modern Islam, in which the female sex is only to be seen in public heavily shrouded and veiled, had not yet come into being.

Although chairs were not unknown in Baghdad in the time of Harun, the chief article of furniture, as to-day, was the " diwan " or low couch. Meals were served on low tables by the side of the diwan. Three meals were customary ; a light breakfast, a dinner at noon, and supper after the " asr," or late afternoon prayers. It was usual to entertain visitors at the two latter only. Various kinds of sherbet, then as now, formed the usual beverage of the household, though the use of wine and intoxicating liquor was not unknown. Guests were entertained by conversation, by recitation and music, or by games, according to their inclinations. Cards and dice were the popular indoor games, but chess, possibly introduced from Persia by Harun, had later a very great vogue. The Arabs possessed a natural inclination towards outdoor sport, and this trait was encouraged and cultivated by Baghdad society. Both horse racing and hunting were extremely popular ; an invitation to the Caliph's hunting party was regarded as the highest mark of social success. Wrestling tournaments, always dear to the Arab heart, were held constantly in the great cities, and archery was practised. Fencing, polo (also a Persian innovation), falconry and spear-throwing were popular sports, and there are references in later authorities to a kind of racquets or tennis, possibly borrowed from the Greeks. Both Harun and Mamun were great polo players.

The business world was extremely active at this time. The consolidation of Arabia, Mesopotamia, Egypt, Syria, Persia and Khorassan into one realm gave manufacturers a large and accessible "home market"; and the excellent system of roads, and the high standard of the facilities for transport by river and canal, rendered the operations of business on a grand scale perfectly feasible. Direct trade intercourse was maintained between Baghdad and Spain, north and west Africa, Sicily, Italy, France, Constantinople and eastern Europe, the shores of the Caspian Sea, northern and southern India, and the distant marches of China. The fact that Harun entertained ambassadors during his reign from both Charlemagne of France and the Emperor of China shows the comparative ease with which long distances could be covered. The merchants of Baghdad, renowned even in the poverty of to-day for their business acumen, and surrounded as they were at this time by the principal manufacturing centres of the world, would not be slow to take advantage of the fact. The Arab trading colonies of the East African littoral, many of which still exist to-day, were due to the enterprise of this time; to Arab merchants is reputed the discovery of the Azores; and coins of the Abbassid Caliphs have been found as far afield as Russia and Sweden. The well-known story of Sinbad the Sailor symbolizes, in a mythical form, the energy and enterprise of the merchants of Baghdad and the seafaring folk of Basrah.

To the great intellectual and literary activity of the age we have already alluded. The picture of the last Mesopotamian civilization that we get is a notable one; a strong and well-supported ecclesiastical State, governed by an autocratic, but usually capable, monarch; a fruitful and well-cultivated countryside, studded, in the case of Mesopotamia, with little manufacturing towns, and held together by an admirable system of roads and canals; a large and brilliant capital, the admitted second city of civilization, and the resort of students and cultivated people from all parts of the world ; a society in which, though demoralization was common and increasing, the ideals of patriotism, of culture and of faith were still honoured ; and a daily life for the ordinary citizen, which was, on the whole, as broad and as full of opportunity as the limited resources of that age could afford. In the time of Mamun, " we see," in the words of a modern observer, " for the first time perhaps in the history of the world, a religious and despotic government allied to philosophy, preparing and partaking in its triumphs."

Mighty Babylon herself could hardly have rivalled Baghdad in the splendour of her streets and the variety of her tastes ; the last of the Mesopotamian civilizations was at least as brilliant as any of her predecessors. It is the remnant of this civilization which, still alive after the slow decay of centuries, the modern world of the West is at last attempting to comprehend ; and the problem of modern Mesopotamia will not be understood unless the Western observer can visualize the country as the seat of a civilization of its own, overturned but not destroyed by the disasters of the Middle Ages ; artificially sheltered for generations from the storms and buffets of the modern world ; though feeble, still actually alive, and still endowed with hopes, beliefs and ideals of its own. On how much the Western world is able or willing to comprehend and to help this alien but actual civilization, will depend the future of Mesopotamia, and the justification for the high mission claimed by the idealistic Imperialism of the twentieth century.

CHAPTER VII

THE COMING OF THE TURK

"At length the wolf-cub will become a wolf,
Even though it grew up amongst men."—SA'DI.

THE fall of the brilliant half-Arab, half-Persian civilization which had Baghdad for its capital did not come about abruptly, or through the operation of a single event; it was a gradual process, extending over several hundreds of years, and apparently liable at any time to be reversed. The great empire did not so much fall, as dissolve into its component parts. The central power gradually weakened, the independence and authority of the provinces gradually increased, until the time came when Baghdad was left as the spiritual capital and the principal commercial centre of a world of little warring states, each nominally acknowledging the sovereignty of the capital, but each acutely jealous of its independence, and fully aware of the fact that its loyalty was a mere matter of form. The last years of the empire offered but another example of the astonishing power of historical ideas. Long after all life had departed from the Caliphate, men looked towards Baghdad as the centre of their world, and to the Caliph as the most influential monarch upon earth. Tradition came to the rescue of the tottering throne, and enabled it to enjoy an influence far beyond its capacity to enforce or sustain.

It is for this reason that the history of the later Abbassids presents such a strange mixture. The Caliph as a man was frequently treated with indignity, and was nearly always notoriously at the mercy of whoever might happen to be the strongest among his nominal subjects; there were even at one time in Baghdad three ex-Caliphs, blinded and deprived of their position by their political enemies, and begging in the streets for their daily bread; and such humiliation and disgrace seems to have struck no one with either horror or remorse. On the other hand, the office of

Caliph assumed a spiritual significance which actually appeared to grow as time went on ; and, as with the Pope in Christendom, the strongest of the Sultans or princes who had set up as independent monarchs in various parts of the empire were never quite secure politically until they could count their letters of patent as having the personal authority of the Pontiff.

It followed that, although the direct administrative influence of Baghdad utterly disappeared, and although the city was not infrequently the scene of violent civil conflicts, the influence of her metropolitan position as the seat of the Caliph continued, as did the luxury and distinction of her life ; and up to the time of the Mongol invasion, which involved the Caliphate and the city in a common ruin, Baghdad probably suffered remarkably little from her many vicissitudes of fortune. The Caliphs did not always accept the decay of their fortunes with equanimity. There were several attempts made by individual rulers to restore the temporal power of their office ; and even a few years before the fatal arrival of the Mongols, it appeared that the monarch might again be able to get the better of his turbulent and quarrelsome lieges. But the trend of circumstances was against the restoration of Abbassid power ; and it would have required a man of very exceptional ability indeed to have stemmed the tide of dissolution in the empire, once firmly set in.

From the first the empire had suffered from two outstanding weaknesses ; its differences of race, and its differences of religious outlook. Under a theocracy of the type of Islam, which presupposes the civil law as a derivation of God's revealed will, the latter difference was probably the more fatal of the two. If the Shiah schism had never arisen, and if the religious genius of the people could have been retained within the fold of the State Church, instead of frittering itself away upon a variety of new and heretical doctrines, it would have been almost impossible to shake the solidity of Islam, for its undoubted power of binding alien races together is remarkable even to-day. On the other hand, the Shiah and other schisms can be easily traced to racial causes ; and the break-up of the Arab Empire seems but one more reminder of the fact that no

Imperial power, even when founded on a common faith, will continue to hold subject races in dependence for more than a limited period of time. The fate of Baghdad was the fate of Rome; she was conquered by her own subjects. Gradually the city became but a cosmopolitan gathering place, a city to inspire wonder and admiration, but in no sense a place to inspire patriotism; for the latter springs from the heart, and it requires some sort of racial background for its growth. The cosmopolitanism of which Baghdad boasted, and to which she owed, to some extent, her existence and position, proved in the long run her undoing; and when at last the foreign invader reached the gates, no one but her own townspeople chose to defend her.

Very soon after the death of Mamun (A.D. 833), the trouble over the differences of race began to assume acute proportions. From the first the Arabs had disliked the influence of the Persians at court, and of the Turks in the army; the growing influence of the latter began in turn to alarm the Persians; and at last the spirit of the haughty barbarians became so unbearable that the whole of Baghdad was roused against them. The nervousness of the old dominant races was indeed little to be wondered at. Year by year, thousands of young male slaves were brought from the borderland of Turkestan; those that were not required in the Guards, were enlisted in the regular army; and such as showed personal courage and military talent could always be sure both of attaining to their freedom and of professional preferment. Very soon not only the Arab troops but even the haughty Arab officers found themselves being replaced in the service and favour of the State by the hardy but stupid men of the eastern steppes; and more and more the Arabs chose to remain among their tribal units in the desert, there to join their aristocratic fellows who, driven from Court life earlier by the favour shown to the Persians, had made an earlier retirement. Thus were the Arabs wholly replaced in the dominant offices of their own empire by the men of the conquered races; and they could retire to muse among the tents upon the strange partiality of Fortune, who had given them an empire with one hand, only to take it away again with the other.

Meanwhile the streets and bazaars of the capital were given up to murmurings against the haughty Turkish soldiery, who galloped unrestrained through the streets, oblivious to the danger to civilian traffic ; and against whose dealings there was apparently no redress. At last an aged sheikh of Arab blood determined to accost the monarch personally, and to make one last appeal for justice and the rights of the people. The Caliph Motasim, the brother and successor of Mamun, was riding in Baghdad one day, accompanied by a small escort. The sheikh, who had long waited for his chance, approached the monarch, addressing him by his ordinary name, in the ancient Arab style. The escort would have set upon him, but the monarch, struck by something in the old man's demeanour, bade them stay their hands, and encouraged the sheikh to speak his mind. " A horde of foreigners," said the latter, " has been planted in our midst ; from their insolence and rapine there is no escape." The inference was unmistakable ; the shot went home ; and Motasim never again rode in the streets of Baghdad. A large country seat had been begun, but never completed, by Harun at Samarra, some eighty miles north of Baghdad on the Tigris, and near the site of the great battle between the Persians and the Romans in which the Emperor Julian had lost his life. Motasim now conceived the plan of completing the palace, and of designing a new capital in the vicinity ; and for over sixty years the government of the empire continued to be conducted from Samarra. The new capital was well designed and expensively adorned ; and the ruins which are visible to-day testify to the solidity and magnificence of the buildings. But the move was fatal to the dynasty. In this small and retired town, far from the traffic of the world and the realities of ordinary life, the monarchs fell more and more under the control of palace cliques and court intriguers ; and as the cliques or groups, whatever their form, were almost invariably Turkish in origin, the Caliph was now practically permanently under the sway of foreign captains. In Baghdad the strong current of public opinion had served to some extent to check the excesses of the aliens and the decay of the throne ; but, freed from the scrutiny of a great city, there was no longer any need to throw a cloak over reality, and the power of the Turkish captains began to be used openly and unmercifully.

It was obvious that such a state of things would not be tolerated for long in the provinces, however they might have to be borne in the nominal capital; and the anger of the provincials took the form of almost continual local rebellions, which ended invariably in the establishment of practically independent principalities. Meanwhile, various religious and social disturbances added to the confusion of the times; there was almost constant trouble with the Shiahs and the Alids; there was a negro revolt at Basra, the suppression of which strained the resources of the Government to the uttermost; and there was an inroad into the southern marches of a peculiar wandering Indian people, who managed to capture and hold a reach of the lower Tigris, and successfully levy a toll for some years on all shipping to and from Baghdad. This little people were eventually transported by the Government through Baghdad (where their passing caused much interest), and dumped over the frontier of the Roman Empire; from whence they wandered eventually all over Europe, under the familiar generic name of "ziganes," or gipsies. Perhaps the most serious of the revolutionary bodies with which the Government was called upon to deal was the organization of Persian communists under the leadership of the infamous Babak. Communism had been strong in Persia from very ancient times, and most of the sects having a communistic basis that have arisen in Islam from time to time can be traced to a Persian origin. Babak and his followers aimed, not merely at adapting Islam to their ideas, but at destroying it utterly, and the civil disturbances of the age appeared to offer considerable hope for their success. Under Harun they had been regarded as simply a local danger, but thirty years later they had managed to secure the control of large portions of Persia and Khorassan. They were, however, eventually defeated by an energetic Turkish general, engaged for the task by the Caliph; and Babak himself had to submit to the unpleasant fate of being paraded through the streets of Samarra on the back of an elephant, after which he was publicly crucified. The incident is interesting, in view of the question, much disputed nowadays, as to the possible political field for communistic propaganda among the people of Asia.

The only Caliph of note during the Samarra period was the orthodox and conservative Jafar al-Motawakkil (" He who puts his trust in the Lord "), the man perhaps more responsible than any other single man for the retrogression and eventual decay of Islam. Orthodoxy was reinstated as the official religion, and a persecution instituted against both heretics and the members of other faiths. Christians and Jews were compelled to wear a distinctive dress, and to nail a figure of Satan to the outside door of their houses ; and at the same time they were removed from all State employment, and forbidden to send their children to the State-supported Moslem schools.

Motawakkil's treatment of the Moslem sectaries was very nearly as severe. The Shiahs were forbidden to go on pilgrimage to the holy cities of Najaf and Kerbela, and the mausoleum of Hosein at the latter place was levelled to the ground, and the site ploughed up. The Caliph's harshness led to several indecisive rebellions, the Shiahs at one time having to be besieged in Kufa, and the combined forces of Syrian Christians and Jews in Homs. The rebellions were suppressed with great severity ; in Homs, all the Christians were banished, and all churches and synagogues destroyed. Nevertheless Motawakkil possessed a certain quality of political perspicacity, and he made genuine efforts during his reign to curb the power of the Turks. New Arab battalions were created as an offset to the Turkish troops, and efforts were made to interest the Arab families in the new capital, and in the affairs of State. But the Turks by this time held the reins of power in their own hands, and the contest between them and the growing feebleness of the Crown was an unequal one. It was concluded, so far as Motawakkil was concerned, by his assassination. He had conceived an aversion to the Crown Prince, who was in league with a powerful Turkish general ; and he arranged a plan with his confidential companion by which the Crown Prince and the Turk should be assassinated in company. But the plot leaked out ; the heir to the throne was informed ; and without hesitation he prepared the murder of his father, together with that of his fellow plotter. It was then conveniently announced to the world that Motawakkil had been assassinated by his bosom companion, who had afterwards fallen under the just wrath of his retainers. Motawakkil's orthodoxy was combined with a moral character of the lowest type, and he has been described by a Moslem writer as " the Nero of the Arabs." His drunkenness and debauchery finally became a public scandal ; and even at the last he was said to have been unable, on account of intoxication, to resist his murderers. His moral delinquencies, however, affected the history of his realm far less than his obstinacy of character. He had not the wit to see that, by re-establishing orthodoxy of the most rigid type, he was permanently alienating the more intelligent of his subjects, and handing religious development over to the tender mercies of ecclesiastical pedants. In spite of the efforts of various reformers, the mantle of rigid orthodoxy, securely re-established by Motawakkil, descended unchanged from his day to the Turkish Sultan of our own.

The power of the Caliphate decayed very rapidly after Motawakkil's death, in spite of the efforts of several able and sincere rulers to stem the tide. The Turkish chieftains themselves soon became the prey of various rivalries and factions, and the unfortunate head of the State was moved about from place to place at the bidding of military or political convenience. Sometimes rival Caliphs were set up by rival Turkish captains ; and furious civil war, in which the city of Baghdad was inevitably involved, was the invariable result. In the disorganization that followed, the independence of the provinces became more and more accepted. Baghdad, though still the nominal capital, had to watch the growth of independent administrations almost at her very gates. For many years Mosul and Hillah remained the seats of powerful principalities, which cut off all direct communication between Baghdad and the west ; and Basrah and the south remained at the mercy of the Carmathians and Fatimides, a combination of sects which led to the rise of the independent Fatimide Caliphate in north Africa and Egypt. Until the last days of the empire the Carmathians remained a menace to society.

THE COMING OF THE TURK

Inheritors of that free-thinking mysticism which has always found a following among the Persian Shiah, they became infamous at this time through the activities of a sub-sect, the celebrated Assassins. The latter, so-called from their belief in the efficacy of "hashish," the Arabic term for hemp, formed a secret society on the Masonic model, and with Carmathian doctrines. Their head-quarters were for many years in an inaccessible and mountainous part of Persia, whence their chieftain gained the popular title of "the Old Man of the Mountain." The great feature of their practice was their readiness to procure the secret death of their adversaries; and so successful were they in this art, that their name has survived, in a similar connection, to the present day. The Assassins were not finally dispersed for some centuries, and there are still a few Carmathian bodies in Persia and India to this day.

The last days of the Caliphate witnessed a turn in the tide and a revival in the central power, not in the persons of the monarchs themselves, but in those of two remarkable families who served them. After a period of disastrous civil war, Baghdad was captured in December, A.D. 954, by a member of the Persian Buyid family, who forthwith took the title of Sultan, reserving to himself and his descendants all the executive power of the Caliphate, and merely allowing the Caliph a salary and a residence in the capital. The Buyids built up a considerable empire, and for a time Baghdad was once more the executive capital of a territory stretching from the Caspian Sea to the Syrian desert. But the Buyid family fell a prey to internal strife, and, almost exactly a hundred years after they had first entered Baghdad, they were driven out by the leader of the Seljuk Turks, the celebrated Tughril Bey. Once more the authority of the Caliphate was re-established by the energy of their Sultans, and Syria, Arabia and west Africa, as well as the whole of the eastern provinces of the old empire, acknowledged the sway of Baghdad. But the Seljuks, like their predecessors in power, soon fell into decline, though they produced several sultans of international fame, notably Malik Shah, at whose Court rose to prominence the celebrated Persian astronomer and poet, Omar Khayyam. But in A.D. 1097, the world of Islam was invaded by an altogether new enemy, from a quarter which, for many centuries, its inhabitants had been accustomed to despise.

Since the decline of the Roman power, no military effort of the first magnitude had been initiated in Europe. The collapse of the Roman Empire, and the dissensions of the various barbarian conquerors, had left the western continent in a state of utter exhaustion ; and the sovereigns of western Asia could at least remain assured that no danger was to be feared from the rude and feeble inhabitants of France, Germany or Great Britain. But in the centuries that intervened, new nations had been growing into manhood on the ruins of the Roman provinces ; and a spark of religious fanaticism proved sufficient to kindle, suddenly and unexpectedly, the united energies of the young peoples. Ever since the capture of Jerusalem by the troops of the Caliph Omar, the holy city, sacred alike to Christian, Moslem and Jew, had rested in the possession of the Moslems ; and Constantinople, for many years the only Christian power of the first rank, had never been able, with the utmost endeavour, to recapture it for the Cross. By a strange fate, the youthful energies of the western nations were now to become attracted to the same ambition ; and western Asia, for close upon three centuries, had to endure the burden and horror of the Crusades.

The Crusades were a remarkable Christian copy of the fanatical wars by which the creed of Islam had successfully been propagated by the original Arab invaders. Every effort was made to stir the greed, the sensuality and the fanatical zeal of the participants. The Crusader, like the Arab invader, was a privileged soldier, entitled by enlistment to many legal advantages, to ownership of anything that he could loot or steal, and, if he met death on the field of battle, to eternal life in Paradise. The Moslems, after five hundred years, were to receive a taste of the misery that had been created by themselves in the old Christian dominions of Heraclius.

The Crusades, though they failed in their immediate object, had one decisive effect. They weakened beyond repair both the empire of Constantinople and the Caliphate of Baghdad ; and thus directly paved the way for the more solid victories of yet another race of central Asian conquerors. The one permanent result of the Christian crusades was the establishment of the Moslem Turks in possession of the dominions both of Constantinople and of Baghdad.

Though they did not actually touch Mesopotamia, the holy wars are important in Mesopotamian history for yet another reason. They mark the first attempt of modern Europe to interfere in the internal affairs of western Asia. Hitherto, for some centuries, the tide of offensive power had been flowing from Asia into Europe, sometimes even threatening to inundate it altogether. The Crusades mark the turn of the tide. Europe has come to life again. Henceforth the tide is to flow from Europe into Asia, until it culminates in the conflagration of 1914, and the total collapse of Islamic civilization.

The immediate results of the holy wars were naturally the first discernible. The effort required to ward off the attacks of the European invaders utterly crippled the Islamic world, and emphasized the divisions into which that world was decaying. Only successful adventurers, such as the famous Saladin in Egypt, were able to ride the flood; and the way was paved for the arrival of a power which was already beginning to make itself felt in the heart of the Asian continent.

The origin of the Mongol power is still obscure; but by A.D. 1220, this exceptionally warlike and savage midAsian people had succeeded, under the able rule of their great chief, Jenghis Khan, in conquering an empire which stretched from the borders of Manchuria to the southern marches of European Russia, and which threatened to engulf the whole of Asia. The Caliph at that time, Nasir by name, was a clever and ambitious man, and he had been successful, by taking advantage of the general confusion of the times, in re-establishing the control of the throne over all the old central provinces. Sure of his position in Mesopotamia, he began to turn his attention to Persia; but he found there, in a powerful native principality, an obstacle which he had not the strength to tackle singlehanded. In an evil moment, he besought the assistance of the barbarian and heathen Mongols; and thus set the stage for the final extinction of his house and throne.

The Mongols obeyed the summons with alacrity; and already at the end of Nasir's reign were becoming too formidable on his own frontier for him to wish to encourage them further. But the mischief was done. The Mongol hordes, tempted by the vast wealth and the comparative helplessness of the Persian and Mesopotamian plain, determined upon a general invasion; and, though efforts were made to ward off the attack, the dawn of the year 1258 found Hulagu, the grandson of Jenghiz Khan, at the gates of Baghdad.

The reigning Caliph, who rejoiced in the singularly inappropriate name of Al-Mostasim b'Illah ("He who clings for protection to the Lord"), was an irresolute and avaricious dotard, who was totally unable to deal with the grave dangers of the time. Baghdad was the scene of continual disorder; the various schools of the orthodox faith quarrelled and argued in the streets; the Shiahs fought with the Sunnis, and both with the Christians and Jews; the wealthy merchants and the working classes went in hatred of each other; and the rabble of the great city, taking advantage of the general confusion, were banded together against everyone. No concerted effort was made to resist the attacks of the barbarian chief. The Caliph, careless of his dignity, and thinking only of his considerable private fortune, offered to surrender on disgraceful terms; at Hulagu's demand, every man capable of bearing arms was handed over to him; and the city, together with the women and children, was given over to the plunder of the barbarian hordes. The Mongol, with grim humour, refused to allow the unhappy ruler to reap the benefit of his pusillanimity; and the Caliph, having confessed under torture the whereabouts of his considerable private treasure, was ignominiously put to death.

The inhuman Hulagu gave up the captured city for four days to the murderous pleasure of his troops. All the appalling scenes of ancient barbarian conquest were re-enacted upon a mediæval stage. Large numbers of people were put to the sword, merely to serve the pleasure of their Mongol masters; and the waters of the Tigris ran red with blood for days. The bazaars, the mosques, the colleges, the palaces of the mighty city of the Abbassids

THE COMING OF THE TURK

were committed to the flames; the artistic accumulations of five hundred years of brilliant effort were destroyed in a few hours. Baghdad, like modern Petrograd, descended in a few days from the position of a great metropolis to that of a city of the dead. The fairy town of the Arabian Nights disappeared for ever before the fierce breath of the dreaded scourge of Asia.

But the fall of Baghdad was only typical of a far greater disaster which now befell Mesopotamia, and put an abrupt end to an economic prosperity of several thousand years. The Mongols, satiated with the pleasures of the fallen capital, and seeking new worlds to conquer and destroy, pressed on westward; and as they went, they destroyed the canal system on which the prosperity of Mesopotamia had, from time immemorial, been built up. The sun beat down as fiercely and as fruitfully as ever upon the plains by the banks of the two rivers; but the water, which had fertilized the hungry soil into life, came no more. Henceforth one of the most fertile countries in the world was reduced to the condition, except on the immediate banks of the rivers, of a howling wilderness. From this unparallelled disaster Baghdad and Mesopotamia never recovered, nor were they destined to be free from other invasions, as fierce if not as destructive as the first. The vast empire of Jenghiz Khan and of Hulagu broke up as suddenly as it had come into being; but Baghdad remained in the possession of the descendants of Hulagu for a hundred and fifty years, during which period it was visited by the celebrated Italian traveller, Marco Polo. Islam was now making great progress among the Mongols, and the Ilkhans, as the descendants of Hulagu were called, were Moslems and men of considerable cultivation. Before the termination of the fourteenth century, the government of the Ilkhans had been swept away by another Mongol invasion under Timur (the Tamerlane of European song). Timur was very far from the old type of merely destructive Mongol savage, and he laboured hard to re-organize and re-settle the vast empire which he conquered; but the general confusion of the times was against him, and Baghdad soon passed into the hands of a local sultan, who was expelled in A.D. 1417, by Kara Yusuf of the "Black Sheep" Mongols.

Fifty years later it was again besieged and captured by a foreign invader; on this occasion Uzun Hassan of the "White Sheep" Mongols.

Meanwhile the condition of the city and country went from bad to worse. The total collapse of civilized conditions in the hinterland of Persia and Khorassan had ruined the trade of Baghdad; and the countryside, in its helpless and decayed state, was more and more becoming the prey of the great Arab tribes, who began to encroach from the Syrian desert, and convert what had lately been cultivated land into pasture for their sheep. The control of these great wandering bands was quite beyond the primitive organization of the various little Mongol states; and as time went on the tribes grew bolder and more enterprising, and there arose settlements of tribes and sub-tribes all over the country between the two rivers, and even east of the Tigris. From this period dates the rise of the influence of the great Mesopotamian tribal confederations, especially those of the Shammar in the north and the Muntafiq in the south, an influence which still remains powerful to this day.

But gradually out of the chaos of conditions in the Near and Middle East there arose two powerful States which were destined to continue into modern times. Persia had, ever since the collapse of the Abbassids, been governed by a number of local princes or khans, who were submerged temporarily in each great Mongol invasion, but who emerged again when the hordes had passed on. As time went on the power of Persia began to become more centralized, and the nation as a whole began to make its influence felt; and the movement reached its culmination at the beginning of the sixteenth century in the person of Ismail Shah, the first of the dynasty of the Safawids, or Sufis, a Shiah sect of ultra-mystical proclivities. In A.D. 1503, Ismail Shah began to take advantage of the weakness of his neighbours to increase the influence of the new Persian realm. He had already been successful in conquering a large part of Turkestan and Afghanistan; and the presence of the holy cities of the Shiah world would naturally incline his attention towards Mesopotamia. He invaded the country, meeting with but slight opposition, abolished the last Mongol government, and entered Baghdad

A RUINED TOWER AT SAMARRA

BABYLON TO-DAY

in triumph. For twenty-five years Mesopotamia remained a Persian possession. Meanwhile on the northern border another new Moslem power had arisen on the ruins of the Caliphate and the eastern Roman Empire. In A.D. 1268, a few years after the destruction of Baghdad by Hulagu, an inconspicuous band of four hundred Turkish horsemen, of a rude and obscure tribe, had been allowed by a local chieftain to settle near Angora in Asia Minor. The local chieftain passed away, but his clients flourished surprisingly, and in less than two hundred years their descendants had accomplished the astonishing feat of conquering the whole of Asia Minor. In 1295 the name of their chief Osman, or Othman was substituted for that of the Seljuk sultan of Asia Minor in the weekly service, an acknowledgment that the followers of Othman, or Ottomans, were now the leading power in this portion of the Moslem world.

Meanwhile, the power of Constantinople was rapidly on the decline; every kind of vice, political and moral, disgraced the so-called capital of Christianity; and the Christian nations in the west, then as now, were too preoccupied with their own rivalries to come to the rescue of their Christian brethren farther east. Surrounded by enemies, and aided only by degenerate subjects, the Emperor of Constantinople led a vain effort to check the rising power of the Ottomans; but when the latter had succeeded in capturing the European possessions of the Empire, and thus in surrounding the Imperial city on every side, the prospect of salvation appeared hopeless. Nevertheless, the contemporary Constantine and his few faithful followers proved themselves not unworthy of their Roman name and of the ancient Imperial tradition; a final desperate stand was made in the ramparts of the beleaguered city; and when the conquering Sultan Muhammad II. entered Constantinople, the body of the last of the Cæsars could be seen among the fallen.

The Ottoman Turks, having thus succeeded to the civilization of Rome, were soon to combine with it the tradition of the Prophet Muhammad. After the conquest of Baghdad by Hulagu and his assassination of the last of the Abbassid Caliphs, a younger scion of the house had escaped to Cairo, where, under the care of the local Sultan, he had been solemnly acclaimed as Caliph of the Moslem world. This purely spiritual position his descendants continued to hold until the capture of Cairo, and with it the Caliph, by the Ottoman Sultan Selim in A.D. 1517. The Caliph had no heir, and the last of the Abbassids was easily persuaded to resign his office to the triumphant Turkish conqueror. The sacred banner and the relics of the Prophet were carefully removed to Constantinople; and the sultans of Turkey have ever since been accepted as the Caliphs of the faithful. Thus, by a strange turn of fortune, the descendants of an insignificant tribe of Turkish horsemen inherited two civilizations that had been enemies and rivals for seven centuries.

It was inevitable that the Turkish ruler, having obtained the title and dignity of Caliph, should feel his imagination drawn to the city of his Abbassid predecessors. After the death of Ismail Shah, the Persian hold on Mesopotamia had waned; and a period of anarchy set in, during which the country was practically divided between the larger local tribal groups. In 1528 Baghdad fell to a Kurdish tribe, but was almost immediately afterwards recaptured by the Persians; and six years later a Turkish army appeared before the city, headed by the son of Selim, the famous Suleiman the Magnificent. The Persians, torn by internal dissension, were in no position to offer an adequate resistance to the finest troops of the age; and in 1534 the city was captured by Suleiman, and the boundaries of Mesopotamia and Persia became very much what they are to-day.

Suleiman subdued the whole country and showed the strength of his arms on the Persian Gulf; and for the first time since the days of Trajan the palm-girt shores of the Indian Ocean were under the same government as the cool uplands of the Bosphorus.

Thus Mesopotamia entered upon another phase of her long history. The Mongol invasions, terrible and destructive as they were, proved to be but an interlude; the flood passed away as quickly as it rose. The fall of the Arabs led directly to the rise of the Turks; and the gradual fall of the Turks, the inheritors of all the Near Eastern empires of the past, paved the way once more for the arrival of the European.

CHAPTER VIII

THE COMING OF THE ENGLISH

" He hath subjected the sea to you that ye may eat of its fresh fish and take forth from it ornaments to wear, and thou seest the ships ploughing its billows, and that ye may go in quest of His bounties."—THE KORAN (xvi. 14).

THE three and a half centuries which divide the capture of Baghdad by Suleiman the Magnificent in 1532 and the arrival of the celebrated vali Midhat Pasha in 1870 mark, for Mesopotamia as for the rest of the world, the great period of transition from mediæval life and conditions to those of modern times. In 1532 the Turkish Empire was at the height of its power, and the permanent existence of a powerful Moslem state in the Near East, carrying on the tradition and the civilization of both ancient Constantinople and ancient Baghdad, might have been regarded by the political observer as a reasonable probability. But in 1870, at the dawn of the modern age in Mesopotamia, the picture has completely changed. Near Eastern civilization, as such, has crumbled hopelessly to pieces, and the ancient lands which once led the world have now degenerated into mere bones of contention between the " Great Powers " of Europe. The three and a half centuries which brought Europe all her modern strength, wealth and power, held nothing for the Near and Middle East but ever increasing feebleness and decay.

The period is dominated, so far as Mesopotamia is concerned, by three great movements, the eventual direction of all of which still remains undetermined. The first of these movements is the decline of the Turkish power, gradual at first, but rapidly increasing in momentum with the passing of time; the second is the reappearance of that European influence which had been previously driven out by the invading Arabs in their victories against the Roman Emperor Heraclius, and which the Crusades had tried in vain to revive; and the third is the unexpected appearance in the field of a reborn Arab nationalism, which seeks to claim for the Arab race something of its ancient position and eminence. Upon a combination of these three forces has been raised the precarious structure of modern Iraq.

The decay of the Turkish power became apparent in Mesopotamia at an earlier date than in any other province of the cosmopolitan and far-flung dominion that had been built up by the descendants of the first tiny band of wandering Ottomans. As early as 1623 A.D., Baghdad had to be surrendered to the Persians, who, under the energetic control of Shah Abbas the Great, were undergoing one of their periods of intermittent national revival. The city was retaken by the Turks, under circumstances of the utmost barbarity, fifteeen years later, but the control of the Ottoman Government was not very certain for many years, and early in the eighteenth century an enterprising local Turk, Ahman Pasha, was able to defy Stamboul and to set up for himself as an independent ruler, with Baghdad as his capital. So strong, indeed, was his position, that, when attacked by heavy Persian forces under Nadir Shah (afterwards famous for his victorious campaigns in northern India), he was only forced to leave Baghdad for a few months and in a short time he was in full control again of central Mesopotamia. But his position was a very local one. The growing power of the Muntafiq tribes in the south practically cut him off from Basrah and the sea; and the equally formidable Shammar, who had not long before migrated from their original home in Arabia, barred him on the north from communication with Syria or Asia Minor. The end of the eighteenth century saw a slight recrudescence of the power of the central Turkish Government, which, by playing off the various local chiefs one against the other, managed to reoccupy Baghdad and secure some sort of authority over the whole country. This authority, however, remained very largely nominal throughout the whole of the period that we are now considering.

The return to Mesopotamia of the European influence, at first so slight as to be hardly noticeable, increased continually throughout this time, until to-day it has become the most important single force bearing upon the future of the country. The increase of this influence was due to the

THE COMING OF THE ENGLISH 105

paramount position which Europe, for the first time in history, was able to assume. There had been periods before, such as during the supremacy of Alexander, and, later, of Rome, in which it appeared for a time that Europe would succeed in obtaining control of all the civilized world; but in practice she had never succeeded, in the last event, in achieving such a dominant position. There had always been a power in the Near or Middle East, Parthian, Persian, Arab or Turkish, strong enough to ward off the violence of the European attack, and to divert the ambitions of that restless continent into some easier direction. But with the decay of the Turkish power, Near Eastern civilization collapsed, apparently irrevocably; and a portion of the earth which had inherited a system of living and a family of ideas dating back to the dawn of history, became a mere suburb of northern Europe. Such a complete collapse is unparalleled in history.

Direct influence from Europe may be said to have been first felt, during the period we are considering, in A.D. 1498, when the great Portuguese navigator, Vasco da Gama, doubled the Cape of Good Hope, and demonstrated the possibility of trading direct with India. As the Portuguese power grew in the East, more and more of the Indo-European trade tended to use the new route, and Mesopotamia's age-long position as one of the trade routes to the Far East was seriously challenged. The commencement of the decline of Mosul as a business centre, a decline which was finally completed nearly four centuries later by the opening of the Suez Canal, dates from this time. From their great Indian capital of Goa, the Portuguese colonized the port of Hormuz at the entrance to the Persian Gulf, and completely overturned the mercantile position of the Arabs, who had enjoyed a practical monopoly of sea-borne commerce in the Indian Ocean for many centuries. For a hundred years the Portuguese practically undertook the whole of the carrying trade between India and Europe, and much of the overseas trade of Persia, which had in the past used the route via Mesopotamia and Syria, was diverted to Hormuz. The latter city was ruled nominally by an Arab prince, but the Portuguese were responsible for the administration, and they retained control of the customs.

About 1600, however, the waters of the Indian Ocean began to be invaded by another European intruder. Portugal had come under the political control of Spain, and the Spanish king, in an ill-advised moment, had forbidden the merchants of the Netherlands the use of Portuguese ports or ships. The people of the Netherlands, who already possessed a very considerable Eastern trade, worked via Lisbon, were compelled to attempt the opening up of direct communication with the East in their own ships. A successful initial voyage from Amsterdam to Java resulted in an outburst of Dutch commercial adventure, and in a few years there were scores of Dutch boats fighting their way out to India and the Spice Islands, and returning home laden with treasure. But the commercial results were not always satisfactory to the shrewd merchants of the homeland, who realized that the business, to be made profitable, must be organized on a more ambitious scale; and the result was the appearance in the field of the famous Dutch East India Company, with its capital in Java, and its ramifications all over the Orient. The Portuguese trade disappeared rapidly in the face of this energetic competition; and a rival station to Hormuz was established at Bander Abbasi, a new port which had been created on the Persian Gulf by the fostering care of Shah Abbas.

But hardly had the Dutch established themselves than a new and far more formidable competitor appeared upon the scene. In 1579 the first Englishman reached India. From Goa he wrote home such glowing accounts of the country and the trade that others of his island countrymen were tempted to seek their fortune in the East. In 1583 four English merchant adventurers came overland through Mesopotamia, probably the first men of British blood to set eyes upon the land of the rivers. On arrival at Hormuz they were promptly imprisoned by the Portuguese; but eventually they were successful in obtaining their release, and were permitted to go on their way to India. One settled in Goa, and another entered the service of the Great Mogul, and thus became the first Englishman to serve as an Indian public servant. Meanwhile the attention of Queen Elizabeth had been drawn to the desirability of trading direct with the East Indies, and in 1600 the

THE COMING OF THE ENGLISH 107

English East India Company was formed, thus actually anticipating the Dutch creation by two years. The first enemy to be attacked was the Portuguese, whose jealousy the English merchants found against them at every step; but the issue was decided, so far as Persia and Mesopotamia were concerned, in the early months of 1622, when the English and the Persians in co-operation attacked, and finally captured, Hormuz. In this action, incidentally, fell Baffin, one of the greatest of early English navigators. England was technically at peace with Spain (which then controlled Portugal) at the time, and great indignation was aroused by the incident in Spanish court circles; more especially as the heir to the English throne was then seeking the hand of a Spanish princess in marriage. But the directors of the East India Company were shrewd men of the world, quite capable of handling so delicate a situation. The powerful Duke of Buckingham received a gift of £10,000, as part of the spoils of war; and there is strong reason to believe that King James secretly received an equal sum. The incident was smoothed over at the Court of Spain, and nothing more was heard of it.

This event marked the final ruin of Hormuz as a great trading depôt; henceforth both the Dutch and the English conducted their business with Persia and lower Mesopotamia through Bander Abbasi; and after 1651, when the Portuguese were driven away from the opposite coast of Oman by the rising power of a local Arab state, their ships were seen no more in the Gulf.

But in the men of the Netherlands, men equal to them both in determination and in knowledge of the sea, the English found very much sterner competitors; and the influence of the Dutch East India Company was not finally extinguished until the invasion of the mother country by the armies of revolutionary France, nearly two hundred years later. All through the seventeenth century the Dutch remained the unquestioned premier sea power of the world, and, alike in the East and West, the English found themselves everywhere sorely harassed. The summit of prosperity for the Dutch East India Company was reached in 1670, when it is said to have possessed a hundred and fifty trading ships, forty ships of war, and nearly ten thousand soldiers, and to have paid a dividend of forty per cent. Previous to that time the Company had succeeded in driving the English entirely out of the Malay Archipelago, and in confining English trade practically to the continent of India and the Persian Gulf. Throughout the period of its greatness the Company continued to maintain a factory and a trade commissioner at Bander Abbasi.

But the star of the English was in the ascendant, and by the middle of the eighteenth century Dutch influence on Mesopotamia had been completely eclipsed by that of their island rival. In 1766 the last Dutch settlement on the island of Kharak was captured by the Arabs, and ships from the Netherlands practically disappeared from the Gulf. In the meanwhile the English were steadily consolidating their power, not only commercially but politically. As early as 1622, after the capture of Hormuz from the Portuguese, they had concluded a defensive agreement with Shah Abbas, by which the East India Company agreed to maintain two men-of-war constantly in the Gulf for the protection of shipping. This agreement marks the first attempt of the English to obtain a political status in the Gulf, and forms the beginning of that English political influence over both Persia and Mesopotamia, the end of which has not yet been reached. The year 1622 may therefore be legitimately termed the birth year of the British Mesopotamian connection. But if the English ever entertained the hope that by the elimination of the Portuguese and Dutch they were to be left unchallenged masters of the field, they were soon to be undeceived. As the Dutch power waned, an even greater menace to English supremacy arose from the sudden enterprise of a very old enemy, the French. For centuries within the narrow confines of western Europe the English and the French had fought for superiority. There had been times when the English appeared to have all the cards in their hands, and when the French seemed on the border of a hopeless and permanent collapse; but the net result of six hundred-odd years of fighting and rivalry had been French victory all along the line; and in the seventeenth century the English, who had at one time conquered half

THE COMING OF THE ENGLISH 109

northern France, did not possess a single acre of French land. The ancient battle was now to be transferred to a wider sphere. Both the French and the English had entered the field of colonial adventure at a later time than the Spanish, the Portuguese or the Dutch; but, once there, they showed far more ability and resource than their earlier competitors, and from A.D. 1700 onwards, for more than a hundred and fifty years, the French and the English remained the only two European powers that counted on the distant seas. All over the known world, in north and central America, in India, along the African coast, in the near Mediterranean or the far distant China Sea, these two ancient enemies swept the other maritime powers before them; and when the Portuguese and Dutch had been finally driven from the field, they were left once more alone and face to face. From that day to this the ancient rivalry, transferred from Europe to a wider sphere, has continued unabated; and, by a strange coincidence, the two rivals find themselves in our own time in precisely the same position as two centuries ago. The World War has eliminated Russian and German competition, just as the earlier wars eliminated Portuguese and Dutch; and once again the situation in the Near and Middle East is dominated by the always existent, but seldom acknowledged, rivalry between the English and the French. It would appear that not even yet has the time arrived for the settlement or the dissolution of this age-long feud. But if the French were successful in driving the English out of continental Europe, the English came within an ace of being equally successful in driving the French out of their newly acquired colonial interests. In spite of the terrible disaster of the American revolution, a disaster which might easily have crippled a less resolute people for ever, the English steadily increased their political and commercial influence throughout the eighteenth century; and before the end of the period, they had successfully crushed the French power in India, and had seriously crippled it throughout the East. With regard more particularly to the Persian Gulf and Mesopotamia, French enterprise dates from the formation, in 1664, of the French East India Company, and the creation of a French factory at

Bander Abbasi. From this port direct trade relations were established with Basrah. French missionaries had already, some thirty years previously, obtained a footing at the latter place; and thus the foundations were laid of that French cultural influence which has had such a strong effect upon the building up of modern Mesopotamia.

On the purely political side, however, the English in the Persian Gulf and the adjacent countries were soon successful in obtaining a predominant position, and by the end of the eighteenth century their ascendancy had become unquestioned. Several things combined to give them this position. The development of their sea power in the Gulf and the Indian Ocean had brought them in very early days into direct touch with the Arabs, who retained the profitable coastal trade of that area in their hands. The Arabs are natural colonists, and Zanzibar and the east coast of Africa have always contained as many Arab merchants as Mesopotamia and Arabia themselves. From the day that the English began to take a prominent part in the traffic of these waters, they were forced, not only to come in contact with the Arabs, but to become themselves involved to some extent in the local politics of the various Arab countries fronting the Persian Gulf. From the capture of Hormuz to the present day, almost every decade has seen some increase of English interference in the affairs of these countries, some situation arising in which the English have been compelled, often against their own inclinations, to take decisive action either for or against some local potentate. It was the English, for example, who were responsible for putting an end to the lurid activities of the infamous Jawasimi pirates, the terror alike of their own countrymen and of the foreign trader; it was English influence that secured the restraint and practical disappearance of the slave trade; and to the support of the English the little independent Arab monarchs along the coast owe their safety against the imperialistic designs of the states of the interior, or of Turkey.

In addition to this growing tendency to interference in local political controversies, another and immediate cause of the growth of the British Mesopotamian connection was the increasing importance to England of quick and direct communication with India. The long struggle between England and France which followed the French Revolution of 1791, and more particularly the dramatic campaigns of Napoleon in Egypt and Palestine, gave the English serious cause for alarm with regard to their communications with their great Eastern dependency, and led them to explore the possibility of obtaining a nearer and more accessible approach than either the Cape or the Egyptian routes could offer. In 1839 the English were able to consolidate their position on the latter route by the occupation of Aden; but there were obvious advantages in the more direct way through Syria and the valley of the Euphrates, and in the Napoleonic wars the mails to India were frequently despatched by this route. In 1835, or four years before the occupation of Aden, an Englishman, Colonel F. R. Chesney, acting under instructions from his Government, successfully carried out the experiment of transporting a steamer overland from the Mediterranean, reassembling it on the Euphrates, and performing the journey down the latter river to the Persian Gulf. Six years later the East India Company announced their intention of maintaining a fleet of steamers on the Euphrates, for the purpose of fostering trade by this route; but experience soon proved the unsuitability of the river for navigation, partly owing to the very large number of artificial obstructions caused by the ruins of the dams of former days. In 1870 Midhat Pasha attempted to solve this difficulty by destroying many of the dams, and for awhile, under his energetic rule, regular steamship services were maintained by the Turkish authorities; but meanwhile the proved success of the new invention of the railway as a means of transporting passengers and goods over long distances had diverted men's minds into quite a different direction. Thus it will be seen that the connection of the English with Mesopotamia was an inevitable corollary of their powerful position in India and the Persian Gulf. The power responsible for the surveying, lighting, sanitation and policing of the Gulf—duties which were assumed by the English at the close of the eighteenth century—could not escape entering into political relations with Mesopotamia, whose chief port of entry and egress lies on the Gulf. Thus the connection of Mesopotamia with Britain is not, contrary to the popular view in England, a thing of yesterday; it is three hundred years old. The capture of Hormuz in 1622, and the consequent political agreement with the Persian Government of the time, led inevitably to the invasion of 1914, and thus to the present situation to-day. It is only by keeping this important fact in mind that any reasonable and just consideration of the present Mesopotamian problem can be obtained.

The first official recognition by the English of the political value of the Mesopotamian connection came in 1798, when the East India Company appointed a permanent Resident in Baghdad, with a view to counteracting the growing influence of the French. Thirty-six years afterwards the post was officially recognized by the British Government, and the Resident vested with consular powers. In the same year (1834), special privileges for navigation on the rivers were granted to an English firm, and the monopoly of these rights, except as regards local and Turkish firms, was officially confirmed by the Turkish Government some thirty years later. Until 1881 the British Resident, with the exception of the French agent, continued to be the sole official representative of an European Power in Baghdad. The large and extensive British Residency became the social centre of the European colonies; the Resident maintained his own guard of British Indian troops, and his own gunboat, flying the British flag, on the river; English post offices were opened in Basrah and Baghdad, and an English camel post connected Mesopotamia with the Mediterranean. The position of privilege of the English in Mesopotamia was unique, even in the territories of the decadent Ottoman Empire; and it is small wonder that the local inhabitants came to believe that, in the event of a final break-up of the Turkish dominions, Mesopotamia would automatically become a portion of the British Empire.

But, taking a broader view of the situation, the influence of the English was perhaps not quite so strong as their powerful political position would assume. Their old rivals the French, though beaten politically, were extremely active culturally; and though there was never any question of Mesopotamia becoming so permeated with French influence as the neighbouring land of Syria, still it became obvious in the nineteenth century that French interest in Mesopotamia was by no means dead. It would appear to be a truism in colonial circles, that what the French lose in direct political control, they not infrequently regain by the spread of their language, culture and point of view; and the impartial observer in Mesopotamia will be compelled to admit that such refinement and local culture as exists to-day owes far more to French than to English inspiration. The influence of the French missionaries, resident in the country for over three hundred years, has by no means been confined to the spiritual sphere; and what little of the spirit of civilization has been kept alive in the land of the rivers owes its existence to the efforts of these admirable people. It would be strange indeed if there were to be no material reward for the self-sacrificing labours of these gallant sons and daughters of France, during a period of three hundred years; and it is no mere chance that, until the invasion of 1914, French, and not English, was the accepted European tongue of Mesopotamia. Of late years the French cultural influence has been offset to some extent by the renewed effort of the English language and manner of thought to establish themselves in the Near and Middle East; but this effort has been directed, not by the English themselves, but by their co-heirs in the English tradition, the Americans. Indeed it would appear that as colonists the English, brave and able in war, strong in the political and commercial spheres, are yet weak in their general civilizing influence. Their generals and proconsuls, to whom in practice they entirely trust the direction of their colonial policy, are usually men of narrow intellect, highly trained professionally, but badly educated generally, and as a consequence they have seldom realized to what an extent political and commercial power must owe their strength to cultural and social causes. The English possess the talents, and at the same time the weaknesses, of the pioneer; in a raw country, among raw people, their civilizing power is unique; but when once that raw country has reached the stage of desiring and needing cultural and refining influences, the English appear incapable of adapting themselves to the new situation. It is a strange comment on the English control of Egypt, for example, that, after forty years of unexampled peace and prosperity due entirely to English government and guidance, the Egyptian masses still remain nearly as illiterate and as wild as on the day on which the English first arrived.

The same peculiarity of policy was, before the World War, visible in Mesopotamia. For a century the English had been, to all intents and purposes, the only European nation exercising political power in the country; yet one small missionary school remained the sole outpost of civilization associated with the English name; whereas several large French and American institutions had gained for themselves a reputation which was gratefully acknowledged, not only in Mesopotamia itself, but in the adjoining countries as well.

The opening of the nineteenth century saw the arrival on the horizon of a new competitor for the hegemony of the Middle East. The youthful state of Russia, but recently built up by the unrivalled energy of her ambitious rulers, commenced her expansion in the Near and Middle East at the expense of Persia; and, if she was late in the field, she made up for it by the exercise of a vigour equal, if not superior, to that of any of her competitors. By 1830, Russia had annexed Erivan, had conquered Caucasia, and had made herself supreme on the Black Sea and the Caspian. By the middle of the century she was completely committed to the dream of Eastern expansion. In a few years she had covered the whole northern frontier of Persia, had reached Afghanistan, and, foiled in that direction by the opposition of England, had quietly spread herself across the whole of Central Asia to the shores of the Pacific. With the exception of the United States, there is no parallel in modern history to this ranging of a people across a whole continent within a space of little more than fifty years.

Nor was Russia's political ability less marked than her colonizing power. The growing weakness of Constantinople gave her the opportunity of making her influence felt throughout the whole Turkish Empire; and she was able to exercise an indefinite but considerable weight in Mesopotamian affairs, which grew with the increasing consolidation of her power in Persia. But her interests in the Turkish Empire, and her assumption of the position of protectress of the Christian population, brought her into direct collision with France; and Mesopotamia, like a second Belgium, slowly developed into a debatable ground, on the borders of which hovered the eastern ambitions of all the Powers. Thus the political power of the English, enforced through the Resident in Baghdad, found itself faced year by year with the growing cultural influence of the French and the Americans, exerted through the medium of missionaries and schools, and the indefinite influence of Russia, hovering on the Persian border, and ready always to throw her weight into the scales on the side which might suit her best. Under the blight of these secretly warring European interests, with all their attendant little strifes and jealousies, the political and economic condition of Mesopotamia and the adjoining countries grew steadily worse and worse.

Meanwhile the world outside was witnessing an absolutely unprecedented movement of expansion on the part of the nations of Europe. For three hundred years the latter had been slowly gaining a predominant position in the more accessible parts of the whole world; but the poverty of their resources, and the bad quality of their equipment, little better than that of the various native races, prevented them for some time from reaping the full reward of their natural enterprise. The latter half of the eighteenth century, however, had seen, particularly in England, an enormous development of the new invention of steam power, and this was followed in the nineteenth century by the revolutionary arrival of railways and steamships. From this time the nations of Europe literally leapt ahead of their contemporaries in other continents; and by 1850, Europe had attracted to herself such a proportion of the power, wealth and invention of mankind as had never been seen in any one quarter of the earth before.

Naturally this great material expansion had an immediate effect upon the colonial situation. Journeys to the East which had previously occupied three months or more, could now be done in under one; Europeans of all classes who had hitherto kept themselves to their own country or continent, began to travel, and to realize the advantages of Imperial connections. As a result, there ensued a rush on the part of the various European Governments to secure overseas possessions and to imitate the example of the English, who, having been the first to realize the logical outcome in the colonial field of the birth of the new age, had already established themselves in most of the key positions of the world. A large proportion of the Near and Middle East was still attached politically to Turkey, and therefore any open attempt to seize territory in that quarter was doomed to failure. But the European Powers, soon made the important discovery that open political control is not the only form of control, and, by a dexterous use of their merchants, travellers, and missionaries, they were soon able to divide helpless Turkey into " spheres of influence," which meant in practice that various provinces of the Empire were allotted as monopolies to certain Governments, in exchange for similar favours elesewhere. This arrangement led to endless complications, and the history of the Turkish Empire, including Mesopotamia, in the nineteenth century is largely the history of the disputes and intrigues of the various European Powers and of the hopeless protest of the resident population against their intervention.

But, in the sphere of human affairs as in that of mathematics, action inevitably produces equal and opposite reaction. The Near Eastern answer to European aggression was bound to come. When it did come, it came not from the Turks, but from a far more widely spread and representative people.

Ever since the collapse of the Abbassids, the Arabs had been declining to the culture and level of semi-barbarians. Arabia itself, hopelessly shattered by the Carmathian disturbances, had split again into small tribal units; and it appeared that the task to which the Prophet had set his hand, of welding the tribes into a single Arab nation, had proved itself, in the light of experience, an impossible one. In the eighteenth century the Arabs, but lately the masters of the Middle Eastern world, were more helpless and more amenable to the pressure of outside enemies than they had been thirteen hundred years before.

But in the middle of this historical century, so fraught with fruitful changes for all parts of the world, there arose

THE COMING OF THE ENGLISH 117

in Arabia one of those remarkable religious movements, which appear to have more influence in stirring the Semitic races to political action than any merely worldly inducement. In the early days of the century, a quiet student of Nejd in Central Arabia, by name Muhammad Ibn Abdul Wahab, after completing his studies in Basrah and Damascus and making the pilgrimage to Mecca, became consumed with the idea that Moslems were not, in these latter days, following the Prophet's teachings, but were honouring a religion so changed and so overcharged with outside beliefs as to render it practically a new faith. He felt a strong urge to undertake the missionary task of leading his countrymen away from the complicated doctrines of the present age and back to the simple Puritanism of their forefathers; and he forthwith set about his self-imposed work, advocating a complete return to the simple doctrine of the Prophet as set down in the Koran and the Traditions, and the abolition of the abuses which, during the course of the ages, had invaded the practice of the faithful. For a time his doctrines were as unpopular as similar exhortations to simple living and clear thinking have ever been in Christendom; but in 1742 he was successful in converting an important local sheikh, Muhammad Ibn Saud of Dereiya, and the immediate result was a religious crusade of such success that in twenty years practically the whole of central Arabia was united once more in a single principality, under the spiritual leadership of Abdul Wahab, and the temporal sway of Ibn Saud. Thus came into being the memorable sect of the Wahabis. By 1785 not only was the reformed faith accepted far beyond the borders of Nejd, but a number of raids on the pilgrim caravans to Mecca had been successfully undertaken, and the authority of the Sultan of Turkey as Caliph and Defender of the Faithful thereby seriously challenged. Before the close of the century a Turkish force was despatched against the Prince of Nejd, but its subsequent failure to achieve any definite result merely increased the prestige of the new Arab Empire.

After the dawn of the nineteenth century, the attacks of the Wahabis began to grow both in boldness and in range. Saud, the grandson of the original convert, was the most successful Arab conqueror of modern times. He invaded Mesopotamia, captured the Shiah holy city of Kerbela, destroyed the shrine of Hosein (repulsive to the Puritans owing to the saint worship associated with his name), and returned to the heart of Arabia with the spoil of the town, accumulated from thousands of pilgrims during hundreds of years. But an even more startling success was soon destined to attend his arms. Taking advantage of the weakness of the Turkish power, he invaded the holy land of the Hedjaz itself, captured Mecca, and shortly afterwards Medina. The treasures of the two cities were removed; the tombs of the saints and all likely objects of veneration were destroyed; and all ceremony savouring in any way of idolatry was sternly repressed.

Meanwhile the Moslem world outside Arabia was bringing pressure to bear upon the Turkish Caliph to take action; and the Porte, hopelessly involved at the moment in European complications, was forced to commission Mehemet Ali, the celebrated Pasha of Egypt, to reconquer the holy land for the Moslem world. A seven years' war ensued, in which the Egyptian troops were repeatedly defeated in the field, but eventually succeeded, by dint of superior discipline and generalship, in crushing the Wahabi power. But the revival of Arab nationalism, which had been heralded by the rise of the Wahabis, was not so easily to be overcome. The Egyptian hold on Arabia soon began to weaken; and on the ruins of the Wahabi empire arose a new state in Jebel Shammar, under the leadership of the Ibn Rashid family. By the middle of the century the Wahabi influence itself was beginning to revive; and the struggle for supremacy between these two small powers, headed by the dynasties of Ibn Saud and Ibn Rashid respectively, forms the pivot of modern Arabian history. Meanwhile, their complete success in freeing themselves of any vestige of Turkish or other foreign control sent a thrill of hope through the whole Arab world; and the revival of the Arab national spirit, which has become so marked a feature of our own times, is directly traceable to their example.

However, the internal history of Mesopotamia in the nineteenth century remained unprogressive and uneventful. After the collapse of the Wahabi power, and the reconquest by the Turkish Government of the independent pashalic of Baghdad, some attempt was made by Constantinople to increase and consolidate its authority in the country, the strength of which became more noticeable as the century wore on. A great effort was made in the early years of the period by Doud Pasha to revive the city and province of Baghdad, but he was hindered by the feebleness of his home government and by the depredations of the Shammar, who roamed all over northern Mesopotamia, and claimed tribute from the settled peasantry, and even from the towns. Ali Pasha later succeeded in dividing the Shammar into two parts by means of a successful intrigue, a division which remains operative to this day. It has not, however, always proved efficacious in securing peace, for rivalry between the groups has threatened from time to time to cover the whole of the north with civil war and desolation.

In the south, civilization remained at a low ebb. Over long periods Turkish authority was practically non-existent, and as late as 1777 Basrah enjoyed the doubtful privilege of being besieged and captured three times in one year, by a wandering army of Persians, by its rightful Turkish owners, and lastly by the Muntafiq confederation, who, from their new capital of Nasriyah, were engaged in extending their control over all the inhabitants of the marsh country. In 1831 Mesopotamia was desolated by plague and famine, and Baghdad at this time is said to have contained only fifty thousand inhabitants.

The arrival of Midhat Pasha as vali of Baghdad in 1870 marks the dawn of a new era. Mesopotamia was emerging at last from the long night of the Middle Ages. Even the Turks were beginning to wake to the material possibilities of this ancient land; schemes of irrigation, of reclamation, of railway enterprise were in the air. The period upon which we entered at the commencement of the chapter is over; the three great movements, whose various ramifications we have attempted to follow, have completed their work. The Turkish Empire, apparently so strong and solid when Suleiman the Magnificent entered Baghdad, has decayed beyond repair; the European influence, so long jealously forbidden the fair lands of the Near East, has returned in overwhelming power; the tender spirit of a reborn Arab nationalism has reared its youthful head. Such are the insecure foundations of modern Mesopotamia; and meanwhile the development of new means of communication is beginning to give rise to the hope that the country will soon once more be brought into touch with the great world outside. With the arrival of Midhat Pasha we enter upon a period which marks Mesopotamia's open appearance upon the stage of modern world politics, and her inevitable preparation for participation in the universal disaster of the World War.

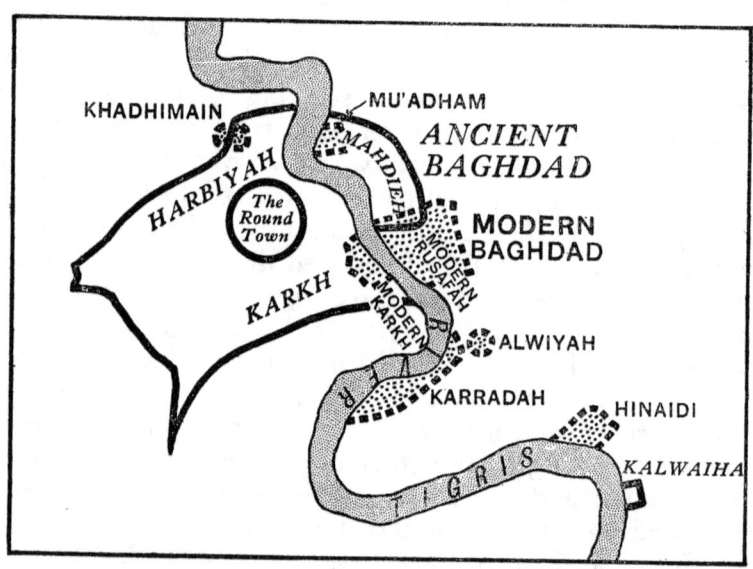

ANCIENT & MODERN BAGHDAD
(*After Le Strange*)

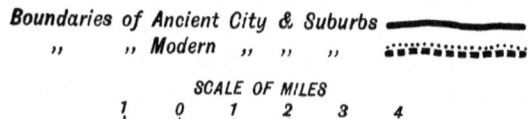

CHAPTER IX

THE COMING OF THE GERMAN

" Who plays at butting with a ram,
Will quick enough a broken forehead rue."—SA'DI.

THE modern age in Mesopotamia was ushered in by a man who was curiously illustrative of the effect that recent European material progress was having on the usually conservative and unyielding mind of the Turk. Midhat Pasha, before he received the appointment of vali of Baghdad had shown distinct administrative talent in various provinces, and under the most adverse conditions. By the influence of his official enemies, who mistrusted equally his perfect honesty of purpose and his faith in European methods, he had more than once been sent to quieten rebellious districts in outlying portions of the empire, and to reorganize their administration ; and, so sincere was his patriotism and so striking his ability, he had invariably succeeded in accomplishing the particular task allotted to him. In fact, certain of his administrative reforms had proved so successful in local spheres that they had been adopted by the Sultan as a standard for the whole empire. The task of reorganizing and pacifying the Mesopotamia of 1870 might well have appalled even so distinguished a proconsul ; but his rule was directed with such ability during the short time he was allowed to remain that there is very little doubt that he would have proved successful even in this unpromising sphere, had he only been permitted sufficient time. As it was, it has to be acknowledged that at no time during the last six centuries has Mesopotamia ever had a fairer chance of re-establishing her ancient fame and fortune than under the enlightened and benign rule of Midhat Pasha.

The state of the country at that time was such that drastic measures of some sort had to be taken to revive even the shadow of Turkish authority over the land. The big towns contained Turkish garrisons, and were reasonably safe; though the holy cities of Najaf and Kerbela, with their large and growing Persian population and Shiah proclivities, were nearly always in a state of unrest under the heavy hand of their Sunni Turkish governor. Outside the towns, the great tribes ranged the country at their own sweet will. In the north the Shammar, periodically moving up and down the land between the two great rivers, levied a toll on the settled Arabs in the district, and on the smaller towns as well; and at times approached so close to Baghdad as to terrify the timid inhabitants of the capital. To the west of the Euphrates ranged the almost equally dreaded Anaza, and on the other flank of the Shammar could be found the powerful Tai. Each of these tribal confederations held in their power several of the smaller tribal groups of the country (of which at this time there were nearly sixty), and each was in touch with, and affected by, the political changes of Arabia proper, an area practically outside Turkish official control. To the south-east of Baghdad, again, came the Beni Lam, and south-west of the Euphrates the equally troublesome Dhafir. In the marsh country between the lower reaches of the two rivers lived a dark, non-Arab people, popularly known as Ma'adan Arabs, a people absolutely lawless and wild, and equally antagonistic to the great Arab tribes and to the central Government. The chief asset of the Ma'adan lay in their skill as river pirates, which not infrequently took an immense toll on river traffic passing to and from Baghdad. Finally, claiming the whole south country, Ma'adan and all, as their province, came the great Muntafiq, perhaps the most powerful of all the tribal confederations, who had not only on one occasion captured Basrah itself, but had succeeded in holding it for a considerable period against all the forces that the Government had been able to bring against them.

But the administrative difficulties of modern Mesopotamia were not, and are not, confined to the tribes. Dotted about the country were a number of completely foreign groups, whose importance and economic value enabled them both to preserve their national existence and to assert their own importance. In the south, on the edge of the Ma'adan country, was to be found a small community of so-called "Sabians," inheritors of an old Egyptian faith and culture. Retaining their own religion, and speaking their own language, this curious people had maintained themselves precariously against the hatred of the Arabs by their skill as boat builders, carpenters and silversmiths, in all of which trades they possessed useful secrets. In the north, in the low mountain range to the south-west of Mosul, lived an isolated Kurdish people, the famous "Yezidis" or Devil-worshippers, whose peculiar religion rendered them subject to persecution alike from Moslem and Christian. Several groups of Christians, Chaldeans, Assyrians and Armenians, were to be found in various parts of the country; and the town of Mosul appeared to be rapidly becoming an exclusively Christian centre. All the little Christian bodies maintained their own culture, and to some extent their own languages; as did the Jews, of whom there still remained many thousands in Baghdad alone. The predominant Moslem section of the population was itself divided racially into Arabs, Kurds, Turks and Persians, and the Arabs were again sub-divided on religious grounds into Sunnis and Shiahs.

The task of controlling and assimilating such a multitude of antagonistic nationalities, opinions and religions might well have appalled a patriotic Turkish governor, full of modern ideas regarding the suitable government of subject provinces, and endowed with the qualities of honest purpose and ambition. Nevertheless Midhat Pasha tackled the problem of settling and developing the country with energy and resource. By a series of successful intrigues, he managed to neutralize the power of the Shammar in the north, and to render that portion of the country reasonably secure; and, to strengthen the hand of the central power, he established permanent barracks in Baghdad, and stations in the smaller towns, for the accommodation of the Turkish garrisons. The solid if unprepossessing buildings which afterwards became so familiar to British troops in the World War, owe their creation to his enterprise. In the south, although he found the penetration of the marshes and the extinction of the power of the river pirates beyond his means, he managed to clear the main traffic routes; and it became possible to travel up and down the Tigris and Euphrates with more security than had been possible for some centuries.

Directly he had made his control of Mesopotamia reasonably certain, Midhat Pasha began to turn his attention to the Nejd country, across the border of Arabia proper. He realized, as every governor of Mesopotamia is forced eventually to realize, that political control of that country can only be assured by the possession of a certain amount of influence over the Arab motherland to the south. The rivalry between the two principalities of Ibn Rashid and the Wahabi Ibn Saud had reached a critical period, and the former made an appeal for help to Midhat. The chance was too good to be missed. Hastily assembling a strong Turkish force, Midhat invaded Nejd, and announced the establishment of a Turkish province. But Midhat's success in this direction brought him into immediate conflict with the English, who were disposed to regard the establishment of a strong Turkish outpost on the Persian Gulf as a threat to their supremacy in those waters; and friction between the Turkish and the English authorities, at times cleverly utilized by the various Arab potentates for their own ends, was continuous from this time to the outbreak of the World War. Midhat's ambitious schemes were frustrated by the inability of Constantinople, worried over the European situation, to spare him more troops; but his policy in Arabia was continued by his successors, and an attempt a few years afterwards by the Turks to seize Bahrein was only prevented by the actual intervention of a British gunboat.

Nor were Midhat Pasha's interests wholly concerned with politics. He had a keen admiration for the mechanical discoveries and refinements of Western civilization, and he fully realized their value in the rapid development of a barren country. He was responsible for the introduction into Mesopotamia of large quantities of machinery of various kinds, and for the building of the tramway to Khadimain, a suburb of Baghdad and a place of Shiah pilgrimage. Indeed it may truthfully be said that the few constructive measures which can be found in operation in Mesopotamia in modern times owe their inspiration, if

THE COMING OF THE GERMAN

not their actual origin, to the genius of Midhat Pasha; and from his time onwards the Turkish Government made genuine, if not wholly successful, efforts to pacify and redevelop what had once been the garden of the world.

Midhat Pasha's attempt to restore the navigation of the Euphrates was inspired to some extent by the opening of the Suez Canal, which threatened to deprive Mesopotamia of the remnants of the trade between India and the west, of which she had once enjoyed almost a monopoly. The project for a canal connecting the Mediterranean and the Red Sea was the work of a group of Frenchmen, and, as such, was regarded with extreme suspicion by the English authorities; and in 1856, when the French group repaired to Constantinople to obtain the necessary permission of the Sultan for the construction of the new waterway, they found themselves completely surrounded by the hostility of the British. The chief engineer thereupon travelled to London, where he was informed by Lord Palmerston, then one of England's leading statesmen, that it was the considered opinion of the British Government that the canal was an engineering impossibility; that its construction would ruin British maritime supremacy in the East; and that the whole idea was, in fact, merely a cloak for French political interference in what England regarded as her own particular "sphere of influence"!

In spite of the opposition of the British, however, the canal was built, and in 1869 was opened for traffic. Temporarily defeated in this direction, the British now turned their attention hopefully towards the Euphrates valley, where Midhat Pasha was busily engaged in his ambitious schemes for re-creating the prosperity of the ancient river. It soon became obvious, however, that not the river but a railway would prove the best means of opening up a new route to India, and of combating the insidious ambitions of the French in the isthmus of Suez. As early as 1857 an official report on the question of an Euphrates Valley Railway had been presented to the British Government by two officials, one of whom was that same Colonel Chesney, who, twenty years earlier, had made the experiment of navigating the Euphrates by steamer. Peculiarly enough, it had been the report in 1830 of the feasibility of the Suez

Canal project by this adventurous Englishman which had led the French engineers originally to consider the scheme, and he was always referred to by them as the "father" of the canal.

The railway which Chesney proposed would have left the Mediterranean at Alexandretta, striking inland via Aleppo to the Euphrates valley; proceeding down the valley through Anah and Hit, it would have crossed to the Tigris at Baghdad, and thence followed the course of that river to Basrah. In 1872 the project was carefully considered by a Committee of the House of Commons, specially appointed for the purpose on the advice of a prominent Indian railway official, who even committed himself to the statement that the security of British interests in India depended upon the construction of such a railway, and its retention in British hands. But, though the Committee's report was favourable, nothing was done immediately to further the scheme; and three years later the British Government purchased the Egyptian Khedive's shares in the Suez Canal Company, and thus secured a voice in the control of that undertaking. In consequence the Euphrates Valley Railway, was, as far as the British were concerned, abandoned altogether.

Meanwhile in the extreme north of the Sultan's Asiatic dominions a little railway was being constructed which was soon fated to assume an importance altogether out of proportion to its size. The Sultan Abdul Aziz had a favourite shooting-box at Ismid on the Sea of Marmora, which was handicapped by its inaccessibility from the capital; and in 1871 the monarch conceived the idea of inviting a distinguished German engineer, who was at the time engaged in constructing railways in European Turkey on behalf of a German financial house, to build a short line from Haidar Pasha, an Asiatic suburb of Constantinople, to Ismid at the expense of the Turkish taxpayer, thus guaranteeing His Majesty speedy and comfortable access to his favourite retreat. The line was built, and sixteen years afterwards a German syndicate approached the Turkish Government for a concession to take over the little railway, and extend it to Angora, an additional length of some 300 miles. The combined system became known as

THE COMING OF THE GERMAN

the Anatolian Railway; British capital was at first represented in the company, but eventually the British interest was bought out, and the line, which was completed in 1893, became wholly German. In the year of its completion a further concession was obtained to extend the system from a point on the Angora line to Konia (the ancient Iconium). This extension was opened for traffic in 1896. In the same year a very much more ambitious concession was obtained for the extension of the line to Kaisariyah and Diabekr on the Tigris, and so down to Mosul and Baghdad. Thus was born the famous Baghdad Railway. At first the new scheme did not arouse either the interest or alarm with which its successor of some six years later was destined to be welcomed. Both the British and the French, it is true, owned railways and concessions in Asia Minor and Syria, but the proposed new railway passed far to the east of any of them, and in no way compromised a possible future English or French railway down the Euphrates valley to Baghdad. Moreover the German Government had not at the time given any official support to the policy of the "Drang nach Osten," and there seemed no reason to suppose that the railway was anything but a commercial speculation of a group of private German capitalists. However, a more startling turn was soon to be given to events, firstly by the unexpected opposition of Russia, and secondly by the dramatic personal intervention of the German Emperor.

The Russian Government had for some time past been acting in collaboration with France, with a view to checking the Imperialistic designs of England. The old disagreement over the position of the Christians in the Turkish Empire had been patched up, and joint anti-British action had been agreed upon through the medium of the existing French control of Indo-China and the Russian control of eastern Turkey, Persia and Afghanistan. For the security of this control, it was important that no new non-Russian railway should pass within striking distance of the Turco-Russian frontier, and a railway through Diabekr would obviously come under this heading. Accordingly, very strong opposition was offered by Russia, who possessed great influence at Constantinople, against the scheme ; and the company, probably acting upon the suggestion of the Turkish Government, abandoned the project and prepared to await the trend of events.

In 1898, two years after the completion of the Anatolian Railway to Konia, Europe was startled by the news of a second State visit to the Sultan of Constantinople on the part of the able and versatile German Emperor. Much had happened in the eight years since 1892, when the same monarch had aroused mild surprise in diplomatic circles by his first visit to the capital of Islam, the first occasion upon which any modern Christian monarch had been the guest of the Caliph. England, which at the time of the first visit had been extremely friendly both to Germany and the German Emperor, had in the following years become alarmed at the growing manifestations of colonial ambition in Germany, and by the latter power's bid for a strong navy. In January, 1895, had come the famous declaration by the German Emperor that " our future is on the water " ; and at the end of that year the Jameson Raid telegram from that monarch to the President of the Transvaal Republic, publicly congratulating him upon preserving the independence of his country " without appealing to the help of friendly powers." In 1897 had occurred the Kiao-Chow incident, resulting in the creation of a German port in Chinese waters ; and the Emperor's orations on this occasion, which included the famous " mailed fist " speech, had given considerable cause for alarm not only to England, but to various other European powers as well.

In the Turkish Empire, too, the situation had changed, and changed considerably for the worse. From 1890 onwards Crete and Macedonia remained in a chronic state of revolt; and at the other end of the empire the Arabs were seriously beginning to assert themselves, and the incessant disturbances in Sana cost the central Government many thousands of lives and much treasure. Worse than all, the Armenian massacres of 1895 had sent a shudder of horror through Europe, and had even shaken England's traditional support of the Porte in Near Eastern affairs. The commission of inquiry into the Armenian atrocities included English, French and Russian officers, but no

THE COMING OF THE GERMAN 129

German; and it was possibly this obvious slight that encouraged the Emperor to intervene more actively in the affairs of a Turkey which might at any moment collapse into hopeless confusion.

The State visit of 1898 was planned with singular directness, and revealed Germany for the first time as a serious competitor in Near and Middle Eastern affairs. Regardless of the feelings of Christian Europe, only recently horrified by the state of religious animosity revealed in the Armenian atrocities, the great German Emperor treated the aged Sultan as a personal friend and equal, craved from him a plot of ground in Jerusalem for presentation to German Christians, and publicly announced himself as the protector of the hundred million Moslems throughout the world. This latter announcement, and the theatrical laying of a memorial wreath upon the tomb of Saladin at Damascus, caused a storm of protest even in Germany itself; but the gifts which the Emperor brought back with him were too tempting to be resisted, and the commercial classes of Germany soon forgot their righteous indignation in their admiration of their Emperor's solid business acumen. First among these gifts was a new concession for the Baghdad Railway.

The new concession proposed a railway which should leave the existing Anatolian Railway at Konia and cut transversely across Asia Minor to Aleppo and Nisibin, crossing both the Taurus and Amanus ranges, and following in general the historic highway of the Cilician Gates. From Nisibin the line would continue to Mosul and thus via the course of the Tigris to Baghdad; and a German cruiser was, it was announced, to make an immediate journey to the Persian Gulf, hitherto an exclusively British preserve, to inquire into the possibility of a suitable terminal in the south. The full scheme was made public in November, 1899, by Dr. Siemens, the chairman of the Anatolian Railway; but the concession was not formally confirmed on the Turkish side until early in 1902, when an *iradé* of the Sultan, dated January 16th, put the seal of Turkish official approval on the new scheme. This concession was never destined, however, to be carried into effect; for in March, 1903, it was superseded by a new one, in which the Baghdad Railway Company was created as a separate entity from the Anatolian Railway, and its proposed main line increased by an extension from Baghdad to Basrah. Including the existing Anatolian line to Konia, the whole system to Basrah involved a mileage of some 1,800, exclusive of branch lines.

The concession of 1903 marked the actual commencement of the new Baghdad Railway, and the final disappearance of the old northern scheme for a line through Diabekr. The change of route had immediate political consequences, which were emphasized by Germany's increasingly aggressive attitude. Had the promoters been able to adhere to their northern route in spite of the opposition of Russia, they would have secured the neutrality, and probably the indifference, of the French and English, whose "spheres" in Syria and the Mediterranean littoral would have remained untouched. Indeed, there would have been nothing to prevent the eventual construction by England of her favourite Euphrates Valley scheme, connecting at Baghdad with the German system, and thus offering the choice of two routes from Europe to the City of Peace. By moving the course of the Baghdad Railway southward, the promotors escaped Russian opposition only to encounter the violent hostility of France and England. From henceforth Germany took the place of England in French eyes as the great enemy in the Orient, and for the first time since the disappearance of the Dutch power, English and French were to be found working in close co-operation in Levantine and Middle Eastern waters. Meanwhile Germany, who had done her best to conciliate Russia at the risk of offending France and England, soon found that even the Muscovite power was growing suspicious of her intentions. The open alliance between Russia and France, and the growing friendliness between Russia and England, which eventually found expression in the Persian agreement of 1911, finally left Germany completely isolated in the Near East, relying only on the feeble and precarious friendship of Turkey.

At the same time, the new route gave Germany very solid and undeniable advantages over her rivals. By crossing southern Asia Minor and northern Syria transversely, the new line practically ensured the domination of the railway system of all Turkey in Asia; for the French and English systems were effectively confined to the coast, and could only develop inland by joining the Baghdad Railway at some point. In addition, by the proposed extension to the Persian Gulf, Germany would control the sole existing railway route from Europe to the western gateway of India; and by the proposed branch from Samarra to Khaniqin, on the Mesopotamian border of Persia, she would be in an excellent strategic position for a railway invasion of the latter country.

The terms upon which the new company obtained the concession were extremely favourable. Both a traffic guarantee and a construction guarantee were granted, a sum covering the construction of each section of the line being placed at the disposal of the promoters by loans issued and guaranteed by the Turkish Government. Material for the railway entered the Turkish Empire free of import duty, and for the most part would be of German construction. Thus in practice the German promoters would be enabled to construct a railway of paramount political importance to Germany at Turkish expense and out of material purchased in Germany; with the additional advantage of securing German control for the line for a period of ninety-nine years. The sole return which the Turkish Government exacted was that the officials and workmen employed on the line were to be Turkish subjects, with the added proviso that, in the case of the few European experts who would be permanently needed, the wearing of a fez as head-dress should be obligatory!

It must in common fairness be admitted that the German syndicate showed no desire to confine the ownership of the line to German nationals. Several attempts were made, both by the promoters and by the German Government, to induce French and English capitalists to interest themselves in the scheme, and Dr. von Gwinner even went so far as to write an article in an English periodical encouraging co-operation. But suspicion of German motives had by this time become general in both France and England, and the invitations to invest in the undertaking were merely regarded as a move on the part of

Germany to quieten suspicion while, at the same time, obtaining foreign capital for the futherance of her own plans. In the direction of a large enterprise, far more depends upon the attitude of the directors than of the shareholders ; and, as five out of the eleven directors were to be nominated by the Anatolian Railway Company (already under German control), and three were to be Turks (regarded also as under German control), the fears of the French and British publics appeared to be justified. Both M. Delcassé, then Minister of Foreign Affairs in France, and Mr. Balfour, then Prime Minister in Britain, recommended the acceptance of the German offer with a view to safeguarding, to some extent, existing French and British interests in the Near East ; but public indignation at the German success was very great in both countries, and the Governments were forced to break off all negotiations on the subject, although the German Emperor, on the occasion of his visit to England in 1899, was rumoured to have obtained a promise of a free hand in Asia Minor from Mr. Chamberlain. Though it is not difficult to sympathize with the indignation of the French and British publics over the extremely favourable terms granted to the Germans, it is unquestionably a pity that the German offer to make the concern an international one was not taken up. The presence of large groups of French and English capital would undoubtedly have tended towards more amicable relations over Near Eastern questions, and might even have given Germany more cause for reflection before embarking on the policy of the World War. Even as late as 1903, the German Chancellor publicly declared that the railway was being built for commercial and not for political ends ; and it would probably have been wiser for the French and English to have taken such an assurance at its face value. In 1910, French public opinion had so far relented as to allow the capitalists associated with the Imperial Ottoman Bank to take up thirty per cent. of the capital, and in 1914, just prior to the World War, England and Germany were believed to have arrived at an understanding over the whole question ; but these events happened too late to stem the tide.

Meanwhile the English, realizing their inability to

THE COMING OF THE GERMAN

control the new railway project at the northern, or Constantinople end, determined to make certain of their hold on the southern, or Mesopotamian, end. The publication of the German scheme was the signal for the opening of a period of great English activity in the land of the rivers, to some extent overshadowed by corresponding efforts on the part of the Germans. The situation had been complicated by the sudden appearance of Russia in the rôle of competitor for the trade of the Persian Gulf, thus making the contest a three-cornered one; the ancient rivalry with France having been largely modified by the spirit of co-operation which followed in the wake of the " Entente Cordiale." Russia had opened a consulate in Baghdad in 1881; and from that time onwards she had continued to employ her influence against England both in Persia and on the banks of the Tigris. It was this English obsession which blinded her to the growing menace of Germany, and allowed her to remain neutral during the latter's railway invasion of southern Asia Minor, once she had gained her point with regard to the northern half of that area. At the beginning of the new century, Russian policy became more active. In 1900, the Russian Steam Navigation and Trading Company, subsidized by the Russian Government, commenced to run a direct service of steamers between Odessa and the Gulf ports, and persistent efforts were made by the Tsar's Government to obtain a naval station in the waters of the Indian Ocean. All through the last decade of the nineteenth century Franco-Russian co-operation in the Gulf had also continued strong, and in 1896 a subsidized steamship service was instituted by the Messageries Maritimes. When the period of co-operation with England was entered upon, both these services were withdrawn.

Meanwhile events in Arabia itself began to play an important part in the tangled situation. We have followed in an earlier chapter the rise of two Arab kingdoms in central Arabia, the Wahabi sultanate of Nejd, controlled by the dynasty of Ibn Saud, and the amirate of Hail, controlled by that of Ibn Rashid. Ever since the time of Midhat Pasha's intervention in central Arabian affairs, the latter family had continued to be friendly with the

Turkish Government, and they remained meanwhile at the height of their power. The fortunes of the family of Ibn Saud were at a correspondingly low ebb. Their inheritance had been dissipated by unsuccessful wars against Ibn Rashid and by dynastic quarrels; and, at the beginning of the century, the rightful heir to the sultanate had long been a fugitive at the court of the independent sheikh Mubarak of Koweit. The ancient quarrel between these two little central Arabian principalities was now to become a matter of world politics, for it was through the amirate of Hail that the German group at the back of the Baghdad Railway commenced to cast about for a suitable port for the railway on the Persian Gulf. The eventual destination of the railway had been at first left conveniently vague. The main line was to end at Basrah, but a branch was to be constructed from Zobeir (a town near Basrah, and the site of the ancient Bassorah of Sinbad the Sailor) to a point " to be determined "; the right of navigation on the Shatt-al-Arab, the estuary through which the two great rivers run out to the Gulf, being allowed to German ships. This, it will be remembered, had hitherto been an exclusively English privilege. Thus the original proposal left the Germans a free hand to explore the upper reaches of the Gulf in harmony with the Turkish authorities at Basrah, until they could select a port likely to be suitable for their purpose.

It soon became evident that their choice had been made. A short distance south of Basrah, and due east of the dominions of Ibn Rashid, lay Koweit, a port with a large and increasing local trade, carefully fostered by the independent sheikh Mubarak. The ruler of Hail had long coveted this important harbour, through which much of the trade of his inland dominions must pass; and the German railway magnates saw in the port, possessing an excellent situation, and easily connected with their main line, exactly what they desired. Turkey, in addition, had wished for some time past to assert her position more successfully among the semi-independent Arab chieftains of the Gulf Coast; and thus both the Germans and the Turks realized the advantage to be gained by joining forces with the Amir of Hail with a view to furthering their own particular objects. In 1901, an open quarrel arose between Sheikh Mubarak and the Amir of Hail; the latter was immediately supported openly by the Turkish Government; and a Turkish force, under Ahmad Feizi Pasha assembled at Basrah. Sheikh Mubarak thereupon appealed to Great Britain, and the appearance of a British gunboat made any direct seizure of Koweit out of the question.

Meanwhile Mubarak was able to enlist the services of a romantic but hitherto unknown figure. The heir to the Wahabi throne, who had been so long a fugitive dependent upon Mubarak's hospitality, was a man of great piety but of no conspicuous energy, in striking contrast to his youthful son, who burned even as a boy to return to his own land and assume the leadership of his people. Trouble in the Wahabi capital of Riyadh at length brought about his opportunity. His father, wisely recognizing the political talent of his son, resigned all right in his title to him, and one night the youthful Abdul Aziz arrived in disguise, with a few faithful followers, in a suburban garden of Riyadh. During the night the guard was overpowered and the city entered; and next day the delighted populace secured the surrender of the city, almost without a blow, to the rightful head of the house of Ibn Saud. From that day the young ruler never rested until he had made himself secure, and had laid the foundations of a new epoch of Wahabi power.

Sheikh Mubarak, who for so long had offered the hospitality of his house and court to the exiled members of the Ibn Saud family, was now to reap his reward. Abdul Aziz was quick to see the opportunity afforded him of appearing in opposition to the power of Ibn Rashid, whose empire had in the past been largely created at the expense of his own; and he was soon able to enlist the aid of the powerful Muntafiq in lower Mesopotamia, who were suspicious of any attempt on the part of the Turkish authorities to assert their power in the Basrah area. The three allies, Ibn Saud, Mubarak and the Muntafiq, backed by the "moral support" of Great Britain, now attacked and utterly defeated Ibn Rashid, and captured several of his towns. Turkey made several attempts to protect her protégé, and Ahmad Feizi Pasha once advanced from Basrah with a considerable force ; but the Arab revolt in the Yemen, on the other side of Arabia, which occurred about this time, compelled the Turks to hold their hand, and the Arab contestants were left to fight it out amongst themselves.

Meanwhile Great Britain, temporarily successful in checkmating the German railway advance through the victories of her local allies, determined that the situation, in so far as her position in the Gulf was concerned, should be defined once and for all. In 1903 Lord Lansdowne, speaking on behalf of the British Government, laid it down that " we should regard the establishment of a naval base or a fortified port in the Persian Gulf by any other power as a very grave menace to British interests, and we should certainly resist it by all the means at our disposal." This declaration was formally reaffirmed by Sir Edward Grey in 1907, in a despatch to the British ambassador at the Russian capital, the further statement being added that " His Majesty's Government will continue to direct all their efforts to the observance of the *status quo* in the Gulf, and the maintenance of British trade ; in doing so they have no desire to exclude the legitimate trade of any other Power." These declarations were regarded as a direct hint, not only to Germany, but to Russia and France ; for it was largely French influence which was responsible (supported to some extent by English arms manufacturers) for the maintenance of the dangerous arms traffic in the Gulf and the countries adjoining, which had caused both the English and the Persian authorities considerable anxiety. But the creation of the Entente Cordiale, soon to be followed by the Anglo-Russian understanding, practically eliminated both the French and the Russians from the Gulf for the time being, and left England face to face with Germany.

England had undoubtedly scored a point over the proposed terminus of the new railway, for the German promoters were forced, by their failure to secure Koweit, to remain content with Fao, an obscure port lying between the former and Basrah, and completely covered, in the event of future hostilities, by the British control of Koweit.

THE COMING OF THE GERMAN 137

But they continued the struggle with some determination, and a German line of steamships was put on from Europe to the Gulf ports, and German merchants actively encouraged, and with some success, in the best strategic points for local trade. Nor were the French or English idle. Rival schemes were rapidly promoted for a system of railways connecting with the French railways in Syria, running via the Euphrates valley to Baghdad and Basrah (the latter stretch to be under English control), and with a branch from Baghdad to the Persian border, to connect with a Russian railway from Teheran. These plans were submitted to the Turkish Government in 1909, but the half-heartedness of Russia, who, for political reasons, did not actually wish to see any railways constructed connecting direct with Persia, and the strong opposition of Germany, who refused to surrender the Baghdad-Basrah concession to England, prevented their acceptance by Constantinople. An independent American project for a similar group of railways was defeated at the same time. The situation was not finally clarified until 1914, when an agreement covering the whole area had been negotiated between the English, the Germans and the Turks, in which, it is believed, the right of Great Britain to maintain her supremacy in the Gulf was not seriously challenged.

Meanwhile the actual construction of the Baghdad Railway was being slowly undertaken. In October, 1904, the first section from Konia to Bulgurli (125 miles) was opened for traffic. The second section proved more difficult, owing to the mountainous country encountered, and to the general political uncertainty in both Turkey and western Europe, especially after the Turkish revolution, which rendered the financial and administrative work extremely difficult and arduous. For some months no work was carried out on the line whatsoever, and it was not until 1914 that the section Bulgurli-Adana, also of 125 miles, was completed. Construction had also now been commenced at the Baghdad end, and the line Baghdad-Samarra (75 miles) was opened in 1914. Of the remainder of the great project, the stretch Adana-Aleppo-Nisibin was completed during the war, and the short length Samarra-Shergat was built by the British after their conquest of

Mesopotamia; the remaining section Nisibin-Mosul-Shergat still remains uncompleted. The southern extension from Baghdad to Basrah was constructed after the Armistice by the British; and the great railway from Constantinople to the Persian Gulf thus only lacks 175 miles of its whole length of 1,875 miles to make it at long last a reality.

Meanwhile the discovery of oil in Persia, and a growing recognition that petroleum was likely to become the fuel for ships of the future, once more served to emphasize the importance of the Persian Gulf and its adjacent countries to British interests. The oil industry in Persia owes its inception to a grant made by Shah Muzzaffar-ad-Din in 1901 to a British subject for working petroleum in all its forms in southern Persia. The initial venture of the promoters was not a success; hope, however, still clung to the enterprise, and additional capital was secured by interesting the Burmah Oil Company, a powerful Scotch group operating in the East, in the new scheme. In 1909, it was recognized that a field of much promise had been found, and steps were taken to form an independent company to take control of the operations. A refinery was built at Abadan, on the Shatt-al-Arab, and a pipe-line laid to it direct from the fields. The British Admiralty had by this time decided that a safe and ready supply of oil fuel for the British navy was a necessity, and Mr. Winston Churchill, then First Lord of the Admiralty, suggested the securing of control in the new company by the purchase with Government money of a large block of shares. The project was carried into execution; and the Anglo-Persian Oil Company (as the new concern was termed) agreed to accept a number of directors appointed by the British Government, and to hold itself in readiness to supply British national needs, when called upon. Early in 1914 the pipe-line was doubled, and the resources of the refinery largely increased.

After the Turkish revolution of 1908 the international situation in Mesopotamia became distinctly easier. No attempt was made by the Germans to take up the concession for the railway from Baghdad to Basrah; Russia withdrew her opposition to railway construction in the Near Eastern area, and even agreed to consider a Persian system to connect with the Baghdad Railway; and farther north the concessions held by the Russians in Asia Minor were turned over to a French company. British sentiment was flattered by the appointment of an Englishman (Sir William Willcocks) as irrigation adviser to the new Government in Turkey, and by the decision to act upon his suggestions in Mesopotamia, and to construct the new Hindiyah Barrage, at the junction of the Babylon and Hindiyah branches of the Euphrates. It appeared at last as if the material development of the Near and Middle East was to proceed along settled, peaceable and friendly lines. Mesopotamia was beginning once more to fulfil its historic rôle as the meeting place of the nations; but in this age it was to be a friendly meeting place, in which various clearly defined " spheres of influence " were to recognize each other's boundaries.

The years immediately preceding the World War saw, on the whole, a gradual recrudescence of British influence in Mesopotamia, in spite of the activity and growing prestige of the Germans. In the towns the latter were popular; they were clever, they were energetic, they pulled well together and they had money to spend; they mastered the language and habits of the country quickly, and they mixed freely with the people. The British, whether engaged in official duties or in business, appeared somewhat aloof and careless, and the impression grew among local business men that the representatives of English firms did not care very much whether they sold their goods or not, so long as they were left in peace to enjoy quiet and gentlemanly lives adorned with all that a good name, a regular salary and a host of native servants could provide. The quick-witted German soon began to make serious inroads into the trade monopoly which the English had held for two hundred years, and he used all his wiles to play upon the imagination of the ignorant but by no means dull inhabitants of the Mesopotamian towns. England was represented by him as decadent, over-comfortable, a power of the past; Germany as the " modern " nation, alive, energetic, up-to-date, the very embodiment of all that twentieth-century hustle and activity which has so great a fascination for active minds imprisoned by fate in old and backward countries. The military power of Germany, her aggressiveness, her hardness, her cruelty were left out of the picture ; and it was as a sort of Europeanized American that the German came to Mesopotamia, full of schemes for setting the country on its feet, full of modern democratic notions, ready to mix with the people as an equal, the apostle of " push and go " as against the maddening, if gentlemanly, indolence of the Turk and the Englishman. The German told of his country, raised from a position of impotence to that of a great power in forty years ; of her inventions and industries, which were sweeping British goods from all the markets of the world ; of her cities, which had grown at a speed that America herself could not rival ; of her mercantile fleets, which had challenged the proud English on their own element, and had challenged them successfully. The thoughtful Mesopotamian became more and more convinced that if his country was ever going to be resuscitated, the German, and not the Englishman or the Frenchman, was the man to do it ; and he turned more and more away from the cultivation of the lordly English sahib and the cultured French missionary to the companionship of this novel commercial gentleman from Berlin. The younger generation, permitted a freedom of travel which their fathers had never possessed, chose to go to Germany rather than to France or England for their travels or their studies ; and in a surprisingly short space of time the German might congratulate himself upon having achieved a position in Baghdad equal, if not superior to that of the French and English.

But if the German success in the towns was marked, it was limited in effect very largely to the towns. The modern German is essentially a townsman, and his whole scheme of Imperial penetration partook largely of the nature of a town-bred idea. The Englishman, on the other hand, remains at heart largely a countryman or a man of the sea, with the ideals, the manners, the limitations, but also the attractiveness of the sailor, the rancher or the country squire. Amid the rather squalid and second-rate cosmopolitanism of modern Baghdad, with its conflicting communities and large foreign interests, the Englishman remained uncomfortable and isolated to some extent from the general life of the people; but in the country or the desert, in the tents of the sheikhs or on the estates of the country proprietors, the Englishman was in his element. It was the old story of the pioneer over again; as long as the civilization around him was of the paternal order, of the country variety, the Englishman, strong, truthful and reliable, stood supreme; but in quarters in which civilization had reached a more complicated stage, where knowledge, tact and unscrupulousness are the necessary weapons of existence, the Englishman appeared to be outplayed.

But Mesopotamia is a land in which, on the whole, the influence of the country on the national existence largely outweighs that of the towns; and in the country districts in Mesopotamia, as in Arabia proper, the Englishman continued to hold the confidence and even the affection of the Arab to a degree to which no other European even approached. Moreover, in the few years preceding the World War the English as a race had become genuinely alarmed, and had wakened to a realization of their declining position; and in 1913 something of the same sort could be witnessed in the Middle East as was noticeable in other parts of the world, in a steady and not unsuccessful British attempt to meet the German menace, both in trade and politics, by the adoption of more modern methods and a more liberal outlook. It could truthfully be said that, in spite of the remarkable effort made by the Germans to gain supremacy in Mesopotamia, the opening of the World War found the British in the more advantageous position of the two.

Meanwhile, the spirit of Arab nationalism, reborn in the Wahabi campaign of a century earlier, was steadily but quietly growing in strength. The return of the Ibn Saud dynasty to power in central Arabia, under a young and capable ruler, and the obvious helplessness of the Turks against the rebels in the Yemen and other parts of southern Arabia, had begun to revive the hope of Arab independence; and the growing alertness of the Arabs in Syria, owing to the educational advantages of that country, had made Damascus a veritable hotbed of Arab nationalist propaganda. The failure of the revolutionary

Turkish Government to carry out their promises, and their increasingly open attempts to impress the Turkish character upon the subordinate nationalities, gave an immense impetus to the spread of the pan-Arab idea; and, alike in the bazaars of Aleppo and the tents of the *Ahl Bedu*, the gossip round the coffee hearth turned more and more towards the fate of the people of the Prophet, their long history, their strange alternations of fortune and their possible destiny. The restless and unconquerable spirit of Arabia, which countless times before had covered Syria, Egypt and Mesopotamia with the results of its own strange political upheavals, was beginning to stir again.

CHAPTER X

THE WORLD WAR

" Our wearisome, pedantic art of war,
By which we prove retreat may be success,
Delay best speed, half loss, at times, whole gain."—BROWNING.

THE World War, so far as Mesopotamia was concerned, proved an almost irreparable disaster. In 1914 the prospects of the country were brighter than they had been for many centuries ; a large irrigation scheme, which included the celebrated Hindiyah Barrage, had actually been undertaken ; the Baghdad Railway was in process of building ; everywhere men's hearts rose at the thought that at last the land of the rivers was to have a chance of that material development and progress to which her natural resources entitled her. Hardly had these hopes been formed when they were destined to be dissipated by the whirlwind of the World War. Nine years afterwards Mesopotamia, in the indecisive grasp of post-war England, had lost all hope of material development in the immediate future. The Baghdad Railway was still uncompleted, and, what was worse, likely to remain so ; no further irrigation works of any magnitude had been attempted ; the conquering power had spent many millions of treasure in achieving little or nothing ; and Mesopotamia was beginning to learn the slow and painful lesson that in a post-war world of poverty and exhaustion, nobody was likely in the long run to help her but herself.

The World War, in so far as it touched the land of the rivers, opened almost unobtrusively. For the first three months Mesopotamia remained outside the region of hostilities ; for the secret treaty existing between Constantinople and Berlin was unknown in Europe generally, and it was the beginning of November, 1914, before the British Government found cause to declare war formally on Turkey. It had become obvious somewhat earlier, however, that the entrance of Turkey into the war was possible, and in the middle of October a brigade of the sixth division (British Indian Army) had arrived in the Persian Gulf, where they held a watching brief with a view to future developments.

Action was not long to be denied them. On November 5th, the British Government declared war on Turkey; on the 7th, advanced troops from the sixth division arrived at the mouth of the Shatt-al-Arab. The small fort at the mouth of the estuary was easily overcome, and the soldiers disembarked on the right or western bank of the stream. Soon afterwards came the news of the cutting of the Persian oil pipe-line by hostile tribesmen, and the consequent despatch of troops to Ahwaz. The train of events set in motion by the storming of Hormuz nearly three centuries earlier had reached its inevitable conclusion.

The news soon spread through the land that the English and Indians had come; and Turkish forces were hurriedly assembled and marched downstream from Basrah. Meanwhile the remainder of the sixth division had arrived from India, and on November 17th the Turks were completely defeated, and the way thrown open to Basrah. The latter city was occupied on the 21st, and the Turkish forces retired to Qurnah, an unprepossessing spot at the junction of the two great rivers, traditionally but illogically supposed to contain the site of the Biblical Garden of Eden.

The Turkish forces were badly supported, and their line of communication was long and inadequately served; and the British and Indian troops had little difficulty in cutting them off higher up the Tigris, and in securing the surrender of Qurnah (December 9th).

Meanwhile, heavy Turkish reinforcements were being hurried down from Baghdad, on either bank of the Tigris; one body on the left bank aiming at harassing the right of the British-Indian forces, and at menacing the oil pipe-line through southern Persia; the other on the right bank at stirring up the powerful Muntafiq tribes round Nasriyah, and thus threatening the left flank of the invading army. But the Turkish forces, though considerable, were not strong enough to give effective trouble, and the invaders were practically left unmolested until the spring of 1915.

Thus ended the first phase of the British invasion, with the port of Basrah, the Gulf coast and the pipe-line in the hands of the invading army, which was faced by a nebulous combination of Turkish and Arab forces of unknown strength, practically devoid of transport facilities.

In spite of the melancholy and much-quoted declaration of the late Mr. Bonar Law, that he " wished we had never gone there," no serious criticism of the wisdom of the first invasion of Mesopotamia, from the British point of view, has yet been made. The official reasons offered for the initiation of the campaign were three : the protection of the oil pipe-line and other plant of the Anglo-Persian Oil Company in southern Persia and the Gulf, a protection vital to the British navy ; the occupation of Basrah and its environs, with a view to making this protection effective by securing the principal enemy port ; and the " moral impression " upon the local Arabs, which, it was thought, could not fail to have an echo on the Egyptian border, and might even have some effect upon the attitude of the Moslem population of India. But in fact, as we have seen, the invasion of Mesopotamia by the British, at any rate in its original form, was inevitable ; it had been made inevitable by the assumption of authority by the British in the Persian Gulf, by the discovery of oil in southern Persia, and, finally, by the decay of the Turkish Empire, and the knowledge that sooner or later, if the British were unwilling to interfere in Mesopotamia, there would not be found wanting other powers willing and even anxious to do so. If the British had not invaded the seaboard of Mesopotamia in 1914, they would have been compelled to do so at a later period of the World War ; and the invasion later might have been neither so easy nor so successful.

Meanwhile the position of the small force in front of Qurnah was by no means a comfortable one. The strength of the Turkish forces, which were known to be gradually reassembling, could not be ascertained with any approach to accuracy, and the loyalty of the Arabs within the zone of conquered territory must, while the success of the occupation was uncertain, remain an unknown quantity. In addition, there were two distinct directions by which the Turks might approach; following the course of the Tigris; or, leaving the river at Kut and turning down the Shatt-al-Hai (itself an old bed of the Tigris) to its junction with the Euphrates, and thus menacing the British left from the direction of Nasriyah. It soon became obvious that to ensure a proper hold on the territory already conquered, some further advance would have to be undertaken, and it was therefore decided early in the new year to raise the strength of the invading force to that of an army corps. The command was now taken over by Sir J. Nixon, General Townshend arriving at the same time to take charge of the sixth division.

Meanwhile efforts were being made on the political side to strengthen the British position with the Arabs, and a British agent had been appointed to the court of Ibn Saud of Nejd. The latter was about to open a campaign against his ancient rival Ibn Rashid, who had again allied himself with the Turks. Alliances were sought by the British with the various tribes lying between the present front and the towns of Amarah, on the Tigris, and Nasriyah, on the Euphrates; but the Arabs, who realized that their own future depended upon their skill in backing the winning side, showed no great eagerness to commit themselves, especially as during April, 1915, the Turkish forces began to show marked activity, and even at one time threatened to cut the Persian pipe-line.

By the beginning of May, however, the situation had materially improved from the British point of view. Turkish attacking forces had been twice beaten off, and a serious offensive was being organized against Amarah. The offensive was successful. On June 3rd, General Townshend entered Amarah; and on July 25th, Nasriyah fell to the British forces, nearly 3,000 prisoners resulting from the two engagements. A decisive blow to local Turkish prestige was meanwhile being dealt in central Arabia by the total defeat of Ibn Rashid by Ibn Saud, the British agent being unfortunately killed in the battle. By the capture of Nasriyah and Amarah the British secured control of both the river approaches to Basrah from the north, and moreover held a position extremely difficult of approach from the Turkish side, for the country north of

BASRAH

BASRAH

both towns is wild and desolate, and inhabited by a turbulent and difficult population.

Much was meanwhile being accomplished in Basrah itself towards accustoming the population to the new regime. The sanitation and the policing of the town had been an immediate care, as much on behalf of the invading troops as of the inhabitants; and, with the press of liners in the river and the congestion of motor traffic along its tortuous streets, Basrah might regard itself as busier than at any other time since the days of Sinbad. Serious difficulty was soon experienced in the matter of provisioning the troops, owing to the scarcity of local supplies; but every effort was made to induce the people to cultivate such produce as could be easily and quickly grown, and any hardship which might have resulted to the civilian population in the matter of shortage of food was practically eliminated by careful organization. On the whole, the British military administration could congratulate itself at the end of 1915 upon having completely restored Basrah's normal life, and greatly increased her prosperity.

Meanwhile the possibility of a further advance was being considered, both at Simla, the head-quarters of the invading force, and in London. The reasons which prompted the consideration of a further advance have been much discussed since the Armistice, and need not be considered in detail here. Probably those that were accepted as decisive were, firstly, the obvious political effect on the general war situation of a further successful advance; and, secondly, the notable success which had already been accomplished with inferior forces and under difficult conditions, which possibly misled the British authorities into believing that the Turkish forces which could be put into the field in Mesopotamia could never be either large or effective. This belief, if it ever existed, was soon to be very severely shattered.

By the month of August, 1915, London and Simla had reached agreement upon a very much more ambitious programme in Mesopotamia than had been contemplated nine months earlier. It was decided that, as a first step, the town of Kut al Amara should be occupied, there being obvious advantages in its capture whether the campaign was developed further or not; for it is here that the Shatt-al-Hai leaves the Tigris and cuts across country to the Euphrates, and the possession of Kut would thus offer complete protection both to Amarah and Nasriyah, by cutting off the best means of approach to both of them. Moreover, Kut was reasonably close to the Persian border town of Khanikin, and from it there would be a reasonable hope of eventually establishing contact with the Russian forces operating in northern Persia, and thus making the "Eastern front" at last continuous.

Meanwhile information was received by the British that a considerable Turkish force was concentrating at Kut, under Nur-ed-Din Bey. In the autumn of 1915 General Townshend advanced rapidly up the Tigris, and on September 15th defeated a Turkish outpost at Abu Rimman, some fifteen miles below Kut. Soon afterwards his outposts came into touch with the Turkish entrenched positions at Es Sinn, and on the 28th he attacked and completely broke them, taking nearly 1,700 prisoners. The town of Kut now fell to the British, and the Indian cavalry in their pursuit of the enemy penetrated half way to the city of Baghdad, a success which possibly suggested a further move forward. At any rate, the British troops were hardly given time to consolidate their position in Kut before the idea of attacking the defences of Baghdad was being persistently mooted.

There were obvious reasons why such a dramatic effort, even if attended with considerable risk, should possess some attraction for the British authorities. The Gallipoli expedition, which had aimed, by the capture of Constantinople, at effecting a junction with the Russian forces and thus isolating the central powers from the outside world, had proved a failure, and the evacuation of the peninsula was admitted to be only a question of time. The Palestine expedition was not yet in full swing. There was obvious need of some stroke which should weaken the Turks and in addition rehabilitate the honour of British arms in Asia. Moreover, increasing evidence was reaching the British authorities of the success of the unscrupulous German propaganda in Asia, especially in Persia, which might easily, if not counteracted, have very serious consequences. Consistent efforts were being made by German emissaries to enlist the support of the Moslem world, even to the extent of spreading the interesting information that the Emperor had been converted to the faith, and was now known as " Hajji Wilhelm."* The danger that Persia, through her fear of both Russia and England, might be persuaded to join forces with Hajji Wilhelm was in 1915 a very real one ; and if Persia had declared for the Central Powers, Afghanistan almost certainly would have followed suit, and the British authorities would have been faced with the immense problem of a defensive campaign on the north-west frontier of India. The seriousness of the situation was revealed by the capture of several finely illuminated letters on vellum addressed to the Amir of Afghanistan and various Indian princes, signed by the German Foreign Secretary himself. As it was, several British vice-consuls in isolated towns in Persia were murdered, and German influence in the district left supreme. In considering the pros and cons of the advance to Baghdad, the Persian problem should not be overlooked.

In addition, it must be remembered that some consideration was due to the Christians of the eastern portions of the Turkish Empire, who had openly declared for the Allies.

From the early part of 1915 onwards, the Assyrians of the hill country of Kurdistan were engaged in fighting both Turks and Kurds, the latter having, on the outbreak of war, thrown in their lot with the Turks on both sides of the Turco-Persian frontier. Farther north, the Armenians were making a desperate struggle for existence. Both Assyrians and Armenians were in touch with Russian forces, but it was obvious that the more pressure that could be brought to bear upon the Turks from the south, the greater the chances for success in the north for these little Christian communities. Finally, it had to be recognized at the time that, with Gallipoli evacuated, Mesopotamia became actually part of the long eastern battle-

* A " Hajji " is one who has performed the haj, or pilgrimage, to Mecca. The German propagandists omitted to state how the versatile Emperor had managed, in so short a time, to undergo conversion and to perform the pilgrimage, but, doubtless, such a point was overlooked by their ignorant audience.

front; and that therefore, from a purely military point of view, it was necessary to exert all possible pressure upon the enemy, there as well as elsewhere.

Meanwhile an interesting situation was developing across the Arabian desert. The Sharif of Mecca, as traditional guardian of the holy cities of Islam, had enjoyed under Turkish rule a position of extra-territorial independence, although the Hedjaz, the country in which the two sacred cities of Mecca and Medina are situated, was for administrative purposes, a Turkish vilayet, or province. For many years the Stamboul Government had been striving to make its authority in the holy land more secure, and the Hedjaz Railway, running from Damascus to Medina, and nominally built for the convenience of Moslem pilgrims, was intended to serve this end. The Hedjaz as a vilayet possessed many privileges. Not only were the sacred cities exempt from taxation, but they actually received a subsidy from the Government, as did also several minor sheikhs of the Beni Harb, who inhabit the country bordering on the main pilgrim road, and therefore possess the power to attack the pilgrim trains at will. The whole vilayet was also immune from conscription, though an abortive attempt was made in 1914 to enforce it. The position of the Sharif of Mecca was a purely spiritual one, but his secular power was in practice considerable, and he was allowed to maintain agents of his own at Medina and Jidda, the port of Mecca on the Red Sea, in addition to his extra territorial privileges in Mecca itself. In the hands of a clever and far-seeing man, the position practically ensured the control of the country, for the Turkish officials were isolated from everybody but their own small garrison, and the Sharif was in nearly every case their go-between in dealing with the local population.

In 1908 there succeeded to the Sharifate Hosein Ibn Ali, a man of considerable ability and wide ambition. The Turks had supported his nomination on account of his pacific and pro-Turkish views, and for some years they had no reason to regret their choice. Hosein's sons, Ali, Abdullah and Feisal, were sent to Constantinople to be educated, and in 1910 the latter, at his father's instigation, personally took up service with the Turkish forces fighting against the Arab rebels of the south, and rose during the campaign to the command of a division. In the same year the Sharif took up arms against Ibn Saud of Nejd, whose anti-Turkish attitude was well known. Up to the year 1913 the Turks had every reason to congratulate themselves upon the staunchness of their ally. But in that year the Sharif conspicuously shifted his ground. Whether this was due to a long-conceived plan, or whether events had occurred to make the Arab prince change his mind, it is impossible to say with any degree of certainty. It is probable, however, that the obvious feebleness of the Turkish Government, demonstrated during the campaign against the rebels in southern Arabia, as well as the growing strength of Ibn Saud, with his British alliance, on his flank, may have induced him to some extent to look with favour on the Arab nationalist cause. Whatever the reason, he now commenced to pursue an openly anti-Turkish policy, actively agitating against the extension of the Hedjaz Railway to Mecca, secretly receiving leaders of the Arab nationalist movement from Syria, and utilizing every opportunity of increasing his own influence at the expense of the central Government. In the latter project he was helped largely by his considerable wealth, drawn chiefly from his estates in Egypt; for the Sharif had long been reputed to be the wealthiest of all the Arab princes.

In 1915 word was received by the British authorities that the Sharif had definitely committed himself to a policy of revolt against Turkish authority, and the former thereupon agreed to support him with money and supplies. This was the beginning of that Anglo-Arab campaign that ended in the capture of Syria, and became so memorable to the outside world through the romantic exploits of the young archæologist, Colonel T. E. Lawrence. The knowledge that a revolt of considerable importance was shortly to be expected in Arabia itself undoubtedly had some effect in influencing the authorities in favour of a further advance in Mesopotamia.

Kut secure in his grasp, General Townshend had for some weeks been feeling the ground in front of him towards Baghdad. He reported the Turks as far less disorganized than at first supposed, and his own troops as weary and short of establishment. In view of the length of his communications and the fact that they depended entirely upon water transport, with the exception of a short length of narrow gauge railway, and in view of the complete isolation of his force, he not unnaturally deprecated any further advance. He was, however, finally overruled, and early in November a forward movement was ordered.

On the 21st of the month a Turkish force was encountered and driven off, and soon afterwards the British troops came in sight of the historic ruins of Ctesiphon, the old capital of pre-Arab days. Here the Turks were found in force and strongly entrenched; the bulk of the British forces were accordingly led up under cover of darkness, and the attack launched at dawn. At first the battle went with the British; two lines of trenches were carried, and many prisoners captured. But strong Turkish reinforcements arrived while the fighting was in progress, and by the 25th of the month the Turks had regained all the ground they had lost. During the night the British commenced to retreat. After much weary marching and heavy fighting, the little force reached Kut again on December 3rd, having lost 4,500 men, but bringing in 1,600 prisoners. Five days later the town was invested by the pursuing Turks.

A superior to Nur-ed-din Bey now appeared in the field, in the person of the German Field-Marshal von der Goltz. Under his direction several attacks were immediately launched against the isolated British garrison, but all were unavailing. The Turkish forces were then moved south of the town, and elaborate defences constructed against the possible attack of a relieving force. General Townshend was thus completely cut off from his base and the remainder of the British forces.

The opening of the new year saw a determined effort to break the blockade and rescue General Townshend and his garrison. During the first few days of January, the Turks were successfully driven out of their forward positions and compelled to fall back upon a new line not far distant from Kut itself; but all British efforts to pierce this line met with complete failure, and the casualties were so numerous that the attackers had to pause for reinforcements. Meanwhile the supreme command of the Turkish forces had devolved upon Khalil Pasha.

An abortive attempt was made on the night of March 7th to break through the investing lines, after which no further movement was undertaken till April; during that month, however, strenuous efforts were undertaken to rescue the beleagured British troops. On the 5th of the month, part of the Turkish line was successfully penetrated; but several heavy attacks against other portions were repulsed with heavy losses. The position of the force in Kut was now known to be desperate. After a local success on the 17th a great attempt was made on the 22nd, which came within an ace of success. On the night of the 24th a steamer attempted in vain to run the blockade, a last desperate effort to reach the little garrison. On the 29th the garrison capitulated.

The fall of Kut for the first time brought the Mesopotamian campaign before the public attention of Europe, and, coming as it did within four months of the final evacuation of Gallipoli, it had in England a profoundly depressing effect. This was aggravated by the tales of inefficient medical attention and supplies for the wounded, which now began to filter through to India and thence to England. In addition, the serious effect of a second severe British reverse in the Near East on the world in general had to be recognized by the British authorities, and it at once became obvious that Kut would have to be re-captured, even if a very much larger force had to be concentrated in Mesopotamia than had previously been considered desirable. Fortunately, the Turks showed no disposition to follow up their successes, though they developed great activity against the Russians in Persia, driving them out of Kermanshah and Hamadan, and practically confining the Russian forces to the extreme north and east of Persia.

In June, however, the whole situation began, from the British point of view, to clear. The long-expected rebellion of the Sharif Hosein in Mecca broke out at last, and by the end of the month the Turks had been driven out of Mecca, Jidda and Taif, and the Sharif had proclaimed himself independent of Ottoman control. Later in the year he assumed the title of "King of the Arab lands," a style which was afterwards changed to that of "King of the Hedjaz." As such he was formally recognized by the Governments of Great Britain, France and Italy, but his progress was watched with noticeable lack of cordiality by his neighbour Ibn Saud of Nejd, and the strong feeling henceforth existing between the two Arab leaders was destined to give considerable trouble to their common ally, Great Britain.

In Persia, too, the situation was improving. Under the indomitable leadership of the well-known Persian expert, Sir Percy Sykes, who had been vested with considerable power by the British Government, a ragged and heterogeneous force of Persian gendarmerie was gradually transformed into a reliable and pro-British force; the old Swedish gendarme officers, who were pro-German, were forced to flee, and the more important roads and trade routes in southern Persia were opened up to the British once more. The British hold on the country, so vital owing to the oil question, was gradually re-established, and the danger of German propaganda reaching the countries farther east became much modified.

In Mesopotamia itself, the late summer saw a complete reversal of the situation existing earlier in the year. Heavy British reinforcements arrived in preparation for a new offensive, the landing and transport facilities were greatly increased and improved, and considerable railway track laid down. In August the Mesopotamian force was taken over direct by the British War Office in London, and the inconvenient control from India abolished; at the same time a new commander-in-chief arrived in Basrah, in the person of the afterwards illustrious General Maude.

No outward effort was made to advance until the close of the year, although the intervening months were by no means empty of achievement. Determined that there should be no question of past failures being repeated owing to weakness of organization or supply, the new general laboured night and day to transform Basrah into a really efficient jumping-off ground for the new campaign. When he did strike, he struck with effect. A few Turkish positions were suddenly carried on December 13th, and, despite heavy opposition, the succeeding weeks witnessed continuous British progress.

By the middle of February, the whole of the Turkish defences covering Kut had been enveloped, and by the end of the month the town itself was once more in British hands. Nor was this all. By March 4th, the British forces had advanced to the ill-omened site of the battle of Ctesiphon, the high-water mark of their previous advance; but on this occasion the Turks had already retired farther back, and were now entrenched behind the Diyala river, a tributary of the Tigris immediately covering Baghdad itself. Here the Turks made a determined stand, but their efforts were unavailing against the pressure of the attacking host; and before the middle of March Baghdad itself had fallen into British hands, and General Maude had made his historic entry into the city from the Bab-al-Muadham. Still further successes soon crowned the British arms, and by the coming of the hot weather the country had been cleared of Turks as far north as Samarra, and as far east as the Persian border.

In under five months the reverse at Kut had been wiped out, and practically the whole of central Mesopotamia, including the historic capital, captured by the British. The ill-odour which the land of the rivers had already obtained in the minds of the British public, owing to the Kut disaster and the scandals associated with it, perhaps blinded them somewhat to the brilliance of this achievement, which was unique in the long tale of the World War, at any rate so far as British arms were concerned.

Nor was General Maude content merely to rest upon his military laurels. The condition of the captured country from an administrative point of view was very bad. The officials under the old regime had been almost entirely recruited from Turks and pro-Turkish local families, and they had all fled, taking with them the whole of the official documents; moreover, for centuries no effort had been made to improve the material conditions of the inhabitants, who were cut off from even their usual food supply by the operations of war. The country had to be reorganized, fed and run by the British army, at short notice, and while itself engaged in a strenuous campaign the issue of which was still doubtful. In the course of a few months a system of administration and justice was devised, courts of law set up and judges appointed, railways opened to civilian traffic, farming encouraged, roads mapped out, and towns which had been destroyed by the operations, such as Kut, entirely rebuilt. The city of Baghdad itself, covering an area of several square miles and containing a population of two hundred thousand people, was cleansed, lighted, endowed with a new system of street and house numbers, and generally reorganized on modern lines. Seldom or never has a modern army been called upon to tackle such a variety of tasks as befell the British Expeditionary Force in Mesopotamia. In the storm of criticism to which the Mesopotamian campaign has been subjected, since the termination of the World War, in the English press, the remarkable variety and success of the British accomplishment ought not, in common fairness, to be overlooked.

The capture of Baghdad had an immediate political effect, the full result of which could hardly be foreseen at the time. The prestige of the Sultan of Turkey as head of the Moslem world was now seriously endangered ; in 1916 he had lost Mecca, the home of the faith ; in 1917 Baghdad, the fabled capital of the most notable Moslem epoch. The strong pan-Islamic party in the Turkish capital now began to press for the use of every available Turkish force for the recapture of Baghdad, and in this they were supported by the German element, who were still hypnotized by the " Drang nach Osten " and the alliterative cry of " Berlin to Baghdad." Thus, at a critical moment of the war, large Turkish forces were withdrawn from the Egyptian front for use in Mesopotamia, and the dramatic successes of the British arms in Sinai became possible.

By the middle of the year the Turkish leaders had realized that a successful British advance through Palestine and Syria would prejudice the Turkish prospects in Mesopotamia, by cutting off communication down the upper reaches of the Euphrates ; and an offensive on a large scale was planned by Field-Marshal von Falkenhayn, then in supreme command at Aleppo. But it was already too late ; by the time the Turkish forces were ready to assume the offensive, the British were attacking ; and by the beginning of November the Turkish front in southern Palestine was broken. In spite of stubborn rearguard actions, the British progress went forward from this point with dramatic completeness ; Jaffa being captured by the middle of the month, and Jerusalem itself being seriously threatened. On December 9th, Izzet Bey, the last Turkish mutasarrif of Jerusalem, was compelled to evacuate the city ; by midday British soldiers had reached the Jaffa Gate ; and on December 11th, General Allenby, the commander-in-chief of the British force in Palestine, entered on foot the sacred city of three great religions. The Ottoman power thus lost the last of the numerous cities in its dominions with sentimental religious associations.

But in Mesopotamia the year which had showered such a profusion of gifts upon the British force was to end in mourning for the man who, more than any other single man, had made such gifts possible. Rumour of the Turkish plans to recapture Baghdad had reached Mesopotamia ; but once again the British struck first. Late in September a brilliant success in the upper Euphrates country was gained by the capture of Ramadi, and a month later the British forces on the Tigris pushed on north of Tekrit. But at the beginning of November the news began to trickle through that General Maude was seriously ill, and on the 10th of the month, to the consternation of his subordinates and soldiers, he died. The ostensible cause of his sudden death was cholera, but it was widely believed for some time afterwards that he had been poisoned, a belief in support of which considerable proof was unofficially produced. The official report of his death, however, held to the original designation of cholera as the cause of death, and it has never been contradicted. Nevertheless, the very general alarm excited on the spot by the general's death only very slowly subsided. Few leaders in the World War attained to such a position of personal ascendancy over the troops under them as did General Maude, and his sudden passing was widely mourned, on personal as well as on national grounds. He was buried in the British cemetery at Baghdad North, which contains a handsome cross to his memory.

The year in Persia also witnessed a considerable improvement in the British and Allied position, an improvement which was, however, offset by the Russian withdrawal. The advance of General Maude towards Baghdad made the position of the Turkish forces in Persia a very difficult one, and the Russians, who had been driven back the year before, to Kazvin, were now able to turn the tables on their opponents. By the end of March the Turks had been driven across the Mesopotamian frontier, and on April 2nd, a squadron of Cossacks came in touch with the British forces at Qizl Robat, between Baghdad and Khanikin. For the first time in the war, the great Eastern front was joined, and the central powers surrounded.

But the month which saw the capture of Baghdad also witnessed the abdication of the Tsar of All the Russias. During the summer demoralization set in among the Russian troops in Persia, and by the autumn the whole front from the Baltic to Mesopotamia had collapsed. The gateway to India and central Asia lay once more open to German and Turkish forces. During 1918 several small but notable efforts were made by the British to stem the tide of Russian disintegration, and to secure the influence of the Allies in central Asia. British troops were sent to occupy Kazvin; a small force in motor-cars crossed to Baku, and for a time successfully occupied that well-known oil centre; and a military mission was despatched to the countries bordering the northern shore of the Caspian, to assist the Russian Menshevists. The Assyrian Christians who had been left stranded by the retreat of the Russians, were rescued by the efforts of the British forces, and brought in safety to Mesopotamia; a special "city of refuge" being provided at Bakubah, near Baghdad, for their accommodation. Conditions in Persia as a whole remained unsettled for the remainder of the war though the presence of large British detachments helped to maintain order in certain districts.

In Palestine and Syria the British advance continued steadily throughout 1918, in spite of the fact that the serious position of the Allies in France led to the withdrawal of several divisions of experienced English troops, and their substitutition by new, and in some cases inexperienced, Indian troops. Local captures took place throughout the summer, including the important seizure of Jericho; but the Turkish forces were considerable, and some months had to be spent in preparation before the British front in Palestine could be advanced as a whole. The advance, when it did commence, was brilliant. Nazareth was captured on September 20th, Nablus on the 21st, and Damascus entered on October 1st. Tyre was occupied on the 4th, Sidon on the 6th, Beirut on the 8th, and Tripoli on the 18th. The end of the month saw Aleppo occupied by the Arab forces of the Hedjaz, who, under the command of the Amir Feisal, were co-operating with the English, Indian and Australian forces; and by the time of the Armistice, the Turkish troops had been entirely swept out of even northern Syria.

Nor did the British remain idle, in these closing months of the World War, in Mesopotamia itself. Kifri, near the Persian border, was captured in January, Hit, on the upper Euphrates, in February, and Kirkuk early in May. The small British force sent to Baku proved unable to hold that city; and on the fall of the oil centre to the Turks, the British forces in Mesopotamia were ordered to occupy Mosul. The campaign was not recommenced until October 23rd; but two days before the Armistice, the last Turkish army was completely defeated at Shergat, close to the ruins of the ancient Assyrian city of Assur. The way to Mosul was now open. At the time of the Armistice, the British, by a magnificent feat of arms, had made themselves masters of all Mesopotamia, of Syria, of Palestine and of large portions of Persia; and British garrisons dotted the entire length of the country from Cairo to the shores of the Caspian Sea. For one fleeting moment the whole of the Middle East was united once again under the control of a single power.

The Middle East in general, and Mesopotamia in particular, waited anxiously to see what that Power would do with her conquests.

CHAPTER XI

THE YEAR OF HOPE

" We said to the lion, ' Art thou a lion ? ' and he replied, doubtfully, ' Perhaps I am,' or ' I seem to be.' "—MEDITATIONS OF MA'ARRI.

THE year 1919 dawned full of hope for Mesopotamia. The World War was over, and it had ended in a fashion entirely agreeable to the more intelligent portions of all the various Mesopotamian communities. They had long prayed in secret for some form of European or American intervention which should release them from the hopeless serfdom of Turkish control, and put them once more in direct touch with the life of the great world. For generations they had been accustomed to look to the British more especially as their connecting link with the vigorous life of the West, only inclining latterly towards the Germans because of the apparent decay and lassitude of the British themselves; for it is obviously of no use for a weak and dependent people to give their loyalty to a Power, however friendly or familiar, that is apparently either standing still or going backwards. But to their delight, and also no doubt to their surprise, the British Empire had arisen in the war phœnix-like from its own ashes, had shaken off the sloth and carelessness of age, and had shown something of the energy and virility of its earlier years. Directly they had made sure, in common parlance, " which way the cat would jump " (a political proceeding despised by a strong, but absolutely necessary to a dependent people), the inhabitants of Mesopotamia lent themselves whole-heartedly to the British cause; and, the stress of the World War over and past, they naturally looked to see the reward for their fidelity in the material development, so long overdue, of their country.

It is not easy for those who have lived all their lives in the stimulating atmosphere of the West, where progress, both material and intellectual, forms the natural background

THE YEAR OF HOPE

of life, to realize the attitude of mind of an intelligent citizen of a backward and artificially stilted country. Picture the feeling, say, of an inhabitant of Mesopotamia who feels himself to be young, strong, energetic and capable of great things, and whose home life has kept him, through the medium of foreign newspapers and the travels of his parents, in touch with the developments of the modern world. There are many such youths among the more fortunate classes of all communities in Mesopotamia, more particularly among the Christians and Jews. Grown to manhood, such a youth finds but two courses open to him; to stay in his own country and face intellectual and moral stagnation; or to emigrate to some more fortunate land, and indulge his ambition for a normal and progressive career at the expense of his love for his country, a love which is natural in every healthy man. Many and many a Mesopotamian has been driven by the blighting misrule of the Turk to face just such a decision; the United States, the wide plains of the Argentine, and, in a lesser degree, the cities of Europe, are full of the sons of Mesopotamian families who have been compelled to turn their backs on their country in order to give themselves the chances that their talents deserved. Not a few Mesopotamians have risen to eminence in the country of their adoption, the most notable, perhaps, being the members of the great Sassoon family of Baghdad, who both in India and England have shown themselves capable of filling the highest positions that the business and political worlds of their adopted countries could offer them. Hundreds of cities and towns in the United States and South America contain Arabs, Jews and Chaldeans who have been driven to seek their fortune in the great world, but who still conceal in their hearts a haunting love for the once great but now desolate land of the rivers.

But at the beginning of 1919 there was a feeling abroad that all this was over. The Turks had gone; the British were in charge; Mesopotamia would be developed just as India and Egypt had been developed; the rivers would be harnessed, floods prevented, irrigation perfected; roads and railways would appear; in a few years Mesopotamia, with its almost perfect winter climate, would become not only a great agricultural country, but a tourist resort rivalling Egypt in the variety of its attractions and the luxury of its appointments. The time that every loyal Mesopotamian had dreamt of for years had come at last; Basrah, Baghdad, Mosul, the unkempt, dirty cities that he knew so well, would rise, under the magic of the British touch, to some semblance of their former greatness, drained and rebuilt and adorned with all those refinements and conveniences that a modern city expects. And then there was talk of oil—that magic fluid that even recently had galvanized the most lonely parts of Texas into feverish life. The wild tribes of the country would be disciplined and gradually led into the paths of progress; to compensate them for the loss of their lives of lawless but attractive freedom, the British would offer great material chances, great careers; the naked lad of to-day, running to the river bank with a primitive bowl to fetch water for his mother, would perchance be the business leader or the distinguished lawyer of to-morrow. At last Mesopotamia would take its rightful place in the world, the place to which its long history, its soil and its climate undoubtedly entitle it. It seemed in 1919 that a fairer day had dawned for Mesopotamia than she had known since the times of Harun the Good.

Alas, for these vain hopes! No one could foresee the depths of anarchy to which the whole Near East would soon be driven by the incredible folly of European politicians; no one could foresee that the credit of the victorious associated Powers, apparently unassailable after the downfall of their enemies, was resting actually on such insecure foundations; no one could foresee that the British people, having spent a vast amount of money, time and energy in securing Mesopotamia as a " sphere of influence," and latterly in conquering it, would be chiefly concerned in the next five years in a feverish attempt to get rid of it again. Truly the ways of the European are strange, and " Allah is the only knowing one " !

The British in 1919 were faced with the practical outcome of their general policy for the last three hundred years. The prophecies of the more politically minded Mesopotamians had come true; they had always said that in the first great war Mesopotamia was bound to become British, and here it was so. The British were finding out, to their cost, that it was impossible for them in the long run to ensure the control of the Persian Gulf and the Persian oilfields without a footing in Mesopotamia. The land of the rivers, now as always, holds the key to the whole Middle East. And the development of a "sphere of influence" must inevitably eventuate in conquest. But the capture of a country, whether carried out by the wishes or against the wishes of its inhabitants, immediately foreshadows a far more serious problem; the future administration of it. In 1919 it was already too late for the British to discuss the advisability or the reverse of conquering Mesopotamia; they had already conquered it. It lay now at their feet, helpless, divided in many directions against itself, deprived by the sudden collapse of the Turkish Empire of even the vestiges of Government machinery. What would the British do with it?

Two courses lay open to them; they could treat it as territory acquired in war and immediately annex it to the British Empire; this was the course generally anticipated by the world, and, on the whole, sincerely desired by the Mesopotamians. Alternatively, they could arrange an immediate withdrawal from the country, after setting up some sort of local Government which should be reasonably agreeable to the people; this was the course clearly hinted at in General Maude's speech on the entry into Baghdad eighteen months earlier, and thoroughly in accord with the sentiment of the post-war world. There was a general weariness not only of war, but of what was conceived to be the chief cause of war, Imperialistic ambition; and there was a natural and overwhelming desire among the common people of the Western countries, on whom the brunt of the war had chiefly fallen, to allow the backward races of the East to work out their own salvation, in their own time and in their own way. The practicability of such a course of action did not, in the general joy over the termination of the war and the birth of a new era "fit for heroes," arouse either doubt or discussion.

Thus the project of transforming Mesopotamia into an independent state was largely born of the generous, if unpractical, feeling of the time, a feeling which had been admirably expressed by the American President Wilson's doctrine of "self-determination." Ignorance of the Near and Middle East in general, and of Mesopotamia in particular, was, and is, very common among the so-called statesmen of the West; and no one questioned the possibility of a literal interpretation of the doctine of "self-determination" to an area containing numerous different hostile communities, possessing strong national feelings, but extremely limited in size. It was assumed that, Mesopotamia being an "Arab" country, it would be quite easy to set up an Arab state which would be acceptable to the people and at the same time in consonance with the secret pledges given during the war by Great Britain to the new King Hosein of the Hedjaz; pledges which Great Britain had already cynically violated by other secret undertakings with France. The future, then, of the land of the rivers was to be decided in accordance with Mr. Wilson's twelfth point, which laid down for the non-Turkish nationalities of the old Turkish Empire "an absolutely unmolested opportunity of autonomous development." How such an ideal was to be squared with the obvious necessity of the British to retain some sort of control over their old "sphere of influence," no one attempted to explain; and the history of post-war Mesopotamia is, in the main, the history of the attempt to associate these obviously dissimilar objects. The British administration in the country has always been handicapped by the necessity for this double loyalty, which has negatived all enthusiasm and paralysed all action.

Meanwhile a further suggestion of President Wilson, a suggestion which was soon to have a far-reaching effect upon the future of Mesopotamia, had been received with acclamation by the public of Europe. This was the idea of a "League of Nations," an international organization endowed with super-national powers, and based on the principle that the various states and governments of the world should be prepared to submit themselves to the discipline of a system of law and order, in the same way that they require a similar submission on the part of their own subjects within the confines of their own national

THE YEAR OF HOPE

borders. The idea was not a new one; it had in fact appeared in some shape or form at the close of every great European war for some centuries past. Conspicuous modern examples had been the Holy Alliance of the mystical Tsar Alexander at the close of the Napoleonic wars, and, on a smaller scale, the Concert of Europe in the middle of the nineteenth century, which had been responsible on several occasions for the settlement of awkward international disputes by the argument of joint force exercised in co-operation by the leading Powers. But the enormous increase in international knowledge and international co-operation during the last fifty years not unnaturally led men to believe that such a desirable conception was, to say the least, a good deal easier of accomplishment in modern times than it had been even a hundred years before; and the impression began to grow that, just as the war had, by the numbers of peoples it involved and the vastness of its operations, affected the whole world, so it might be possible to construct a peace of some permanence based on world-wide foundations. Thus the proposal of President Wilson to establish this super-national authority at the time of the signing of the Peace Treaty, and, moreover, to entrust to its care the practical application of the Twelfth Point, was received in every European country with the greatest enthusiasm.

It is possible, and even probable, that the various statesmen concerned were perfectly genuine in their desire for the establishment of real national states in the various portions of the old Turkish Empire containing alien populations; but the practical question which now arose, especially in view of the various and conflicting secret agreements concluded during the war, was one of extreme difficulty. How was the thing to be done? Who was to decide what form the new states should take? How were they to be brought into being? The whole administration, not only of Mesopotamia, but of Syria and Palestine as well, had collapsed on the departure of the Turks. The British army was in occupation of Mesopotamia and of large portions of Syria; the French of the Lebanon; and the Hedjaz Arabs of Trans-Jordania and the neighbourhood of Damascus. The only semblance of a national government was in the latter city, where Ali Riza Pasha ar-Rikabi, a local man with considerable Turkish official experience, headed an Arab administration with the tacit support of the Hedjaz army and of the English. It was obvious that, apart altogether from military considerations, if the countries concerned were immediately evacuated by the conquering armies, only chaos would ensue; and the question promptly arose as to how the actual control of Britain and France over their respective " spheres " was to be legalized, without at the same time fatally prejudicing the chances of the countries concerned to achieve " self-determination." A solution for this difficulty was found in the so-called " mandate system," by which (in the words of the Treaty of Versailles) certain " communities formerly belonging to the Turkish Empire " can be regarded as having " reached a stage of development where their existence as independent nations can be provisionally recognized, subject to the rendering of administrative advice and assistance by a mandatory Power until such time as they are able to stand alone." In plain language, the mandate plan sanctioned the establishment of a system by which a weak or backward nationality could be handed over, for a term of years, to the supervision, but not to the control, of a great Power; the latter taking the rôle, in fact, of a sort of national " guardian," prepared to protect and develop its " ward " by all the means in its power, and without any apparent reward. The obvious weaknesses of the system, which were condoned or overlooked in the period of war-weary sentimentality which followed the Armistice, have since become only too plain; but for the moment it was accepted as offering a fairly practical and creditable way out of the difficulty of creating new states and new governments where none had previously existed.

It was some time, however, before any attempt was made to apply the generous ideals foreshadowed in these various Declarations, at any rate as far as Mesopotamia was concerned. The question of the peace terms with Turkey was not even discussed until May, 1919, and the drafting of the treaty was not taken seriously in hand until the London Conference of February, 1920. On April 24th of that year, a mandate for Mesopotamia was granted to

Great Britain, this being the first attempt, eighteen months after the Armistice, to legalize in any way the British occupation of the country; but it was not until August 10th that the treaty which embodied the recognition of the mandate was signed by the delegates of Turkey, and not until December that a draft mandate was submitted on behalf of Great Britain for the approval of the Council of the League of Nations. In the meanwhile things had happened which served to put a completely different complexion upon the whole state of affairs.

It cannot be said that the proposals of the European Powers which aimed at carrying into effect the principle of the Twelfth Point, so far as the Near East was concerned, were received with anything approaching enthusiasm, or even gratitude, in either Mesopotamia or Syria. What the latter countries desired and hoped for was material development; what post-war Europe offered them was frothy political sentiment. It should never be forgotten, first and foremost, that political idealism of the English Liberal or of the American pattern is almost unknown in the Near East. The idea that a great nation would be prepared to carry out a lengthy and possibly expensive project purely on idealistic grounds would in any case be merely received in the East with cynicism. The latter has a very much longer political history than Europe, and, even more so, than the United States of America; and it is inclined to regard political idealism, unless it is idealism of the most obviously practical sort, as merely a convenient cloak for some other less reputable political object. Its people have, politically speaking, all the ingrained suspicion of the elderly person who has " seen it all before."

Nor can it be said that the people of the Near East have had any great reason to put their trust in the political idealism, or even in the good faith, of the West. They have watched the West interfere in Near Eastern matters times out of number in quite recent years, but always to the eventual advantage of the West. They have seen the British occupation of Egypt and the Sudan, undertaken according to their sponsors from the highest motives and merely for a limited time, turn into Imperial encroachments of an obviously permanent nature; they have seen the same

British, with no excusable object, except that of Imperial ambition, occupy both Cyprus and Aden; and they have seen the gradual French infringement of practically the whole northern coast of Africa. The absolutely wanton seizure of Tripoli from the Turks just prior to the World War did not escape their notice; nor could the obvious European encouragement to Turkey's many Balkan enemies avoid comment. Not unnaturally, it had become an axiom with them that it was only a question of time before the various European Powers would seek still further to divide the helpless body of the Near Eastern world between themselves. Then came the World War, and, following that, the wave of idealism through the West, offering them independence; but in independence, of course, qualified by the acceptance of a mandate. Naturally, the people of the Near East jumped to the conclusion that this was the old system under a new name; it would resemble the British " temporary occupation " of Egypt; they would be, under the mandate plan, free men in theory, but in practice subjects of the Power who held the mandate, a new type of colonial; in fact even possibly in a worse position than the colonial, for they would lack the latter's privilege of being an actual legal subject of the sovereign state. Thus from the first the idea of the mandate system, which aroused such enthusiasm among political idealists in Europe, was received by the public of the Near East with derision; nay, with contempt. There did indeed seem something a little mean about the thing, viewed from a cynical Eastern standpoint; if France and Great Britain desired to chop up the remainder of the Near Eastern world between them, could they not have admitted it openly? Surely they were strong enough! So reasoned the coffee-house politicians of Syria and Mesopotamia; and President Wilson's magnificent gesture was thus thwarted entirely in its appeal to just the very people whom it was most intended to serve.

But, on the other hand, the idea of "self-determination" found an immediate echo among the followers of the Syrian and Arab nationalist schools, which, as we have seen, had been growing more and more powerful through the last years of the Turkish regime; and the existing Arab Government at Damascus formed an excellent focus for their activities. Ali Riza Pasha was soon superseded as the head of the administration by the Amir (Prince) Feisal, the third son of King Hosein of the Hejaz, who had distinguished himself as a soldier, in the Turkish forces during the Asiri revolt of 1910, and latterly, on the other side, in the World War. Prince Feisal was personally popular with the Arab residents of Syria owing to the efforts which he had made, often at considerable risk to his own safety, to secure the reprieve of distinguished Syrian traitors who had fallen into Turkish hands. His intimate knowledge of the French language and of European history and customs had brought him into touch with many European officials, and his friendship for Colonel Lawrence, the romantic English archæologist who had served throughout the war as the chief British officer with the Hedjaz forces, was destined later to have a certain political importance. It was hoped at the time that Prince Feisal might be able in Damascus to act the part of a buffer between the violent anti-European feeling of his retainers and the French and British authorities. Meanwhile in Mesopotamia there was nothing to be done but continue the military administration and gradually, if possible, adapt it to the needs of peace-time life, pending the arrival of a settlement by the Powers. The difficulties which faced the constitution of some form of civil administration were peculiar. A state of war still technically existed; even the documents of the old Turkish administration had disappeared; and no official indication could be obtained as to what was to be the immediate future of the country. In the press of greater events the peace delegates had forgotten Mesopotamia; and it soon became apparent to the British officials on the spot that, in their efforts to set the wheels of Mesopotamian life revolving normally once more, they would have to depend upon themselves rather than on higher authority at home. Meanwhile an immediate problem was raised by the stubborn attitude of the British troops, many of whom had been away from their homes for some years, and who naturally desired to leave Mesopotamia and return to England now that the war was over; for the soldiers were in many cases employed on what would in civilized countries be regarded as civilian occupations, and on their release other substitutes for their labour would have to be found.

Nor were the difficulties of the British authorities confined to the trouble over shortage of personnel, or the uncertainty of the political future. Very large areas of the country were inaccessible, and indeed almost unknown, to them; the British advance up country had been largely confined to the course of the Tigris, and the crowded and important districts of the Euphrates valley from Nasriyah to Fallujah had hardly seen British troops at all. The turbulent and isolated holy cities of Najaf and Kerbela, with their large foreign population, had practically escaped British military pressure; and in the south large areas of the Muntafiq country, and of the wild and difficult area bordering the Shatt-al-Hai, were practically unknown to British administrators. In addition, the military situation was far from sound. Demobilization, in obedience to the insistent pressure of the troops, proceeded at a very rapid rate, and reinforcements were not easily procurable from Europe; no order had as yet been received to withdraw the far-flung British line in Persia, and for practical purposes the eastern boundary of Mesopotamia might be regarded as resting, for the moment, on the Caspian Sea. Nor was any immediate improvement in the military situation to be expected; rather the reverse. The Mesopotamians were almost certain to become restive unless the future of their country was decided within a reasonable time; the Bolshevik power might at any time grow to menacing proportions in Persia; and trouble was sooner or later bound to be experienced from the lawless elements of the large areas of marsh and desert into which the Turkish authorities had never dared to penetrate, but which the British administration were anxious to rope within the body politic. It soon became obvious that the denizens of these parts, to whom taxation is more distasteful than death, would not submit to parting with their accustomed freedom without a struggle, and that they would, whenever they considered the forces at the disposal of the British to be weakened or scattered, try conclusions with their new masters. The rapid growth of the Arab nationalist spirit across the Syrian border, and the almost pathetically sentimental condition of European political thought might also serve to give the British authorities cause for uneasiness; for they were only too well aware of the truth behind the dictum, attributed to a well-known sheikh of the Middle Euphrates, that "the Arab is a slave and requires a hard master; give him the stick first, then the sugar." In view of the fact that the World War had resulted in a general distribution of rifles of modern pattern throughout the Near and Middle East, the reliable information that the tribes were now twice as well armed as they had been before the war was hardly likely to encourage a feeling of confidence. It soon became clear that the military resources at the disposal of the British authorities were not adequate to stem the tide of a general rising, should any unfortunate occurrence bring one into being. Meanwhile the question of general reconstruction was surrounded with many difficulties peculiar to the country and the situation. Nearly all the countries involved in the operations of war had reached a certain stage of material civilization, and had nothing to gain, and in many cases everything to lose, by the occupation of invading armies. In Mesopotamia the reverse was the case. The British forces were more than invaders; they were the vanguard of civilization. They brought in their train, primarily, of course, for their own use, everything that a modern civilized country expects, and which Mesopotamia had hitherto lacked. Railways, roads, telephones, wireless, newspapers, motor-cars, medical aid, education, all either owed their initiation in Mesopotamia to, or had received a great impetus from, the presence of the British troops. Thus the problem in Mesopotamia was not so much one of reconstruction as of construction; civilian life had not merely to be restarted, but it had to be re-created on a modern level.

Quite early in the war it had become obvious that some effort must be made to continue, and if possible increase, the amenities of ordinary life in the areas behind the lines. Departments of civil works, of education, of health and finance were early created as independent bureaux under army supervision; and the Basrah area, with its fine roads, electric lights and improved sanitary conditions, had become, in all but climate, a pleasant, up-to-date Eastern urban area. Money was not grudged in the reorganization of Basrah partly because it was considered necessary to impress the local people with the energy and ability of British administration; and because it had been generally assumed that, whatever eventually happened to the rest of Mesopotamia, Basrah would remain a British possession. The civilian departments of the army were extended afterwards to Baghdad, and ultimately to the whole country; and they formed the basis upon which the civilian administration was eventually built up, and upon which it is operated even to-day.

A large amount of elaborate constructional work, the cost of which was afterwards heavily criticized by the British public, was put in hand in 1919. Undoubtedly a great deal of needless extravagance was permitted in the execution of many of these works; but on the other hand a heavy programme was in any case necessitated by the complete lack of everything that a civilized community needs for the performance of its daily life and work. Baghdad, as well as Basrah, was equipped with an electric lighting plant, at first confined to military use, and an additional one later laid down at Hillah. A system of elementary sanitation was introduced into Baghdad, and a water supply arranged; and efforts were made to complete the new street cutting the city in half, which had been commenced by Khalil Pasha as a war-time measure. The old British Residency became General Head-quarters, and a number of handsome new or adapted buildings housed various departments of the civil or military staffs. The most prominent of the new buildings undertaken were the Government Press, whose imposing exterior covers a medley of old houses behind; and a new residency on a smaller scale, for the accommodation of the Acting Civil Commissioner. Many of the British civil officials found themselves, in the chronic house shortage which arose in Baghdad after the Armistice, quite unable to find a house or even a room; and eventually it was decided to build two bungalow villages in the suburbs, both of which have since done a great deal towards improving the amenities of their own particular districts. An effort was made at the same time to interest the local inhabitants in modern town-planning, and a scheme for a

EAST BAGHDAD

Greater Baghdad was prepared; certain portions of this which were needed by the British military authorities were afterwards executed by Turkish prisoners, and have taken shape to-day in the military suburb of Hinaidi.

The completion of the railway early in 1920 brought Baghdad into direct touch with Basrah and the outside world; and the Mesopotamian capital became for the time being the happy hunting ground of a large number of new business firms from India and elsewhere, who sought to take advantage of the post-war boom which, it was assumed, must result from British occupation. The value of shops and offices in the city rose by leaps and bounds; preparations were rapidly made for the rebuilding of the property ruthlessly destroyed in the construction of Khalil Pasha's new street; and it appeared as if the city were about to enter upon a time of real prosperity. The routes to Persia were secure, and there appeared to be more money in that distracted country than had been the case within the living memory of man; and, in addition, the collapse of Russia practically cut off Teheran from the industrial West on that side, and the whole of the Persian import trade was diverted to Baghdad and Basrah. The British officers and soldiers formed a considerable class of (to the Easterner) fabulously rich persons, with easy tastes and generous habits; and the merchants of Baghdad began to congratulate themselves that the poverty and confinement of Turkish times had indeed given way to a new age.

But the satisfaction of the towns with the British administration was, for a variety of reasons, not re-echoed in the country generally. Some of these reasons have already been mentioned; the tendency of the British to make the strong arm of the law felt where it had never been felt before; the continued delay in any announcement regarding the future of the country; the fear of increased and far more general taxation. A feeling was slowly spreading over the country that in a few years, perhaps in a few months, it would be too late to strike at the invader and to make secure the old licence and freedom; if the British were allowed, in the phraseology of European militarism, to "consolidate," then there would be no getting them out at all. This quite natural and comprehensible sentiment, spreading through the countryside, was responsible for the nearest approach to unification of feeling that has ever occurred in modern Mesopotamia.

The danger of the whole country acting together upon an impulse of general rebellion had never been altogether disregarded by the Turkish authorities, whose modern policy had invariably been to weaken the nation by fostering every local and inter-tribal rivalry or dissension. Such a policy obviously could not be adopted by a civilized Power; and the British were forced, at grave danger to themselves, to suppress the feuds of the tribes as efficiently as they could, and to work for the unification of the whole country. Much of this civilizing work, especially that directed towards the abolition of the blood feud between the tribes, reacted eventually on the British to their own disadvantage. It was an example of the old story, on a larger scale, of the humane man who interferes between a wife-beater and his victim; in nine cases out of ten, his immediate reward will be a joint attack upon him by both of them. Something similar was shortly to be the fate of the British at the hands of those whose best interests they were attempting to serve.

Meanwhile many old enemies were beginning to be reconciled by the hope of advancing their fortunes jointly at the expense of the new invader. The Turks were by no means so desperate or so incapable as European statesmen chose to believe; and large parties of patriotic Turks began to see a possible chance for the revival of Turkish influence through the obvious difficulties under which the new authorities in Mesopotamia were working. The word began to go forth that a new Turkey was arising, which should turn the hated European out of the Middle East and free the Muhammedan populations for their own destiny; and the word was received with acclamation both by the Arab nationalists in Syria, now thoroughly alarmed at the French attitude towards themselves, and by the religious leaders of the holy cities of Kerbela and Najaf, who forgot and forgave ancient Turkish oppression in the face of the common danger of Islam. They on their side had been alarmed and horrified by the British invasion of Persia, and by the complete collapse of that unhappy country; and they were the more inclined to listen to any proposal which should have as its object the final overthrow of the British influence in both Persia and Mesopotamia. Finally the idea of a revived Turkish Empire was received with delight by the large class of minor Government officials, who had held office under the Turk, but had been replaced under the British by the alien and unpopular Indian baboo; and it soon became obvious that a large amount of support could be obtained throughout the country for the project of a rebellion which should result in the downfall of the present administration and the withdrawal of the British.

The holy cities offered an admirable rendezvous from which the operations could be prepared and directed. The population were fanatical and anti-European; and very few Englishmen ever entered the district. In addition, the immediate surroundings of the holy cities had been purposely respected by the British, and their inhabitants were almost innocent of the sight of British soldiers; and it was thus not difficult to persuade them that the latter were not so much to be feared, after all. It is an old Arab adage that "the Arab's sense is in his eyes," that is to say, with him seeing is believing; and it was not difficult to convince the ignorant tribesman, who had seen British troops departing to Basrah for demobilization for many months past, that the British were actually withdrawing, or at any rate were prepared to do so on the application of a little local pressure.

The desertion of the cause of the British administration by the religious leaders of the holy cities was mean-spirited to the last degree. Under the orthodox Turks, the holy cities had been regarded with suspicion rather than with reverence; and no Shiah Moslem had been eligible for any Government office, nor had the Shiahs possessed their own courts of law. The holy cities, it is true, had been exempted during the World War from the operation of the Conscription Act, but only because of their own promptness in organizing a rebellion which gave the Turkish authorities considerable trouble for some weeks; and they possessed in Turkish times nothing but fear and dislike for their masters, both on racial and religious grounds. The British authorities, on the other hand, had freed them in every way.

They had instituted Shiah courts of law, they had guaranteed the integrity of the holy places, they had refrained from garrisoning them, and they had left them off the route of the new Euphrates Valley Railway; in addition, they had abolished the official ban against Shiahs, and had thrown open to them the same chances of a public career as fell to members of the orthodox persuasion. Yet, so great is the power of religious prejudice to blind men's hearts to questions of fair dealing, that the Shiahs deliberately fostered a revolution on the holy ground which their so-called enemies had so chivalrously respected.

Some slight excuse perhaps may be found for the treachery of the Shiahs when the stifling atmosphere in which their religious leaders are brought up is taken into account. The evolution of the Shiahs has been traced in an earlier chapter, and the reasons for their refusal to acknowledge a living Caliph considered. The non-existence of any spiritual Shiah head since the disappearance of the last Imam, and the real need of the mystical Persian for a living ecclesiastical authority of some kind, have led to the development of the power of the *mujtahidin*. The mujtahid is a holy man, to qualify for which office he must, in his own native place, gain a reputation for poverty and virtue; he must entirely eschew the things of this world, and as far as possible concern himself only with meditation on holy matters. After having gained some local reputation on these essential points, the budding mujtahid repairs on foot to one or other of the holy places, sometimes walking to Mesopotamia from the farthest confines of Persia, a journey of many days in extent. Once in the holy city, he must aim at sitting at the feet of the leading mujtahid of the day, and acquiring something of his store of wisdom; a process which at times is estimated to take nearly forty years. During this long period the physical needs of the student are cared for by a special fund, maintained by the gifts of pilgrims and other devout men. For the last ten years or so of his education, he may, if his wisdom justifies it, be promoted to one or other of the executive positions which abound in the holy cities; after which he may choose, clothed with the odour of sanctity for the remainder of his life, to return to his native land. If, however, he is both capable and ambitious, he will remain in the holy city and attach himself as closely as possible to the head mujtahid; whom in the end, if fortune favours him, he may replace.

It will thus be seen that the head mujtahid, who invariably resides in one or other of the holy cities, forms a kind of Pope of the Shiah faith; with the difference that his office is in no way subject to election, he depending for his position merely upon the acknowledgment of the other venerable men about him. He possesses no executive power, but his influence is enormous; a "fetwa" or instruction by the head mujtahid will be obeyed by Shiahs as implicitly as a bull by the Pope was obeyed in early mediæval Europe. There have been able and even broad-minded Shiah *mujtahidin* in modern times, but the system is against their development; thirty or forty years in an isolated desert city of sanctified reputation, living on charity and cut off from all touch with the outside world and the realities of life, may be considered about the worst possible education for a public man wielding a vast responsibility. It can perhaps hardly be wondered at that the influence of the holy cities since the British occupation has been invariably thrown on the side of the violent and reactionary parties.

As time progressed, an unexpected ally for the revolutionary cause was found in the town-living absentee owner of land. To the impartial observer, this class of individual, like the Shiah priest, might seem under some sort of debt of gratitude to the British power; for in Turkish times his title to the land had produced in many cases merely nominal rents, and in fairly numerous cases he did not dare to leave the city to inspect his own country holdings. The British occupation at least made his holding secure, and passage to it possible; and if the authorities were at times obliged to annoy him by preventing his exploitation of the luckless country cultivator who worked his land, at least they secured to him the safe and punctual arrival of such rent as was due to him. This class, when they began in large numbers to join the ranks of the conspirators, formed a most powerful addition, for they brought with them in many cases the entrée into influential circles in the large towns; and it gradually became apparent to the British authorities that they might be forced to face trouble, if it came to a head, not merely among the tribes and in the outlying districts, but also in Baghdad itself. It is only fair to add that this class of absentee owner regretted the rebellion when it did come as much as the authorities themselves; for the looting tribesmen showed themselves no respecters of persons, and the property of the coffee-shop farmer proved as fair game to them as that of the British soldier.

In some such fashion, through the tribesmen, the inhabitants of the holy cities, and lastly the well-to-do population of Baghdad, filtered during 1919 an undercurrent of discontent, prejudice, fanaticism and latterly deliberate plotting, which bade fair to make trouble in the immediate future inevitable.

CHAPTER XII

THE YEAR OF DISILLUSION

*"When thou settest fire to the cane-brake,
If thou art wise, shun the tigers."*—SA'DI.

ON the right bank of the upper Euphrates, at a point where the river has long since deserted the sandy plains of Mesopotamia for the broad hills and valleys of eastern Syria, lies the pleasant little town of Deir-az-Zoir. Commanding as it does the gateway to Mesopotamia from the direction of Aleppo, and containing the only permanent bridge over the river at any point south of Asia Minor, the town has within the last twenty years risen to considerable local importance. Its streets and buildings are remarkably handsome, and it has the appearance of a prosperous European country town. Its bazaars, conceived in a peculiar style of plaster Gothic which gives them a fantastic and almost futuristic appearance, serve as an emporium for the trade of the desert round about, which harbours perhaps 100,000 Bedouin inhabitants; and as a link between Europe, the upper Mediterranean and Mesopotamia, the place seems destined to enjoy a considerable future.

Deir-az-Zoir was by the treaty of peace assigned to Syria and the French mandatory sphere; but it had been originally occupied by the British, and continued throughout 1919 to be garrisoned by them. The garrison was, however, for all practical purposes one in name only. A Political Officer, two armoured cars and a handful of Arab levies, then in their infancy as a fighting force, were all that the British administration could muster to guard one of the gateways of Mesopotamia; and the communications between the town and the capital are long and difficult. It is not possible to reach Baghdad by motor-car in under two days; and there are no large towns or centres on the way. Deir-az-Zoir soon occurred to the nationalist plotters as an admirable place on which to try their prentice hand. Its capture, which ought to be effected without great difficulty, must result in increasing their prestige ; and if the British chose afterwards to make serious efforts for its recovery, it could be evacuated easily and without loss. In any case, its seizure would force the hands of the British authorities, and some sort of a decision regarding the future of Mesopotamia would inevitably result.

The nationalist governor of Rakka, the ancient country seat of Harun ar-Rashid, which lies not far from Deir-az-Zoir, was a nominee of the Amir Feisal in Damascus and he was holding the town in his name ; but the latter was far too occupied at the moment in the impossible task of arranging a compromise between his nationalist supporters and the French Government at Beirut to pay much attention to the activities of his outlying subordinates. Syria was rapidly being evacuated by the British ; and, under the pressure of the Arab nationalists on the one hand and the Syrian nationalists on the other—both of whom were anti-French—the whole country threatened to collapse into a state of chaos. When the governor of Rakka, aided by a Kurdish freebooter, attacked Deir-az-Zoir, the Amir Feisal was only able to apologize to the British authorities, and protest his own innocence ; though he did in fact follow up this step by replacing the governor by a new nominee, who, however, proved as disobedient as the old.

The available British forces in Deir-az-Zoir were obviously incapable of holding the town against an outside attack ; and just before the close of 1919 the place was evacuated, to be followed shortly after by Abu Kemal, a small town somewhat closer to the Mesopotamian border. The evacuation followed upon an attack on the town, which had been conducted, at nationalist instigation, by a local tribe notorious among the Arabs for its lack of martial valour ; and thus it was easily made to appear that the British troops were retiring before the onset of a small people, despised as fighters even by their own countrymen. The moral effect of this first nationalist success was very great, and reverberated throughout Mesopotamia ; and the British authorities were warned in person by a friendly sheikh that, unless they took steps forthwith to recover Deir-az-Zoir by military means, they might have to face a general rebellion in the immediate future. No heed whatever was paid to the warning ; and the little desert market town remained in the hands of the nationalists until its eventual capture by the French, who have held it ever since with a considerable garrison.

The year 1920 opened ominously for the Near and Middle East. The Turkish nationalists at Angora were becoming established, and from their stronghold there issued more and more emissaries of trouble for the French and British authorities. Early in the year it was ascertained by the French that the Arab governor of Aleppo, who was an ex-Turkish official, was in communication with the Angora leaders, and in the ensuing weeks several French garrisons and detachments were isolated by rebels and overcome. It became known finally that the Turks were contemplating an invasion of northern Syria in force. Meanwhile the Syrian National Congress, sitting in Damascus, decided to proclaim the Amir Feisal as King of Syria, a decision which was carried into effect early in March. The proclamation caused tremendous excitement throughout both Syria and Palestine ; anti-European feeling ran high, and the Jewish colonists in the south began to fear for their own safety ; and it appeared as if the French would have to meet a nationalistic combination of the Arabs and Turks. During the whole of the early part of the year the French administration was engaged in fighting for its existence ; and parts of northern Syria were not actually pacified until the following year, though by June the French had made their authority supreme throughout the whole of western and central Syria, and were only awaiting a suitable opportunity for dealing the nationalists in the east a final blow, and of overturning the new kingdom of Damascus.

Meanwhile the situation of the new King grew more and more difficult. On the one hand he had to attempt the control of his own supporters, both Syrian and Arab, who looked to Damascus as a centre from which the French might still be driven out of Syria altogether ; on the other, he had to avoid, if possible, any open break with the

French, who were the friends of his war-time allies the British, and whose presence as a mandatory power he had definitely acknowledged. Throughout the Spring of 1920 he was forced to continue the difficult task of attempting to run with the hare and hunt with the hounds; but the time arrived when the French—the situation slightly easier in other parts of the country—were in a position to marshal all their forces against Damascus, and it became obvious that a break was inevitable. In June the French offered to recognize the King and even to grant him a generous subvention, provided that he on his side would openly agree to accept the French mandate and to co-operate whole-heartedly with it; but the nationalists would have none of it, and they were finally successful in compelling the King, under threat of his life, to issue a defiance of the French. In July the French forces approached Damascus; in a series of engagements, the nationalist army was utterly routed; and the new King and his Government were compelled to evacuate the city. The French prepared to consolidate their authority throughout the country, and Feisal withdrew to Palestine, and thence to Europe. The mood of political idealism had quickly passed. The only State in the Near East which, born of the philosophy of "self-determination" and the Twelfth Point, had been actually erected by the people of the country themselves, was destined to meet its end at the hands of the mandatory power!

While the western neighbour of Mesopotamia was thus in a state of almost continual disturbance, the condition of her eastern neighbour was beginning to give cause for alarm. In the middle of May, Enzeli had been attacked by the Bolsheviks and the British garrison compelled to retire; soon afterwards Resht was occupied by the Russians and the British outposts were withdrawn to Kazvin. A panic immediately ensued in Teheran, and the British were largely blamed for failing to "protect" Persia, in blissful forgetfulness of the fact that the Anglo-Persian agreement of the previous year had never been ratified by the Persian people, and that therefore the British were under no obligation to the Persians whatever. Meanwhile the strong anti-British attitude maintained by the Shiah priesthood in Persia, and reflected in Najaf and Kerbela, was beginning to have its effect upon the people ; and it gradually appeared that either the British would have to take steps to control Persia altogether, or they would have to withdraw. For the moment, however, the uneasy balance was maintained ; the British authorities in Mesopotamia still remained responsible for the safety of a military garrison in the highlands of Persia ; and the British taxpayer, for at least another year, had to bear the burden of maintaining British troops in an isolated region completely outside the boundaries of the Empire. The post-war policy of the British Foreign Office in Persia, dictated solely by anti-Bolshevik motives, involved Great Britain in the expenditure of over £100,000,000, the whole of which was both unnecessary and unproductive.

Meanwhile in Mesopotamia itself events were moving rapidly towards the breaking of the storm. The Deir-az-Zoir incident, coupled with the obvious strength and determination of the French in Syria, had decided both the Arab and the Turkish nationalists that Mesopotamia offered the easiest prospect for the achievement of their aims. Preparations were made for an intensive campaign of propaganda, utilizing the active and invaluable aid of the holy men of Najaf and Kerbela ; meetings were summoned in the mosques in the larger towns ; and the disaffected tribesmen were warned to be in readiness to fight later in the summer, once the spring crops had been safely gathered in. In the far north, a process of nibbling at British outposts, on the model of the Deir-az-Zoir incident, was undertaken, at times with fair success ; and at the end of May it became known that a nationalist force was in being in the Mosul district, and was gaining wide support among the tribes. On June 4th, Tel Afar, a small town to the west of Mosul, mainly inhabited by the descendants of the Turkish mercenaries of the Abbassids, was captured by the bedouin Shammar with nationalist support, and the whole of the British garrison put to the sword. Mosul itself was openly disaffected for several days, but the arrival of a punitive column at Tel Afar, and the subsequent collapse of all resistance, served to calm the storm. All through the month of June there were isolated cases of attacks on

British outposts and detachments, and the responsible authorities became so alarmed that the Acting Civil Commissioner, who regarded the situation far more gravely than the newly-arrived commander-in-chief, actually took the step of telegraphing his fears to London. This step was naturally deprecated by the commander-in-chief, who was absent in Persia at the time ; and from this time onwards there developed a lack of co-operation between the civil and military British authorities which never afterwards ceased, and which later became so marked as to be apparent to the public at large.

Another factor had meanwhile arisen which threatened to make the rebellion, if one occurred, even more difficult and dangerous than it otherwise might have been. In the preceding winter permission had been given in London for the wives of serving officers and men to join them in Mesopotamia ; and the spring of 1920 had seen the arrival of a large number of English ladies of all grades of society, new to the country, and in some cases very averse to the rough surroundings inevitable in such an undeveloped part of the world. Two great camps, one at Daurah, near Baghdad, the other at Karind, in the Persian hills, were in process of being laid out for the accommodation of the garrison and their families ; oblivious of the fact, as regards the latter camp, that the site was in Persia, and therefore not technically in British territory at all.

In both cases the initial preparations were on a most expensive and elaborate scale. The pleasantness of the Persian hills in the summer months, when Baghdad is uncomfortably hot, had induced the officials of General Head-quarters to consider the possibility of another summer camp in the vicinity of Karind, for the sole accommodation of the staff ; and accordingly, another small cantonment had been laid out in the neighbourhood, but sufficiently remote from the main camp to ensure the holidays of the staff being uninterrupted by any chance of association with the ordinary rank and file. In spite of the growing and acknowledged anxiety of the civil authorities, no attempt was made to cancel the summer camp project ; and when the storm did burst, the garrison, the married families, and an important proportion of technical staff officers were away in the Persian hills, in an isolated position, and several days' journey from the scene of operations.

The presence of the married families had unquestionably bad effects in other ways. Their arrival very largely helped to consolidate the rebellious elements in the country, for the sight of numerous Englishwomen not unnaturally convinced the people that the British were not only insincere in their promise for the independence of the country, but that they actually proposed to begin colonizing it themselves. In addition, great strength of character and personal restraint are necessary in any European woman undertaking residence in an undeveloped country, especially in the East ; and in the case of a very large body of women drawn from all classes of life, it is not possible to rely on the general existence of these high qualities. There were many married men who had grave cause to regret that their wives had ever been allowed to set foot in Mesopotamia.

The task of the military authorities, in the eventuality of trouble, was in itself a sufficiently grave one. In June, 1920, there were in Mesopotamia, in round numbers, 60,000 troops, of whom no more than 5,000 were British. There were, in addition, another 60,000 Indian "followers," who were employed by General Head-quarters in subordinate capacities in connection with the operation of the various outside businesses with which the British army in Mesopotamia was charged. The country was at this time for all practical purposes largely " run " by the British army ; the electric lighting of Basrah, Baghdad and Hillah ; the cleanliness and hospital arrangements of Baghdad ; the whole movement of Government stores ; the operation of the railways, telephones and telegraphs, and the repair of the country roads ; all these duties and more, had come, as a legacy from war conditions, to be regarded as a part of army routine, though of late an effort had been made to hand over some of them to civilian control. In addition, the army had been compelled by circumstances to organize and operate its own farms, and to maintain its own fleet of steamers on the river Tigris ; and a very large proportion of soldiers at this time was, in fact, engaged upon occupations usually regarded as purely civilian. This state of things was in no way due to a desire on the part of General Head-quarters to absorb all the functions of daily life ; on the contrary, the situation filled thoughtful officers with considerable alarm, and there was a genuine desire to dispose of some of the outside functions on to civilian shoulders, if such could have been found able and willing to undertake the burden. But the civilian authorities themselves were overburdened with the gigantic task of reorganizing the life of a country which, for the time being, had simply come to a standstill ; and, moreover, they possessed no organization with which to face, at short notice, the task of operating large power plants or other works of like nature, in a land where technical labour simply does not exist. Although latterly in control of the railways, they had in practice to borrow English military personnel for their operation ; and as they themselves were legally under the control of General Head-quarters (for the country was still under martial law), there seemed nothing to be gained by transferring departments directly administered by army officials to the merely nominal charge of the civil authorities. To this extent, and to this extent only, the military bureaucracy of Mesopotamia was justified in claiming that the charges of extravagance hurled against it by the British taxpayer were unfair ; for in no country in modern times has the military power been called upon to undertake such a variety of labour outside its own professional work. On the other hand, it is impossible to deny that waste and extravagance were far too common, and financial supervision almost non-existent ; and it is clear that the military authorities, by the exercise of a little more forethought and by a more general willingness to endure the fatigue of detailed work, might have saved the British taxpayer many millions of pounds sterling without in any way prejudicing the eventual issue.

Roughly speaking, then, the military authorities had at their disposal 60,000 soldiers, many of whom were absent from their units on "jobs," and all of whom were scattered over a country of few communications and vast distances, containing a population of nearly three million. The prospect of anything like a general rebellion might well be viewed with alarm.

THE YEAR OF DISILLUSION

The month of June, 1920, was one of quiet, disturbed only by small but suspicious occurrences; but the atmosphere was charged with electricity, and at any time it seemed that the storm might burst. At the end of the month an incident occurred, trivial in itself, which clearly demonstrated the gravity of the situation.

A certain sheikh of the Beni Hachaim, a truculent tribe of the lower Euphrates area to whom taxation had been an unwelcome innovation of the new regime, had borrowed £100 from the Government as an agricultural loan, and had, over a considerable period of time, made no effort to repay it. The fact was reported to the political officer of the division, who ordered his arrest. The sheikh was sent for and detained in the local political office, with a view to his being despatched for the interrogation of higher authority by the evening train. His tribe, however, had already placed their banners out—their formal intimation of war—and some of his men now invaded the political office, rescued the sheikh and killed all the police who attempted to interfere.

Immediately the storm broke throughout the whole area. The railway was promptly cut in several places, reconnoitring trains were driven back, and the town of Rumaithah, containing a small British garrison and a number of British civilians, was surrounded. It was soon noticed that the investing forces were being directed with some skill and knowledge of military science, and it became obvious that the tribesmen were commanded by nationalist and Turkish officers.

The first attempt to relieve the town was completely beaten off, and the authorities were faced with the task of despatching a really large force to rescue the imprisoned garrison. From the first the difficulties of the operation were apparent; the scene of the disturbance was some 120 miles from Baghdad, along a single line of railway through country which, lying not far from the holy cities, was distinctly susceptible to hostile propaganda; news of the siege had been rapidly spread, and its importance exaggerated, over the whole countryside; and the available British troops were scattered in little detachments over a vast and inhospitable area. Orders were at once issued for the concentration at Baghdad of all the outlying garrisons who could conveniently be spared; and the authorities settled down to face a possibly extensive campaign in the middle Euphrates districts.

Early in July the town of Kufa, so redolent of memories of the days of the Arab invasion, now merely a fairly prosperous market town, began to be the centre of wide disaffection; and the small British garrison near Najaf, one of the holy cities, had to be withdrawn. Soon afterwards Kufa became surrounded by hostile forces, and before the end of the month it was invested. But worse was to follow. The column which had been sent out to relieve Rumaithah had achieved its object, but was quite unable to pacify the rising torrent of hostile feeling; and meanwhile disaster had overtaken a small column operating in the Hillah-Kufa neighbourhood, resulting in a loss to the British forces of twenty killed and 360 wounded and missing. The reverse was even worse in that the heaviest losses had been borne by English troops, and it now became impossible to conceal the seriousness of the rebellion either in Mesopotamia or in Great Britain. For some months after this date, eighty men of the Manchester Regiment remained prisoners in the hands of the Arab insurgents.

It was obvious at once that very much larger forces would be needed for the effective handling of the situation than were present in the country; and the British Government, having announced as their immediate policy the suppression of the rebellion first and foremost, sanctioned the despatch of such reinforcements as the commander-in-chief on the spot might desire. Altogether some 5,000 British and 25,000 Indian troops arrived during the course of the rebellion, bringing the total British fighting strength into the neighbourhood of 90,000 men.

Meanwhile in August the trouble began to show itself in two widely different directions. By the middle of the month Bakubah, a small town on the Diala river and the main railway to Persia, was in the hands of the rebels, as was also Sharaban, a town farther up the line; in the attack on the latter an English lady was captured and held captive for several weeks. Communication along the

THE YEAR OF DISILLUSION 189

Persian railway thus became impossible. The town of Khanikin, an important outpost of the Anglo-Persian Oil Company, was in an uproar; and Quraitu, the rail-head for the Karind summer camp and Persia generally, was threatened. For a time the situation was one of extreme peril, not only for the British troops and residents in Persia, but also for the garrison of " wives " at Karind.

In the north, again, sections of the Shammar were beginning to give trouble; the Kurdish tribes round Kifri, ever on the look-out for a chance of loot, were showing signs of restlessness; and fears were expressed for the safety of Arbil. Even in Baghdad itself things were far from reassuring; and the British were compelled on several occasions to make a show of armed force in the streets, an operation which, however, proved quite enough to cool the ardour of the fashionably dressed rebels of the coffee shops. The common people of Baghdad showed no very great inclination to commit themselves; and the ordinary busy life of the metropolis went on with surprising smoothness throughout the entire rebellion. The rebels were, however, successful in procuring the total destruction by fire of the British mechanical transport depôt in Baghdad, involving the loss of the largest store of spare parts and replacements in Mesopotamia. So carefully conducted was the operation that neither the military authorities nor the police were ever able to bring the incendiaries to book; and genuine fear was felt for the other Government stores and places of importance in the vicinity of the city. The precautions which were taken proved, however, sufficient, and the disaster was never repeated.

About the middle of August certain of the tribes to the north-west of Baghdad began to show signs of disaffection, a tendency which was brought to a dramatic head by the infamous murder of the well-known Arabian student and British administrator, Colonel Leachman. The murder was executed in a particularly mean and treacherous manner. Midway on the desert road between Baghdad and Fhilujah, far from all signs of human life except the railway and the telegraph line, stands the police post of Khan Nuqtah, an unpretentious building which has quite obviously seen better days. At this place Colonel Leachman, then the

British political officer of the district, had directed Sheikh Dhari, the official head of a powerful sub-tribe on the upper Euphrates, to meet him, on a certain morning in August. The Sheikh arrived early with two of his sons and some other of his relatives and followers, and he was followed almost immediately by Colonel Leachman in his automobile, which contained, in addition to himself, only his servant and his driver. A friendly business conversation ensued for some time, until another automobile drew up at the khan, containing a party of Arabs who complained of having been stopped and robbed a short distance away. Colonel Leachman immediately despatched a small party of police in the direction of the alleged robbery, and himself retired to the office of the khan. The remainder of the occurrence is obscure; but after some time, it appears, Sheikh Dhari asked permission to interview the colonel again, upon which he was invited into the office. Two men who preceded him into the room, one of them being his son, immediately and without warning shot at, and severely wounded, Colonel Leachman, and Dhari himself completed the dastardly act by thrusting the dying officer through with his own sword. The colonel's death was the signal for a general rising in the district, which for the time being cut off Fhilujah and Ramadi from Baghdad; but fortunately the sheikh of the powerful Dulaim (who range principally to the west of the Euphrates in the neighbourhood of Hit and Anah), stood firm, and the British authorities were relieved of all anxiety regarding the extreme north-western area.

In the south, too, things turned out better than might have been expected. The tribes of the south-east Tigris region, including the wild Albu Muhammad of evil reputation, showed no signs of restlessness whatever; and, above all, the great Muntafiq, who could possibly have isolated the Government completely by cutting off Baghdad from Basrah and the sea, remained in the main loyal throughout. Basrah and its vicinity, too, showed no disposition to sympathize with the rebels; and the trouble in the south was almost wholly confined to the district of the lower Euphrates, in which Samawa was surrounded and invested for nearly two months. For a short time, however, it seemed as if the whole south-western country, Muntafiq and all, might turn against the administration; and the pressure put upon the leading sheikhs and notables by their own countrymen was very great. The pressure on the purely religious side can be measured by the fact that the mujtahid of Kerbela actually publicly performed prayers on the corpse of an Arab killed in action, a ceremony which implies the highest approval of the religious authorities, for by it the warrior is entitled to the crown of martyrdom and to free burial in the sacred ground of the holy cities. Much credit for the comparative quiet of the Muntafiq and Basrah country was due to the local notables, one of whom, Seyyid Talib Pasha of Basrah, was destined to be ill-rewarded by the British authorities a year later.

The rebellion, though so general in scope, was never at any time under the control of one head or one authority; and it soon became obvious that the Government, with all the resources of modern science at its command, and able to communicate by wireless even with its beleaguered garrisons, must prevail against the unnatural alliance of tribesmen, religious teachers, absentee landlords and nationalist politicians, which had been brought into being merely by a common belief in the British weakness. Throughout the latter portion of the year, progress in reconquering the disaffected areas was general; but it was extremely gradual, for not before seven months had elapsed could the Government conscientiously claim that their hold over the country was once again complete. As early as the middle of August, the tide might be said to have turned in the middle Euphrates area; for on the 13th of the month the Hindiyah Barrage was occupied by British troops, and thenceforth the Government held in its hands the control of the water supply of a large portion of the lower country, including that in which the holy cities stood. By the middle of September, communication had been reopened on the Persian railway through Bakubah and Sharaban, and the evacuation of the families from Karind camp to India had begun; and at the same date the trouble in the north-west, which had commenced with the murder of Colonel Leachman, was finally suppressed, and the whole upper Euphrates area once more re-connected with the capital. The operations centring upon Hillah were also being conducted with complete success, and by the middle of October the holy cities themselves could no longer stand the pressure of the Government forces. Kerbela surrendered on the 16th of the month, and Najaf two days later. Kufa and its garrison were relieved on the 17th, and on the 19th the British prisoners, who had been in the hands of the rebels ever since the Manchester disaster in July, were recovered. One only had died in captivity.

Farther south, Samawa had been reoccupied some days earlier; and the smaller outbreaks in the area lying between Baghdad and Mosul had been successfully put down. Block-houses had been erected and garrisoned on the Baghdad-Hillah, Baghdad-Persia, Baghdad-Fhilujah, Baghdad-Kut and Basrah-Nasriyah sections of the railway; and full control by the authorities over their main communications was now assured. The back of the rebellion was broken.

But it could not be assumed with safety that the trouble had been wholly met by a mere, and perhaps temporary, scattering of the revolutionary forces. Far sterner measures were needed to bring home to the wild tribesman, whose "sense is in his eye," and who respects force only when he can see or feel it, the unpalatable fact that the Government was able to bring superior force to bear at any time, and at the shortest notice. Some sort of general punishment was needed which might be remembered by the tribes and by the Shiah religious authorities, if at any future date they might feel impelled to rise again.

It was perhaps inevitable that such a punishment, the lesson of which would have been most salutary, could not in fact be carried into execution. The British Government and people were at last becoming alarmed over the huge cost of their armies in Mesopotamia and Persia, and as their Government had publicly disavowed all intention of occupying the country permanently, it was obvious that the people would never consent to the present military operations being continued for any longer time than was absolutely necessary for the safety of the British authorities and civilians actually in the country. The authorities, therefore, were obliged to content themselves with the visitation of certain areas by troops and with fines in rifles and money, the final total of which amounted to some 60,000 rifles and £54,000 in cash. Even these extremely mild forms of punishment provoked considerable opposition, and the troops had not infrequently to deal with disturbances in the so-called pacified areas later on; and it was not until February of the next year that the operations connected with the rebellion could be considered to have reached a conclusion. The whole affair, involving one of the most difficult campaigns in which the British army has been engaged in modern times, thus lasted over seven months. The futility of the punishment inflicted on the tribes was admitted within twelve months by the authorities themselves, when it became known in General Head-quarters in Baghdad that the rebels had more than regained their pre-rebellion rifle strength, and now actually possessed the advantage of more modern weapons. In the meantime, however, the political situation had changed for the better, and a very definite step forward had been taken by the British Government. Although the latter was, as we have already seen, committed to the policy of "self-determination" for Mesopotamia, no progress whatever had been made, in the two years that had elapsed since the Armistice, in settling the future of that country upon definite lines. Martial law was still in being, and the fountain-head of all law and all government was still the army of occupation; the press and public opinion were muzzled as effectively as possible; and the general dissatisfaction with the status quo had found vent in an open rebellion. The British statesmen began at last to realize that the people in the outlying parts of the world were not prepared to await indefinitely the endless discussions and conferences that followed the conclusion of peace; and it was determined to send to Mesopotamia a British representative possessed of sufficient authority and influence to decide on the spot the nature of the autonomous future government of Mesopotamia, and if possible to arrange for its inauguration. The British Government's choice of an official to attempt this difficult task eventually fell upon Sir Percy Cox, a man of great experience in the Middle East, who had been largely responsible in pre-war days for the success of the British in retaining their position in the Persian Gulf ; and who latterly had been in Teheran as the principal representative of Great Britain in that turbulent capital. Sir Percy Cox was well known personally to many Mesopotamian people, and his arrival in the middle of October brought instant relief to the local political situation. It was followed almost immediately by the public announcement of his mission, and by the taking of the first steps to form a Mesopotamian Government under his presidency. The task of establishing a national State in the land of the rivers, which should incidentally offer a valid test of the new mandate system, was now to be seriously attempted.

CHAPTER XIII

THE PEOPLE OF THE COUNTRY

" In all forms of government the people is the true legislator."—BURKE.

THE ancient land of Mesopotamia was now on the verge of a more important political change than any that had been seen within its borders for many centuries; but before we can rightly measure the importance of that change, or the probable fate of the new forces which were brought into being by it, we must examine to some extent the condition of the people in whose hands, in the long run, the political and social future of the country must lie.

The Moslem population of Mesopotamia numbers roughly 2,700,000, of whom rather more than half are of the Shiah faith; it is drawn from Arab, Persian and Kurdish strains, the Arab largely predominating. There are included in it in addition small bodies of Turks, some of them of Ottoman extraction, but the majority Seljuks, and the descendants of the Turkish mercenaries of the Abbassid Caliphs. The two bodies of the Moslem faith, Sunni and Shiah, are roughly divided by a line running east to west through Baghdad. Kurds and Turks are invariably Sunni, Persians invariably Shiah; the Arabs are about equally divided between the two bodies, with a tendency towards conversion from the Sunni to the Shiah.

In addition to the Moslems there are in Mesopotamia nearly 90,000 Jews, 80,000 Christians of several different races and Churches, and 40,000 adherents of other religions, including Sabians, Yezidis, etc. As religion dominates ordinary life in the Middle East to a far greater extent than in the West, it follows that all the separate communities have their own laws, customs, social habits and deeply reverenced history, and inter-marriage between them is rare.

It has never been found possible to undertake anything but an extremely rough census of the country in modern times, a census being regarded with natural suspicion by the people, as the certain preliminary of taxation and compulsory military service. The following figures,* however, were compiled by the British authorities in 1920, and may be assumed to be within a measurable distance of the actual facts. They are arranged as originally published, by administrative divisions ("liwas"), and by religions.

CENSUS TABLE.

Divisions.	Sunni.	Shiah.	Jew.	Christian.	Other Faiths.	Totals.
BAGHDAD	130,000	54,000	50,000	15,000	1,000	250,000
SAMARRA	66,455	14,215	300	—	—	80,970
DIYALAH	54,953	46,097	1,689	397	900	104,036
KUT	8,578	98,712	381	127	—	107,798
DIWANIYAH	1,000	192,300	6,000	5,000	200	204,500
SHAMIYAH	445	189,000	530	20	5	190,000
HILLAH	15,983	155,897	1,065	27	28	173,000
DULAIM	247,000	200	2,600	200	—	250,000
BASRAH	24,408	130,494	6,928	2,221	1,549	165,600
AMARAH	7,000	284,700	3,000	300	5,000	300,000
MUNTAFIQ	11,150	306,220	160	30	2,440	320,000
MOSUL	244,713	17,180	7,635	50,670	30,180	350,378
ARBIL	96,100	—	4,800	4,100	1,000	106,000
KIRKUK	85,000	5,000	1,400	600	—	92,000
SULAMAINIYAH	153,900	—	1,000	100	—	155,000
TOTALS	1,146,685	1,494,015	87,488	78,792	42,302	2,849,282

The two and a half million Arabs in the country are not only divided amongst themselves by religion, but by widely divergent social and political differences. The Arab of Baghdad and Basrah is very largely, in the wealthier classes at least, "Europeanized": he not infrequently adopts European clothing in its entirety except for the head-dress, which is usually the red fez. An attempt has recently been made to supersede the latter by a new type of national hat, the so-called "Sidarah" or "Feisaliyah," originally worn by the followers of Feisal in Syria. This hat, or rather cap, which is said to have been invented by Jafar Pasha al-Askari, resembles the forage cap of the pre-war British Tommy. Some townspeople of good position, however, retain the more attractive "shafiyah," or head-kerchief of the Bedouin and country Arab. Many of the lower classes in the towns have taken to the European coat and trousers, but invariably retain the shafiyah as a head-dress; the latter is usually of cotton or crepon, sometimes worn plain white as in Syria, but more usually with

* Taken from the "Baghdad Year Book, 1923"; published by *Al Iraq Press*, Baghdad.

THE PEOPLE OF THE COUNTRY 197

a red or blue pattern woven into the material. In the case of wealthy or distinguished men, the shafiyah would be of silk or some costly material. It is worn hanging over the shoulders in the traditional Arab fashion, and is an admirable head-covering for ordinary use in a climate of great extremes, for it is equally effective in shielding the face and head from the scorching sun or the cold wind. The "motor veil" of the European lady is a variation of the same idea. In the country districts, and in Basrah, the shafiyah is kept on the head by an elaborate "agal" or loop of wool or camel-hair, sometimes white, sometimes black; the common Baghdadi, however, is not so careful of his attire, and his shafiyah is usually thrown carelessly round his head in a most inelegant manner. Practically all town Arabs have taken to at least one portion of European attire, differing according to personal taste; thus it is common in Baghdad to see the European coat in combination with the familiar wide Eastern skirt, or, on the other hand, a pair of trousers worn under an Arab shirt and "aba" or dust-coat. Sometimes in Baghdad the round fur cap of the Caucasian is worn in place of the fez or shafiyah, and Christians are frequently to be seen in these caps as well as Moslems. The attire of the poorer classes in the country and desert is not infrequently confined to the shafiyah and a single long shirt, but the sheikhs and headmen sometimes dress most expensively. It is a common practice of the townsmen of all religions to carry a rosary, the beads of which they frequently turn and count in the course of ordinary conversation; the rosary serves them in much the same way as the English walking-stick, as something to carry and occupy the fingers.

Many of the younger Moslems, particularly in Baghdad, within the last few years have come much under the influence of Western habits and manners. They enter public resorts, eat, smoke, and even drink in public; are frequently masters of one European language, and sometimes of two or three. There is a very large variety of complexion and colouring to be seen in the towns, particularly in Baghdad; and many of the faces about the streets are remarkably similar to Western types, there being even in the Baghdad police force two constables with violent red hair. A fair complexion with blue eyes is not uncommon, and, among the artisans especially, there are some strangely English types to be seen.

The country Arabs are very variously divided according to their tribe, their origin, the length of time they have been settled in Mesopotamia, and their social development. Some of the more settled agriculturists or boatmen are indistinguishable, except by their love for primitive methods of work, from the peasantry of Europe; others, such as the dark-skinned and probably non-Arab inhabitants of the marshes, are lawless, intractable and treacherous to the last degree. Some of the tribes are half-settled, half-nomadic; others are completely settled, but retain a certain relationship with their nomadic cousins in the Syrian desert, or in Arabia proper. On the other hand, there are true-blooded Arabs among the peaceful cultivators, artisans and even townspeople of Mesopotamia who have lost all semblance of connection with their old tribal allegiance.

Such are the Arabs of Mesopotamia, the people who form an overwhelming majority of the population; divided into two great religious camps, Sunni and Shiah, into three great social classes, town, country, and bedouin, and into a large variety of types at all levels of civilized development; hardly offering very hopeful material for the making of a new nation. On the other hand, it must not be forgotten that the Arabs are connected by the use of a common language, by common habits of life, by a common tradition, and by that democratic fellow-feeling which Islam has been so much more successful in fostering than any other faith. The natural equality of man is a real thing to Moslems, and particularly to Arabs; there is none of that tendency to emphasize the barriers of race, of colour or of class which has become such a feature of Western civilization. The Arab is, on the other hand, extremely proud of his family and tribe, and is consequently exclusive in matters concerning the marital tie; but that does not prevent him being, in the public affairs of life, democratic almost to a fault. Innumerable examples could be quoted of his free and democratic spirit, but the following, from the pen of a Christian missionary, is typical:

THE PEOPLE OF THE COUNTRY 199

"We sat in the tent of Sheikh Falih, the titular head of all the Muntafiq. At the end of the tent, leaning on a camel saddle, sat the sheikh himself. All around squatted the tribesmen in orderly rows. Suddenly in walked a gaunt bedawee, clad in his one garment. He walked straight to the front of the tent, thrust his rattan cane to within a few feet of the sheikh's face, and said, ' Kef haluk, ya Falih." Then he glanced to right and left, and found a place in the row of sitters.

"After a minute the coffee-bearer came forward and offered him coffee. The bedawee took it, held it high above his head, and flung the coffee on the ground. The hum of conversation stopped at once and Falih said, ' Speak, oh bedawee !' The bedawee came forward again and told how his camel had been stolen in Falih's territory, ' And,' said he, ' until it is restored, your honour is to me as the coffee in the sand !' Within twenty-four hours the camel was recovered, and the bedawee drank his coffee and stalked out again, with never a thank-you nor by your leave."*

How many of the citizens of Western and so-called democratic states would dare to assert their rights before their rulers in so uncompromising a fashion ?

A virtue which is perhaps less evenly distributed among the Arab inhabitants of Mesopotamia is that of personal courage. The tribesmen are undoubtedly usually brave, although several of the Mesopotamian tribes enjoy very evil reputations for treachery, a vice which is more akin to cowardice than courage; the townsmen as a whole are notorious for their lack of heart, and will not infrequently show disinclination even to protect their own immediate belongings. The annual raids southward of the Shammar tribes, even in recent times, used to strike terror into the inhabitants of Baghdad; though that city contained a population of at least two hundred thousand souls, and ought at any time to have been more than a match for a mere

* The Rev. John van Ess in " Historical Mesopotamia." *Times Press,* Basrah.

roving confederation of tribes. The carrying of arms is almost universal in the country as a whole, the townspeople usually keeping a revolver in the house, while the tribesmen are invariably well armed with modern rifles; the World War was responsible for an enormous distribution of modern fire-arms throughout Asia, and fresh supplies are readily procurable.

Nevertheless the individual Mesopotamian of whatever race or religion cannot be convicted of lacking personal courage. In all the modern wars in which the late Turkish Empire was engaged, there have always been large and active contingents from Mesopotamia; and a very striking British tribute to the bravery of the rank and file of the levies, who consist of Mesopotamian personnel under British officers, was paid in 1921 by no less an authority than the commander-in-chief himself. Speaking of the rebellion of 1920, he says:

" No sooner had the insurrection broken out than the rank and file (of the levies), especially those in the Middle Euphrates area, were assailed by blatant propaganda of every kind. In the bazaars and streets they were openly hailed as infidels and traitors; refreshments were denied them at the coffee shops, and in several cases vessels from which they had drunk were ostentatiously flung to the ground and broken. Their female relatives were in the forefront of this campaign of abuse, and exerted all the pressure they could bring to bear to induce the men to desert, assembling in clamorous crowds round the barracks, and calling upon them to come to their protection. Those of the levies who had been recruited from the countryside began to realize that to continue serving with the force meant the end of all relations with their tribe. But what perhaps strained their allegiance more than all else were the reports of assaults on their womenfolk, who in some cases were stated to have been carried off or killed. . . .

" I think in all fairness it may be said that in the annals of the British Empire no young force, a force in this case of only a few months' standing, has ever before passed through so high a trial. Deserters there were a few, for everywhere men of mean spirit will be found; but when the temptations to which the levies were daily subjected, and which almost passed endurance, are weighed against those of them who proved faithless, the number is insignificant."*

High praise indeed, coming from such a source; and the higher when it is considered that the conduct recommended to our notice betokens moral courage, admittedly a finer quality than the mere physical exultation of actual battle.

But the Moslem population, as has been already pointed out, does not wholly consist of Arabs. Just as the Shiah faith is, in its essence, a religious offshoot of the Persian genius, so are many of its followers in Mesopotamia either Persian or of recent Persian descent. As we have seen, the close connection between Mesopotamia and Persia has been, in the history of the former, an only less important factor than the connection with Arabia. Mesopotamia seems destined from its situation to remain the common meeting ground of these two great races; and if we choose to regard it as an Arab country, we must qualify the definition to the extent of admitting a very strong Persian strain. It is not possible to estimate the number of Persians resident in Mesopotamia, but it is considerable, and is constantly being augmented by the addition of pilgrims, who, having performed the necessary rites at the holy shrines, show no wish to return to the land of their fathers. A noticeable proportion of Baghdad labour is Persian; and the holy cities are as much Persian as Arab. The common Arabic of Mesopotamia reflects the Persian influence by its adoption of a number of Persian words and phrases. Another foreign Moslem influence, this time on the Sunni side, is supplied by the Kurds. The Kurds have existed as a race in the fastnesses of the mountains of eastern Turkey in Asia for uncounted centuries. They may be, and probably are, connected racially with some of the famous wild tribes, such as the Scythians, who played such havoc in ancient times with the decaying Assyrian

* Lieut.-Gen. Sir Aylmer L. Haldane, G.C.M.G., K.C.B., D.S.O., in "The Insurrection in Mesopotamia, 1920." Wm. Blackwood & Sons, London.

Empire. Their inaccessibility has largely preserved them from the attacks or the influence of the outside world, and has given them strongly marked characteristics; and though their existence continues to be tribal, their life and inclinations in no way resemble those of the Arabs. They are essentially a hill people, aristocratic, hardy and intractable; by nature reserved and unfriendly, and at times treacherous. For a people of such apparent vigour they have supplied singularly few great figures to the drama of Middle Eastern history; Saladin is perhaps the only historical Kurd who may be said to have attained to international prominence. In recent times they have drifted down into Mesopotamia in considerable numbers, and people of their race can be found in Baghdad in a variety of occupations. They possess a marked mechanical bent, and one station of the Anglo-Persian Oil Company, which employs among its mechanics an entertaining variety of nationalities, gives the first place to the Kurd as a budding mechanical artisan. Much of the unskilled labour in Baghdad and its vicinity is Kurdish, and they are to be found, though rarely, occupying higher positions in the community.

In addition to the Persians and Kurds, there are a large number of non-Moslem minorities in Mesopotamia, which are not only non-Arab, but very generally antipathetic to the Arab on both racial and religious grounds. The most important of these minorities is the great community of the Jews, who number some 90,000 in the whole country, and nearly 60,000 in the capital alone. The community claims descent from the remnants of the Babylonian captivity who did not return to Jerusalem, but the period of its greatest importance was after the destruction of Jerusalem by the Romans (A.D. 70), when the lower portions of Mesopotamia became practically the Hebrew fatherland. Here were developed, under the Parthian and Persian monarchs, two famous schools of Jewish law, and here the main lines of modern rabbinism were laid down. Although it was in Palestine that the Talmud was completed, the better known and more influential version was afterwards produced in Mesopotamia. For many centuries the Jews enjoyed considerable liberty and much influence; their exilarch, or leader-prince, was directly responsible for their welfare and their behaviour to the Persian monarch, and acted as their intermediary in all dealings with the civil authority. In spite of occasional persecution, much of their freedom and influence was retained under the Arab Caliphs. Until the gradual dispersion of the Jews over Europe and the consequent shifting of the Jewish centre of gravity to the West (a movement inaugurated by the Arab conquest of Spain), Mesopotamia continued to be, in a very literal sense, a second Palestine.

The importance of the modern Jewish community in the country is built up, as everywhere else, on commercial power. Though there are many poverty-stricken Jews in Mesopotamia, and many Jews engaged in very humble occupations—most of the shoe-blacks in Baghdad, for instance, are Jewish boys—it is probable that the Jews are much the wealthiest of the various communities. Until the arrival of the European bank, in quite recent times, they controlled the whole of the banking of the country; and a large proportion of the import and export business has always been in their hands. They are large property owners in the towns, and practically monopolize the still very active business of petty finance among the large classes of local people who are ignorant or suspicious of European banking methods. They also control an appreciable proportion of the retail trade of the country, especially in the more isolated districts. As agriculturists they are negligible, and their unpopularity with the tribesmen renders their position in country districts very precarious. They are nevertheless to be found in the most unexpected places, and are by no means confined to the large towns. The Baghdad Jew has, to outward appearance, become far more Europeanized than any other portion of the population. His knowledge is frequently very thorough, and his wholesale adoption of many European habits remarkable. There are many Jewish young men of the " young blood " type, coming from good families who ten years ago would have considered it a breach of propriety of a very grave kind to be seen eating in public, but who to-day patronize the hotels and restaurants of the city with the greatest frequency and enjoyment. Their attitude towards their womankind has, however, remained unchanged; and though the Jewish woman of Baghdad is not isolated to the same extent as a Moslem woman, she has little of the liberty of the European, or even of the local Christian. Nor have the Jews surrendered anything of their ancient obstinacy or dislike of their neighbours. Their contempt for the Arab is obvious and frequently expressed; and there appears little hope at present that they will unbend sufficiently to regard the creation of a Mesopotamian nation with anything approaching enthusiasm.

The Christians form, next to the Jews, the most important non-Moslem minority. There are about 80,000 Christians in the whole country, and these are divided into a variety of sects which differ from one another in questions of ritual, of belief, of language and of nationality. More than half the total Christian population is in or around Mosul, and Christian influence is practically confined to that neighbourhood. The ancient Eastern Churches, the Orthodox (Greek), Nestorian (Assyrian), Armenian and Jacobite are all represented in Mesopotamia, as well as the dissenting bodies from them which have at various times come under the influence of Rome, the Chaldeans, Armenian Catholics and Syrians. The latter Churches acknowledge the spiritual overlordship of the Pope, but retain their own liturgy in their own language. There are in addition a large number of Christians who have deserted their ancient liturgies altogether for that of Rome, and the Roman Catholic, or " Latin " as they are termed locally, churches and schools form the most powerful single Christian body in the country. They are largely staffed by French men and women, and to an extent carry on the political tradition of French missionaries laid down by Napoleon.

There are also small bodies of local Protestant Christians, the fruits of the work of English or American missions, and owing allegiance to the Church of England and various dissenting Churches. Christian Science and the faith of the Seventh Day Adventists are also represented. Some of the Christians are Arab by race, descendants of those tribes who had become Christian before the coming of Islam, and who did not afterwards adopt the new

THE PEOPLE OF THE COUNTRY 205

national faith. Most of them, however, trace their descent back to the Christian populations of Mesopotamia and Syria under the Persian kings and Roman emperors, and their ecclesiastical language is invariably some dialect of Aramaic, carefully preserved by them through the centuries. One or two of the Christian communities, notably the Assyrians and the Christians of Tel Kaif, near Mosul, still preserve living Aramaic languages of their own, the dialect of the latter, known popularly as "Telkaifi," being quite common in Baghdad. The Assyrian or Nestorian Christians have no connection with the Assyrians of antiquity, either by language or, as far as we know, by race; but they themselves claim an historical continuity, and the popular song with which they marched to action in the World War contained references to their desire for Mosul, as the site of the ancient Nineveh. These Assyrians are, incidentally, very much more susceptible to European influence than the other Christian communities, possibly because of the loss of their pre-war home, and consequent direct dependence upon the British Army. The Armenian or Tel Kaifi will, for example, usually retain the characteristic Near Eastern head-dress of the fez even with European clothes, thus resembling the Moslem or Jewish townsman; but the Assyrian prefers to dress himself completely on the English or American pattern, and has even taken extensively to the use of the English cap. If men of a Near Eastern type are seen in the streets of Baghdad in European headgear, it can usually be assumed that they are either Greek or Assyrian.

The Assyrians have latterly been enlisted in special regiments of Levies, and have done fine service under British officers in the turbulent districts of the north-east frontier. With their distinctive slouch hat of Australian pattern, they make smart-looking soldiers, and they have gained several British decorations for individual feats of bravery in action; their good military qualities are compromised, however, by strains of wildness and cruelty, and they are not always to be trusted when garrisoned among a resident civilian population. Large numbers of Assyrians have emigrated to America from time to time, and there is an extensive colony of them in a district of California.

It could hardly be expected that there should be much cohesion or fellow-feeling among the various bodies of Christians, nor in fact is such the case. In 1922 there were eleven different types of Christianity represented in Baghdad, of which nine possessed churches. Some of the native Christians are extremely conservative in thought and habits, while others, on the other hand, particularly the influential minority with American connections, are singularly well-informed and up-to-date. Owing to the great work of the French and American missionary schools, the Christians are now even better educated as a body than the Jews, and the great bulk of the (not very numerous) professional classes is drawn from their ranks; and most of the local enterprises of a Western type, such as hotels and cinemas, are in their hands. On the whole, they are more popular with the Moslems than are the Jews, but their commercial morality is not always above suspicion. Their women, alone among the city women of Mesopotamia, are free to unveil in the streets, and to come and go as they please; it necessarily follows that the majority of professional women, such as teachers, to be found in the country are Christians. The machinations of the Armenian secret societies, which prejudiced the position of the Christians of the old Turkish Empire so fatally, do not appear ever to have extended their operations to Mesopotamia, and as a consequence the Christians have not the extreme horror of the Turks that is possessed by their co-religionists farther north. Incidentally, the unfortunate Armenians appear to be no more popular in Baghdad with the local Christians than they are with the inhabitants of other parts of the world; but they have made a place for themselves in modern Mesopotamia, and they are represented in high positions in the youthful civil service of the country. In many ways both the Armenians and the Assyrians show more strength of character than the Baghdad Christians, who have a reputation for shiftiness and personal fickleness which would appear to have considerable justification.

The violent mixture of Moslem, Jewish and Christian communities in a comparatively small country would in itself offer a sufficiently grave problem to the local statesman; but there are in addition two little peoples who have steadfastly maintained their religious and social independence of the adherents of all three of the world religions. These are the Sabians of the southern Euphrates area round Nasriyah, and the Yezidis of the hilly country lying to the south-west of the city of Mosul. The former profess a religion of great antiquity, but containing additions and adaptations from both Judaism and Christianity in more recent times. Strictly speaking, they are Mandæans, but they are invariably known as Sabians, or, in the popular Baghdad form, "Subbis." By adopting the Sabian title in former times, they secured for themselves the toleration urged by the Prophet upon his followers towards the Jews, Christians and Sabians, as all being " people of the Book." The identity and doctrines of the Sabians intended by the Prophet are obscure, but the same name, curiously enough, was applied by the heathen Arabs to the early Moslems, the description being gained by the importance ascribed in the Prophet's teaching to ablution; the name, in the original Aramaic, meaning " the baptized."

The present Sabians represent only a remnant of the great and powerful community that acknowledged their faith in early mediæval times; under the Abbassids they possessed a large number of places of worship, and even as late as the 17th century they numbered, it is believed, 20,000 families. To-day probably not more than 2,000 of them exist all told. Their men are notable for their handsome and distinguished appearance, which is enhanced by their prohibition of shaving or hair-cutting; and their religion insists on physical perfection in a candidate for the priesthood. The latter office is not confined to men, though women may not rise to the dignity of bishop, an important functionary who possesses full authority over the priesthood, and almost unlimited influence among the people. Curiously enough, a still higher priestly rank than that of the bishop is acknowledged, but only in theory; this archiepiscopal office having only once been filled, it is said, in the last 2,500 years.

The Mandæan religion, in type a form of Gnosticism, is based on the belief that the world was the creation of one of a series of demi-gods, who were themselves emanations from the supreme Spirit. An extremely elaborate hierarchy of gods and demi-gods surrounds the various emanations, who remain in almost as impenetrable secrecy as the supreme Spirit itself, though one of the emanations, known as the father of Primal Life, manifests himself to the souls of pious Mandæans after death. Primal Life, personified, may be said to be the direct god of the Mandæans, and their principal prayers are directed to him. To the belief that his place of residence is beyond the pole star is due their reverence for the north; the pole star being conceived as the central sun around which all the heavenly bodies move.

The Mandæans claim descent from the ancient Egyptians who were saved from the Biblical drowning of Pharaoh in the Red Sea, and they regard the Egyptian king as the founder of their faith. In their hierarchy of gods and evil persons occur representatives of almost all the Babylonian and Palestinian religions, from Bel Marduk to Moses, Jesus and Muhammad. Both the latter are regarded as false gods, and thus Mandæism is hostile to both Christianity and Islam. A peculiar reverence is evinced for John the Baptist, who is represented as an incarnation of one of the Helpers who surround the emanations of Divinity; in the Mandæan story, John is inveigled into giving baptism to Jesus as the Messiah, owing to a mistaken notion of his identity. The final destiny of the world is to be swallowed up by the evil power, the personified fire of hell, and the parent of sons who were afterwards translated by the heavenly powers into planets and stars. The consumption of the earth will herald the end of the evil power, who will burst and fall into the abyss, eventually reaching complete oblivion. Thus the whole universe will then consist of one everlasting world of light.

The reverence expressed by the Mandæans for John the Baptist was responsible for leading a number of early European missionaries in Mesopotamia to consider them as Christians; but there is, in fact, nothing whatever of Christianity in their creed, although there are resemblances between the two religions in small points. Thus the Mandæans observe Sunday as their holy day, and possess a form of service of extra sanctity resembling in many ways the Christian Eucharist, and employing the same elements

KIFL: A TYPICAL EUPHRATES COUNTRY TOWN

THE PEOPLE OF THE COUNTRY 209

of bread and wine. Their most common ceremony is baptism, which is enjoyed by pious Mandæans every Sunday, as well as on other stated occasions. Their places of worship are small and extremely simple, being intended merely for the accommodation of the priest; the worshippers remain outside during the service. Owing to their constant use of baptism, they are compelled always to reside in the vicinity of running water; it was this necessity which eventually secured their release from military service under the Turks. The latter, at the commencement of the World War, attempted to conscript them; but as they refused to serve, on religious grounds, anywhere except in the neighbourhood of running water, and as the military authorities could not possibly in practice comply with such a request, the Turks were compelled to let them go.

Living for the last five hundred years in the midst of the wild tribes of the lower Euphrates marshes, the "Subbis" have escaped complete extermination only by their skill in various useful trades; their principal settlement at Suq as Shevukh, where resides their chief priest, is supported by the building of canoes, in which business they exercise something of a monopoly; they are also skilful house and ship carpenters, and their work in silver has won for itself since the war something of an international reputation. Their great decline in population is only partly due to persecution by the Arabs; they have suffered from many internal feuds, and the meticulously strict way in which their law is administered has sometimes given rise to considerable offence, and some backsliding. Their women especially have tended to leave them by marrying Moslem husbands, and thus becoming lost, with their offspring, to the fold. Nevertheless, procreation is with them a sacred duty, and it is unlikely that, given a reasonable chance of existence, they will die out entirely.

Peculiarly enough, the World War was responsible for bringing them forward in a remarkable manner. Previously, they were practically confined to the neighbourhood of Suq as Shevukh and Nasriyah; but the British capture of Amarah induced many of them to emigrate there, and the unheard-of prosperity which their silver work brought to them soon produced a further stream of emigration. At the present time, not only has Baghdad her regular Subbi quarter, but the Subbis have reached Mosul, Basrah, Bombay and even Egypt; and there are not wanting those among them who are possessed of an ambition to move even further afield. In worldly matters, they are intelligent and keen, with a distinct talent for business; many of their families have grown rich since the occupation of the country by the British. In dress they are indistinguishable from the Arabs, but they always retain the shafiyah and never affect the fez. Among themselves they speak a form of modern Aramaic, but they invariably know Arabic as well, and not infrequently have a fair knowledge of English. They send their boys regularly to the Government schools, and recently there have been some Subbi students in the technical and secondary schools in Baghdad, perhaps the first of their race to receive anything approaching a higher education for a thousand years or more.

In private life, the Subbis are pleasant and sociable, and they will listen with delight for hours on end to descriptions of the great world outside. Their religion, which is tolerant in matters of enjoyment and even expresses disapproval of fasting, does not encourage in them the gloom so characteristic of the pious Moslem, and they have even taken very cordially to the European habit of drinking beer. Their skill as tradesmen has served to educate their faculties, and keep them supple and alert. On the subject of their religion they are, however, extremely secretive, and they do not care for it to be mentioned in ordinary conversation. Bright, vivacious and intelligent, there are many worse companions for an evening's talk than the members of this small and pathetic race, whose origin is unknown, whose present is precarious and whose future, perhaps, is not very bright. Whatever be the eventual fate of the British connection with Mesopotamia, it is to be hoped that the interests of the " Subbis " will receive some protection and consideration at the hands of the powers that be.

The other small nationality in Mesopotamia to which previous allusion has been made is that of the Yezidis, or " Devil Worshippers." They are not in fact so much devil worshippers as devil propitiators. Believing Satan to be endowed with full power for evil in the world, they conceive it their duty to ward off danger by a careful avoidance of anything likely to cause offence to the evil one. Jesus enters into their faith as a prophet, as also does Muhammad; they practise the rites of both baptism and circumcision.

Kurdish in tongue, and probably in race, the Yezidis are far wilder and more unapproachable than the Sabians; nor have the events of the last few years done much towards bringing them into line with the modern world. They have suffered much in the past from the persecution of Moslem and Christian alike, and their isolated situation in the hills largely prevents them from falling under the spell of the outside world. They have shown a tendency of late to accept secular education, but the ability to read and write is with them a highly privileged craft; and, perhaps not unnaturally, their leaders do not look altogether with favour upon the possibility of the spread of general education.

The Sabians and Yezidis do not complete the tale of the minor communities of Mesopotamia; there are still believed to be in existence groups of followers of the new faith of Babism or Bahaism, an offshoot of the Persian Shiah, which has of late years shown such startling vitality in the United States of America. The original founder of the faith, a young Persian Seyyid or descendant of the Prophet, was eventually shot by order of the Persian Government, and his followers gave trouble to the latter for many years; they were treated when caught with atrocious cruelty. For some time the movement centred in Baghdad, where its adherents, on Sunni territory, were safe from the persecution of the Persian Shiahs. Eventually the latter secured their removal, and they were dispersed to Syria and afterwards to all parts of the world; but a remnant of them have lingered on in Baghdad, all their religious services, however, being now conducted in strict secrecy for fear of Shiah persecution.

Such, then, are the various races and religious communities in modern Mesopotamia. The classes and grades of Society, in the towns at any rate, are much the same as in the West, the grading of life being largely, in Baghdad as in London, an economic matter. There are, on the other hand, certain social features necessarily peculiar to such a country, containing ancient and modern elements so hopelessly intermingled, which perhaps deserve rather more detailed notice.

The first is the position of the sheikh, an individual whose life and functions are very largely misunderstood in the West, owing to the spurious popularity which he has recently enjoyed in popular songs and cinema films. On the "movies" the sheikh is invariably a man of prepossessing appearance and inexhaustible wealth, living an idle and pleasant life in the desert in a highly decorated tent, surrounded by tribesmen eager to do his bidding, and with a strongly developed taste for the kidnapping of strange ladies. In ordinary life the sheikh's position is a good deal more precarious, and his life a great deal more strenuous. There are, of course, several varieties of sheikhs. A paramount sheikh of a great confederation of tribes, such as the Muntafiq or the Dulaim, is a man with very large responsibilities. He may control the lives and fortunes of anything from 100,000 to 200,000 people. As the sole fountain of judicial as well as of executive authority, he must always be accessible to the complaints of his men, even when directed against a minor sheikh of one of the various tribes forming his confederation; he is responsible for directing what one may term the "foreign policy" of the confederation; and he must always be ready to battle for his people's interests against those of other tribes, and even possibly against the civil authority. On occasions, as, for instance, if one of his men is "wanted" by the civil police for a theft or murder in a more settled portion of the country, he may have to decide quickly between the claims of the Government and of tribal sentiment; or it may be his duty to urge the claim of some member of his people who has been wronged by other tribes or by a Government official. In addition to his public responsibilities, a paramount sheikh is usually a large landowner, and the responsibility of managing his property profitably may be large, especially in unsettled times; and profit he must have, for his expenses are enormous, and a paramount sheikh, though frequently a rich man, is, equally frequently, short of ready money. His hospitality, much of it forced upon him, must be open and unstinted; and, in addition, he may have heavy dues to pay to the Government on account of land in occupation by his men, or public services, such as irrigation, of which his men reap the benefit. What may be termed the internal taxation system of the confederation, by which he regains some portion of his exterior expenditure from his tribesmen, must, in self-defence, remain his constant care; and the continuance of his power will depend largely upon his ability to give employment to his cultivators, a matter which may involve much labour. The falling into disuse of a canal, for instance, may result in one of his more settled villages suddenly deciding to move, ending in a diminution of his own tribal strength, to somebody else's advantage. The life of a paramount sheikh, tempting as it may seem to the Westerner confined to office, workshop and suburb, is by no means a bed of roses.

The social responsibilities of a sheikh in the matter of hospitality require the maintenance of a very large household staff, and his position will necessitate the retention of a large personal retinue of armed men. Some sheikhs, especially among the Shiahs, whose system of marriage contract is of the freest, have very large families, thirty children being not unusual; one sheikh of the Albu Muhammad who died recently was reputed to have had nearly a thousand. In the smaller tribes, or in the subdivisions of the large confederations, the wealth and the responsibilities of the sheikhs are both materially reduced; but many of them maintain a house in one or other of the towns in addition to their less sedentary country establishments, in much the same way that the bedouin sheikhs of the Syrian desert retain a town house in Damascus.

In modern Mesopotamia, the tribal system is beginning to show distinct signs of corruption and decay, and with the passing of the tribal system the position of the sheikh becomes more and more precarious. Some town-dwelling sheikhs have already altogether lost touch with their original function, and retain the title merely by courtesy; thus one can find in Baghdad sheikhs occupied as wholesale merchants and in other lines of business. The title of sheikh is also very commonly bestowed in the towns upon religious or intellectual leaders of established reputation. With the passing of time the tribal sheikh will tend to become merely a country landowner, much as the aristocracy of Europe has already done; his power and executive functions disappearing with the disappearance of tribal conditions.

If the sheikh represents a social type that is passing, the town artisan represents a novel type that is rapidly increasing in numbers and importance. It might almost be said that the artisan is the creation of the World War. The trades of chauffeur, fitter, vulcanizer, railwayman, electrician, typewriter mechanic, cinema operator and a hundred more of the same sort were practically unknown in Baghdad ten years ago; but the arrival of Western mechanical inventions has been greeted with enthusiasm by the people, and the mechanical services of the community are to-day almost entirely, except in the higher branches, locally manned. This is in itself an achievement which may be regarded as remarkable. Considering that the towns are now largely electric lighted, that the railways are fairly extensive, that there is a public telephone service, and that such privately owned public services as hotels, newspapers, and taxi-cabs are quite adequate to the demand, and that ten years ago such things were hardly dreamt of, it would seem no inconsiderable accomplishment to have procured and trained sufficient local labour to ensure their smooth operation, even on a relatively low standard of efficiency.

The town artisan is thus an entirely new type, and it is too early as yet to say what effect he will eventually have on the life of the country as a whole. That effect in any case must be very considerable. The interest and novelty of mechanical work draws the most unlikely people out of their seclusion, and the bulk of the railway labour in Mesopotamia to-day is coming, not from the towns, but from the tribes. The young man of the local tribe will watch the railway arrive, and thereafter will eye with wonder the daily arrival and departure of the one train that links him with the outside world; and then the lure of it will one day come to him, as it has come to so many in the West, and he will be off to Baghdad to seek employment along the great iron way that has made such an irresistible appeal to his restless love of change. The railway and the motor-car, given time, may yet prove to possess the spell which shall overcome the differences of tribe and religion and draw all men together into one united nation; and the class of artisans, the chief bulwark in Western countries against the oppression of Government or " big interests " alike, may in Mesopotamia prove to be the first to free itself from the desolating rule of tribal ignorance, of political suspicion and of religious intolerance.

CHAPTER XIV

THE CREATION OF THE NEW STATE

" The edifice that has not firm foundations, make it not lofty; and if thou dost, tremble for it."—SA'DI.

THE broad outline of the task to which the British Government had committed itself with regard to the future of Mesopotamia, was summarized in the official announcement of June 20th, 1920, immediately previous to the outbreak of the rebellion :

> His Majesty's Government, having been entrusted with the mandate for Mesopotamia, anticipate that the mandate will constitute Mesopotamia an independent State under the guarantee of the League of Nations and subject to the mandate to Great Britain ; that it will lay on them the responsibility for the maintenance of internal peace and external security, and will require them to formulate an organic law to be framed in consultation with the people of Mesopotamia, and with due regard to the rights, wishes and interests of all the communities of the country. The mandate will contain provisions to facilitate the development of Mesopotamia as a self-governing State until such time as it can stand by itself, when the mandate will come to an end. The inception of this task His Majesty's Government has decided to entrust to Sir Percy Cox, who will resume his position on the termination of the existing military administration as chief British representative in Mesopotamia.
> Sir Percy Cox will be authorized to call into being, as provisional bodies, a Council of State under an Arab president, and a General Elective Assembly representative of, and freely elected by, the population

of Mesopotamia, and it will be his duty to prepare, in consultation with the General Elective Assembly, the permanent organic law.

Such a task might well have appalled even so experienced an Eastern public servant as Sir Percy Cox. Nobody was in a better position than he to know that modern Mesopotamia possessed, in actual fact, hardly even the rudiments of a national spirit, and that the " rights, wishes and interests of all the communities in the country," so glibly referred to by His Majesty's Government, represented about as various an assortment of conflicting desires and policies as could be found anywhere on the earth.

Arabs, Jews, Kurds, Seljuk Turks, Persians, Assyrians, Telkaifis, Armenians—how mould such a composite collection of races into a single nation ? Sunnis, Shiahs, Jews, Christians, Sabians, Yezidis—how to lessen the friction between such a variety of creeds ? How to persuade the tribal sheikh to sacrifice his power for the sake of a non-existing State ? How to persuade the selfish townsman to merge his interests in those of a merely theoretical community ?

New nations in the past have always sprung from some definite and urgent need, some actual basic desire for nationality ; they have represented in a concrete form the feeling in the hearts of a certain number of men and women that they, and they alone, actually represented an unique community, different in its way from every other community in the world. In short, they have been born, and have grown naturally.

But the Mesopotamian nation was to be a new experiment in nation building ; it was to demonstrate the belief prevalent in the West that there is nothing in the world which cannot, if necessary, be made by machinery. No great evidence was forthcoming that the native population of Mesopotamia wanted to become a nation—indeed, large and influential portions of it fought to the last ditch against it ; but the League of Nations and the British Government conceived it as an excellent way of disposing of a country that was threatening to become a nuisance, and which possessed no very clear way of expressing definite opinions of its own.

In deference to this policy, an attempt had been made as early as 1919 by the British officials in the country to obtain some idea as to what form of Government the people really desired. Three definite questions were asked of the local notables and middle-class people, approached by the various district political officers : (1) Should Mosul be included in Mesopotamia ? (2) Should an Arab amir (prince) be given the rule of the country ? (3) If an amir was desired, whom would the people prefer ? The only really definite opinion obtained was regarding Mosul, on which point the educated classes of the country have throughout remained constant ; and it appears to be the decided local opinion that any alienation of that town and district would mean a real loss to the country. In 1919 there was no evidence of any great local feeling in favour of an amir, and public opinion was far from being unanimous on the point even in 1921. In any case, the question of finding out the real wishes of an Eastern community on any subject is surrounded with difficulties quite unknown to the West. The people of the East have been under one foreign master or another for so long a period of time, and have become so accustomed to be controlled by their "superiors," that their first aim is, for the sake of peace and quiet, to propitiate and attempt to please them ; thus they will nearly invariably give to a higher authority, questioning them on any subject, the kind of answer which they conceive that authority to prefer. In consequence, the difficulty of holding anything like a general plebiscite is almost prohibitive ; and the statement that any community in the Near East have "voted unanimously" for any particular person or cause must in consequence always be taken with the proverbial pinch of salt, particularly if it is official.

The first task of the new British High Commissioner was to secure the pacification of the country after the rebellion of the previous year, and to assure its gradual demilitarization. In this he was as successful as the circumstances permitted, and the winter of 1920 and early spring of 1921 passed quietly, and even uneventfully. The last echoes of the rebellion were to be seen in the constant

THE CREATION OF THE NEW STATE 219

movements of the military, followed by the departure from the country of large numbers of English and Indian troops. The railway to Basrah was reopened, and the traffic on it and other lines began to assume a more civilian aspect ; and the country as a whole appeared to be settling itself down to work and normal occupations. There was a sudden and unexpected " boom " in trade, partly due to the large number of extra officers and soldiers who had been brought to the country by the rebellion, and partly to the still chaotic condition of Russia, which left the whole of the Persian foreign trade in Baghdad hands. The sudden access of wealth began to show itself prominently in the latter city, where a host of new shops and hotels suddenly came into being, and motor-cars multiplied almost hourly. A feverish rush to continue the rebuilding of the city followed the inactivity of the previous year, and New Street, the creation of Khalil Pasha, began to assume the appearance of a normal busy Eastern city street. A spirit of progress seemed to be in the air, most gratifying to those who had the future of the country at heart.

On the political side the period was notable for its lack of controversy. Public attention having been largely diverted from politics to the possibility of making money quickly, the High Commissioner was granted a respite in which to complete his plans for the new national Government. The first step was taken in the autumn of 1920, when the local Council of State was organized to assist the High Commissioner in his task of governing the country and of preparing for later developments. The Council of State was headed by Abd-ar-Rahman, the Naqib of Baghdad, an elderly personage, possessed of perhaps wider influence than any other single man in Mesopotamia. The office of naqib is in itself a powerful one, and carries with it many duties, including that of deciding the right of any claimant to wear the green turban which signalizes the descendants of the Prophet. In addition, the present Naqib is the direct descendant of a much venerated Sunni saint of the Middle Ages, whose large and imposing mosque in Baghdad is under his care and administration. The properties of the mosque are considerable, and a large number of Sunni pilgrims are attracted annually to the shrine. The family of the Naqib is a wealthy one, and owns property in both town and country.

In Turkish times the Naqib had not infrequently possessed as much actual power in Baghdad as the Turkish vali, or governor; and the privileges of his position were immediately recognized by the British after their conquest of the country. While maintaining a friendly and helpful attitude he had never ceased to express the hope that the British occupation would end in the political independence of his country; but the rebellion of 1920 and the dissensions which it produced among the Arabs themselves opened his eyes to the extreme difficulty of creating an independent nation out of such diverse elements as go to make up the population of Mesopotamia. The tribesmen during the rebellion had not hesitated to ravage and loot the country properties of their more settled fellow-countrymen; and the latter, including the Naqib and his family, probably realized for the first time that the real spirit of Arab nationalism was at present largely confined to a few of the more disinterested and intelligent members of the educated classes.

The fatal division of the country into complete self-governing religious communities began to appear directly the creation of a national Government became a real possibility. None of the minorities showed any disposition to welcome a local form of control which would, in practice, put them completely in the power of the Arabs; and, owing to the large number of Shiahs among the latter, there was an utter lack of unity even among them. On account of the long Turkish predominance, nearly all the local men with administrative experience were Sunnis; and the Shiahs, forming fifty per cent. of the Moslem population, soon began to assert loudly that the land which contained so many of the Shiah holy places was once more about to come under complete Sunni control.

The alarm of the minorities reached a climax in the case of the Jews, who, directly they realized that the British Government had seriously made up its mind to organize a local form of government, sent a representative to the High Commissioner, and requested, in a body, the privilege of British citizenship. They based their claim on the fact that their country had been conquered by British troops, and that they were actually at the moment Turkish subjects under British control ; and that therefore the British had no moral right to force them to accept a change of nationality, unless they so desired it. They were eventually appeased by the personal influence of the High Commissioner, and by his assurance that ample guarantees would be afforded them by the British Government against any form of local tyranny ; and a prominent Baghdad Jew with considerable administrative experience, and bearing the internationally famous name of Sassoon, was persuaded later to accept office in the Council of State as Minister of Finance. It was, however, significant that the opposition of the Jews to the local application of " self-determination " had to be met by a process of personal and moral persuasion, and that there was in fact no logical argument to be urged against the position which they had taken up.

This point threw an interesting sidelight on to the inherent weakness of the mandate idea, which had been one of the most carefully advocated schemes of the promoters of the League of Nations. Though the theory sounded excellent to a world weary of war and Imperial rivalries and inclined to expect the immediate arrival of the millennium, in practice it was soon found to be the most vulnerable part of the whole organization of the League. The mandate system presupposes that a strong nation will be willing to assume the burden of the guidance of a young State which is admitted by the general opinion of the world to be incapable of standing alone ; and that, conversely, the young State will be willing to permit such guidance, and the consequent continual interference with its internal affairs that such a guidance must assume. The weakness of the system lies in its disregard of the fact that, firstly, no strong nation will be allowed by its own nationals to bear the burden (including probably a heavy financial burden) of guiding the destinies of a smaller State, unless it is allowed very great material advantages in return ; and that, secondly, no small or young State in its turn will be allowed by its own citizens to permit the constant interference of a foreign power. A rich and powerful State cannot " adopt " a poor and feeble State, in the manner in which a rich individual may adopt a poor and struggling youth ; because in the case of individuals the rich man is only doing what he pleases with his own money, but the rich Government has no money of its own at all. The riches of a Government form merely the sum total of what it extracts from the pockets of its citizens by taxation; and the latter will in the long run refuse to provide more than such an amount as they consider necessary for the efficient furthering of their collective interests. The gradual realization of this truth soon commenced to complicate the Mesopotamian situation. The British taxpayer, once he could make his voice heard against the tyranny of the muzzling orders of the war period, began to protest passionately against an arrangement which involved his Government in spending large sums of his money, without being in a position to claim any corresponding advantage, even that of complete control ; and English newspapers and public men started to point out with some truth, that if the British taxpayer was to be asked to finance charity on a large scale, there was plenty of scope for it nearer home.

An additional point which was overlooked by the promoters of the mandate idea, and which the action of the Baghdad Jews had emphasized, is that every small and poor country will inevitably contain an intelligent minority who would prefer, if they are to come under the domination of a powerful foreign State at all, to become subjects or citizens of that State and thus partakers in its inheritance. St. Paul, a Greek Jew, could proudly proclaim " civis Romanus sum," and insist upon a personal trial before the Emperor of the civilized world ; an intelligent Indian, Maltese, or Jewish subject of the British King may compete on equal terms in London itself with Londoners, and even rise to the highest offices of the State. It was hardly to be wondered at that the Jews, together with many of the Christians and Moslems of Mesopotamia, released at last from the deadly inactivity of Turkish rule, should be unwilling to sacrifice the prospects of citizenship in the greatest Empire in the world, for the doubtful benefits of local Arab control.

The only possible hope for the mandate system in practice would appear to be for the League of Nations to administer its mandated territories itself ; this again would depend upon its ability to raise an international army or police force, and to create an international civil service to maintain its obligations in the mandated territories. The system of conferring a mandate upon an outside power can end only in practice either in the mandated territory proving so heavy a burden that the mandate has to be revised or removed (a process which is far advanced in Mesopotamia, and apparently beginning in Syria and Palestine) or in the mandatory power absorbing the mandated territory at the first convenient opportunity (which will probably be the fate of the African and Australasian territories of the late German Empire). No other issues appear to be possible from the much-advertised system which was, in 1919, to pave the way for the emancipation of all the weaker nations of the earth.

The situation in Mesopotamia provided an additional complication in the constant activities of the Arab nationalists. The failure of the rebellion in 1920, and the flight in the same year of Feisal and his followers from Damascus, had led for the moment to the complete dislocation of their plans ; but once they realized that the British Government was sincere in its desire to create an independent Mesopotamia, their hopes of political dominance began to rise again.

It had been recognized by the Assembly of the League of Nations that Mesopotamia was not wholly Arab, and the nationals of the new State were therefore, it was decided, to be designated not Arabs, but " Iraqis " ; an Iraqi being officially described as a former Turkish subject resident in, or proposing to reside in, the portion of the late Turkish Empire now known officially as " Iraq." The double aim of the Arab nationalists now began to be apparent. While welcoming the birth of an Iraq State as the dawn of Arab independence, they never ceased to harbour the hope that the Arab dominion might eventually take a wider scope ; and the agitation for complete Arab independence, which had been previously conducted from Syria, now began to be transferred to Iraq. This indirectly led to considerable feeling between the British authorities in Mesopotamia and the French in Syria, who openly accused the British of fomenting Arab nationalist trouble in the latter country; a feeling which was soon increased by the French suspicion that the British were in secret negotiation with the amir Feisal, whom the French had shortly before summarily driven from Syria. Meanwhile the High Commissioner in Mesopotamia was faced with the added difficulties that the Kurds in the north would be content with nothing short of local autonomy under British protection, and flatly refused to offer their loyalty to the new Iraq Government; and that much of the Arab element of Mesopotamia itself did not want to be regarded as Iraqi but as Arab. Many of the Arab nationalists were, in fact, quite as hostile to the new proposals as the Jews or Kurds, though for a different reason; and, faced with the desire of the Jews and most of the Christians to become British, of the Kurds to become independent, of the Sunni and nationalist Arabs to remain Arab, and of the Shiah Arabs and Persians to be freed from any Governmental authority whatsoever, the British officials in Baghdad had a heavy task to persuade themselves that any genuine Iraqi national feeling existed at all.

But the British statesmen at home were still obsessed with the idea that machine-made nations were possible; and an important step forward in the creation of the new Iraq was taken early in 1921, when the High Commissioner announced the creation of an electoral law, which should form the legal basis for elections to form a new National Assembly, which should in turn evolve an organic law for the new State, and should debate the important question of its possible head. The problem thus seemed at last reduced to something like first principles. An electoral law, a general election, the creation of a constitution, and the election of a president or king. Nothing—on paper—could be simpler.

The electoral law was finished, and under it an electoral roll was, several months afterwards, completed; but that was as far as the British experiment in Iraqi democracy went. Perhaps the " mandatory authority " was not quite sure enough what the result of an election would be; perhaps the sheer hopelessness of attempting to secure anything approaching a general decision on any vital point was realized. At any rate, the elections were never held,

THE CREATION OF THE NEW STATE 225

and the national assembly never met ; and, in the event, the king and the constitution were found to a great extent by the British authorities themselves.

In March, 1921, the High Commissioner left for Cairo, to take part in a conference of British officials called to consider the whole question of the new-conquered territories in the Near and Middle East. The upshot of the conference, so far as Mesopotamia was concerned, was that the whole question of the national assembly was put in the background for the present, and attention was concentrated on the question of appointing an amir or king. It was apparently, and perhaps justly, considered impossible for the people of the country to decide for themselves whether they required a king or not ; and it was hoped, not without some justification, that the appearance in the field of a native or Arab prince would rally local sentiment and aid the formation of some centralizing character in the country as a whole. Accordingly, it was made known that the British Government proposed that the head of the new Iraqi State should be a constitutional king ; that any local or Arab prince who wished might offer himself as a candidate for the new throne ; and that the final decision would rest with the people of Iraq. How this decision was to be expressed in the absence of a national assembly was not explained. At the same time it leaked out that the amir Feisal was about to offer himself for election, and a strong suspicion arose that the British Government were especially inclined to favour his cause, and even that the whole affair had been practically settled already.

Several things tended to confirm this suspicion in the minds of the Iraqi population. Prince Feisal's English friend and companion in arms, Colonel Lawrence, had been present at the Cairo Conference ; the revolt of his father, King Hosein of the Hedjaz, had been unquestionably useful to the British during the World War ; and it was believed in Mesopotamia that feeling between the British and the French was none too good, and that the British had watched Prince Feisal's struggles against the French in Syria with some sympathy. Consequently, when it was publicly announced that the amir was on his way to

Iraq in a British ship to offer himself as a candidate for the throne, with the good wishes of his elder brother Abdullah (who was locally thought at one time to have desired the honour for himself), the people had little doubt as to who was destined to become the first King of Iraq.

The amir Feisal did not, however, have the field completely to himself. Several local people of note were understood to be ready to offer themselves if a suitable opportunity should occur. The Sheikh of Mohammerah, an old ally of the British, a Shiah and a man of great wealth and influence, was considered to be largely acceptable to the Arab and Persian Shiahs; the Naqib of Baghdad, himself acting as president of the local Council of State, was an obvious possibility; and Seyyid Talib Pasha of Basrah, a scion of the Naqib family in the southern city, and a politician with a very lurid past, though a strong supporter of the British, who was ostensibly supporting the cause of the Naqib of Baghdad, was understood to be equally prepared to work in his own interest. In addition to the possible opposition of rival candidates, the amir Feisal had to face the fact that he was not a native of the country, that, as a Sunni, he could not expect a warm welcome from the very strong Shiah community, and that a great number even of Sunnis were inclined to resent the sudden rise to fame during the war of the family of the Sharif of Mecca, resting so largely upon British support and British money. There were a number of the more old-fashioned Sunnis, indeed, who were inclined to consider the rebellion of the Sharif against the Turkish Sultan and Caliph of Islam as a most impious act; and King Hosein, though temporarily successful in his political ambition of creating an independent State in the Hedjaz, had notably failed in his effort to shake the spiritual allegiance of the orthodox world towards the Turkish sovereign.

The partiality of the British Government towards the King of the Hedjaz and his family threatened, too, to involve it in serious difficulties with other, and older, Arab allies, as well as with its own Moslem subjects. We have previously indicated the events which led to the re-creation of a Wahabi State in central Arabia with the youthful and ambitious Abdul Aziz Ibn Saud at its head, and we have touched on

THE CREATION OF THE NEW STATE 227

the close friendship which had existed before and during the war between the latter and the British authorities, a friendship cemented in battle by the death with Ibn Saud's armies of the British representative at his court. We have seen also that Ibn Rashid, the old rival of Ibn Saud, allied himself continually to Turkish and German influences, and would have been, but for the activity of Ibn Saud, a serious thorn in the side of the British forces in lower Mesopotamia. The climax of this ancient feud came in 1921, when Ibn Rashid was utterly defeated by Ibn Saud, his capital taken and he himself made prisoner ; and thus the British victory over the Turk was followed by the victory of their old Arab ally over his pro-Turkish opponent.

But the new victory brought with it considerable complications for the British authorities. Ibn Saud's power and prestige were now greatly enhanced, and, by his latest conquests, his boundary now marched for a considerable distance with that of Mesopotamia ; and the ambition of the able and restless prince unquestionably began to turn towards the fruitful lands to the north, which had been successfully conquered by the Wahabis a hundred years earlier, and which were now in the hands of his all-powerful European friend and ally. For some years Ibn Saud had been carefully consolidating his influence over the tribesmen of all northern Arabia by his clever institution of the " Akhwan " movement, or movement of " Brethren." This institution showed the working of an extremely shrewd and subtle brain, and its influence, which has increased very largely in the last few years, may yet come to play a considerable part in modern Arabian and Mesopotamian history. The Akhwan are banded together by a combination of religious and national motives. On the religious side comes their sworn subjection to the Wahabi creed, which is put before them as the pure doctrine of the Prophet, relieved of all the additions and complications emanating from later prophets and mystics ; on the national side comes the political doctrine that only by combination under an Arab chief can the Arab nation attain once more to the greatness which is its birthright, and which it has once before achieved. The fascination of such a combination of ideas, religious and political, centred in a personality so romantic and so successful as that of Ibn Saud, can readily be seen ; and there are not wanting foreign observers who declare that, if an Arab renaissance is really a potentiality of the immediate future, it will be the strength and coherence of the Akhwan movement which will bring it into being. It had become obvious, in any case, soon after the rebellion of Sharif Hosein in 1916, that Ibn Saud would never tolerate a rival in the struggle for the hegemony of the Arab tribes. The wealth, the immorality and the absence of any real religious belief of Mecca have long been accepted as articles of the Wahabi creed ; and there could never be any real hope that the Wahabis would accept the claim of the Sharifian family to be the leaders of the modern Arab nation, either on the political or the spiritual side.

The difficulty of the British, who were the accepted allies of both parties, will now become apparent. It would have been impossible to invite Ibn Saud to offer himself for the throne of Iraq, although he might without prejudice be considered as easily the most capable and prominent Arab chieftain of the day ; for such a course of action would have provoked an immediate uproar among the Shiahs (who are looked upon by the Puritan Wahabis as idolaters, and who would have every reason to fear the arrival of a Wahabi ruler), and considerable, and probably legitimate, uneasiness among the Christians and Jews. By backing, on the other hand, the amir Feisal, the British would secure the undoubted approval of a certain section of the Iraqi population, and would repay the obligation which they were under to the prince and to his father for their aid at a very critical period of the World War; but they would run the risk of alienating a faithful and far older ally in Ibn Saud, and of sowing the seeds of future strife owing to the unquestioned ambition and ability of this chieftain. The latter, situated geographically between father Hosein on the one side, and son Feisal on the other, and himself harbouring great ambitions, could hardly be expected to sit quietly and watch the growth of Mesopotamia into a modern power, without at some time striking a blow for his own position. Single-handed, and if British support were entirely removed from either combatant, Ibn Saud could feel himself capable of tackling both Mecca and

THE CREATION OF THE NEW STATE 229

Mesopotamia, and of seizing for himself the headship of the Arab nation ; but circumstances were hardly likely to be so favourable to him ten or twenty years ahead, when Mesopotamia, protected by the British during her period of weakness, might have attained to a position of wealth and power far beyond the prospects of his own unfertile and sparsely populated country.*

The final upshot of this struggle has yet to be seen. Feisal was successful in obtaining the throne of Iraq, but his position has had to be guaranteed by the presence in the country of British troops ; on the other hand, Ibn Saud has had to be bribed on more than one occasion with British money to remain quiet, and even to forgo the results of a successful little campaign which he waged in 1921 against King Hosein, utterly defeating the forces of that monarch, and causing undeniable panic even in Mecca itself. If the scales were not weighted with British aeroplanes and soldiers, there is no question as to which is the stronger party of the two ; and, should British troops at any time be withdrawn entirely from Mesopotamia, it can hardly be expected that Ibn Saud will refrain for ever from trying his luck in a contest where the prizes are so great.

The amir Feisal landed in Basrah, with a certain amount of ceremony, in May, 1921. His reception at the port, which is largely commercial and therefore more conscious of foreign connections than national feeling, was not over-cordial ; in the country districts, however, he was well received, and in Baghdad itself with acclamation. In the holy cities anything but a rather chilly and formal reception was hardly to be expected ; but the dignity and attractive personality of the prince, and the memory of his remarkable career, did a great deal to create a favourable opinion. Meanwhile the other candidates for the throne failed to make any great effort on behalf of their claims, with the sole exception of Seyyid Talib Pasha, whose energy and indiscreet frankness eventually led to his seizure and deportation by the British authorities. This rather high-handed action, only too typical of post-war British adminis-

* A Turkish general remarked on this question, " Mon cher, ce n'est pas l'heure pour faire les rois."

tration in the Near East, was carried out in secret, and, owing to the strict surveillance of press telegrams maintained by General Headquarters in Baghdad, was not reported in the London press until many months had elapsed.

That the removal of Seyyid Talib Pasha had an undoubted effect upon the public mind in Iraq and on the eventual success of the candidature of the amir Feisal cannot be doubted, and, indeed, was admitted by many British officials in Baghdad at the time. The Eastern mind is more cynical in political matters than the Western, and will always assume that the Government, as the strongest organization in the community, will in the long run get its own way by fair means or by foul. There appeared, then, nothing very unusual in the British deportation of a prominent local man who might be running contrary to their interests. Such a course was undemocratic and, in view of Seyyid Talib Pasha's admitted services to the British cause in the past, distinctly ungrateful; but, on the other hand, recent events in the Punjab and in Egypt had shown the Near Eastern world that British belief in democracy did not extend very far east of Malta, and gratitude, in any case, is not necessarily a political virtue. When Seyyid Talib Pasha's disappearance and the manner of it became generally known in Iraq, it was assumed by the public that the British had determined that the amir Feisal was to occupy the throne, and that there was the end of the matter. The other candidates withdrew into the background, and the Naqib of Baghdad himself proposed a resolution in the Council of State that the amir Feisal should be regarded as having been chosen ruler of Iraq by acclamation, provided that he would consent to rule under a constitution satisfactory alike to local and to British sentiment. No elections for the national assembly had been held, and therefore no assembly had been called into being; the amir not unnaturally disliked the idea of remaining indefinitely in Iraq without some sort of assurance regarding his position; above all, the British Government, with an anxious eye on the British taxpayer, desired an immediate settlement. A rough referendum of notables, tribal leaders and townspeople was carried out; the result, as was to be expected, was an almost unanimous return in favour of the amir Feisal. The prince subesquently made a series of short visits to the paramount sheikhs of important confederations and received their promise of support ; and, on August 23rd, 1921, he was crowned King of Iraq in the courtyard of the Baghdad Serai, built fifty years before by the Turkish vali Midhat Pasha. Thus for the second time in under two years, prince Feisal found himself "acclaimed" a king.

Though his position on his second throne was infinitely less difficult than on his first, it was still far from easy. The Shiahs, the Jews, the Christians and even important minorities among the Sunnis were far from cordial to the new monarch ; and many of the local tribal heads resented the idea of an Arab ruler being placed over them, even when not impatient of foreign control. "It was not necessary," as an influential local sheikh expressed it, "to pay taxes to the Turks. The British Government are worth paying taxes to, for they bring water, seed and security for trade ; but if there is going to be a local Government in control of my territory I am going to be that local Government." A point of view which commends itself to any practical man.

The commercial communities of the towns, too, were hardly likely to view without anxiety the coming to the throne of a desert prince, experienced only in war and diplomatic negotiation ; while the fashionable coffee-shop loungers of Baghdad could hardly conceal their contempt for a King who steadfastly refused to abandon the ancient Arab costume of the desert for the more flashy European coat and trousers. For some months it became the common talk of the coffee shops that the new kingdom and the new King could not last long ; that the English would soon grow tired of their play-acting ; and that Iraq would either be taken over by the British Empire, or given back to the Turks. Rumours which began to arrive that the Turks were diligently, and not unsuccessfully, preparing for a new offensive against the Greeks, and that they were receiving considerable outside support from the French, Italians and Indians, gave colour to the second possibility, which was carefully cultivated in Iraq by interested persons.

Quiet propaganda of all kinds was greatly aided by the stupidity of the British administration, which continued to maintain a strict censorship of all press telegrams, whether entering or leaving the country ; for it was held to be just as important to prevent awkward news leaking out to London, as filtering in from the outside world. As late as January, 1923, the correspondent in Baghdad of an English newspaper was threatened with deportation on account of an item of news telegraphed by him to London. In Baghdad important news leaked out continually, and on one occasion an official of the telegraph department was seen in a coffee shop with an uncensored copy of a startling foreign telegram, which he had borrowed from the office, previous to its departure to [the censor, for the delectation of his circle of acquaintances. All Baghdad was aware of the fact that the newspapers were under a censorship, with the result that no statements in their columns were believed, even if they happened to be true ; and coffee-shop rumours, always a danger in Eastern countries, naturally gained additional importance, on the score of their being at least as probable as the censored and propaganda news published in the papers. Thus the short-sighted policy of the British authorities completely defeated its own object.

Meanwhile the new King was settling down, with the fatherly aid of the British High Commissioner, to the task of organizing his youthful kingdom. Continuity of administration had to be ensured during the difficult period of the election of a national assembly and the drafting of a constitution ; and it was decided that the tasks hitherto assumed in the provinces by the British political officers should automatically revert to newly-appointed officials of local birth, the British officer remaining as " Adviser." The same system was adopted in the Ministries ; and though it meant in practice paying a double salary for the same work, out of a poverty-stricken Exchequer, it was difficult to see how the creation of a local civil service was to be accomplished in any other way.

The new Ministries, after a certain amount of readjustment, finally resolved themselves into seven : Interior, Justice, Finance, Defence, Communications and Works,

THE CREATION OF THE NEW STATE

Education and Waqaf. Their organization and scope are reviewed in greater detail in subsequent chapters. The new Executive did not, however, completely cover the country; the railways, as the property of the British Government, were administered by the High Commissioner, and several important institutions, such as the electric power-plants of Basrah and Baghdad, remained in the possession of the British army and under the control of General Headquarters. Thus on the purely civil side of life there were actually in operation for some time three distinct Governments, with absolute power in their own respective spheres, and responsible to nobody but themselves; and this serious lack of co-ordination, though not without its humorous side, was badly felt during the opening months of the new King's reign. It was responsible also for a good deal of avoidable extravagance, against which, however, the British taxpayer finally showed some signs of rebellion. The most notorious, though by no means the only, example of this extravagance was the case of the new British Residency. In spite of the fact that two British Residencies already existed in Baghdad, no room could be found for the accommodation of the new High Commissioner and his staff; and an expensive and ill-suited property was purchased on the other side of the Tigris, and adapted, at a cost of some £150,000, for the use of the chief British representative and his entourage. The two older British residencies continued meanwhile in the possession of General Headquarters.

The year which had been ushered in by the coronation passed, on the whole, uneventfully. Some trouble was experienced in reaching an agreement with the Wahabi leader, over the awkward question of the delimitation of the frontier between Iraq and the Wahabi dominions; but the personal influence of the High Commissioner was used to bridge the gap between the claims of the rival Arab monarchs, and Ibn Saud finally signified his intention of entering into a treaty relationship with King Feisal. The new Council of State developed a certain disposition towards political "scenes," and on more than one occasion had to be dissolved and reorganized. Much of the trouble was attributable to inexperience, some of it possibly to the slightly overbearing attitude of the King, who, having been given the position of ruler, soon showed himself determined to rule. His unquestioned ability for affairs, and his experience of foreign methods, tended perhaps to make him impatient of the dilatory methods of some of his Ministers ; especially since he was, far more than they, in a position to realize the backwardness of his country, and the imperative need of getting things done. When the time came to celebrate the first anniversary of the coronation, it could truthfully be said that some progress had been made towards the consolidation of the new regime, and that the King, by his own gifts, had made himself popular with many classes who a year previously had watched his coming with suspicion, and even with dislike. But not even the most hopeful Near Eastern observer would have dared to assume that the new kingdom had as yet shown any signs of permanence, or even of marked stability.

CHAPTER XV

THE ORGANIZATION OF THE EXECUTIVE

*" For forms of government let fools contest ;
" Whate'er is best administered is best."*—POPE.

THE first and most important task which has to be faced by any new Government is the establishment of a system by which the people may be guaranteed a firm and impartial administration of justice. Added difficulty attaches to this question in any Near Eastern country, on account of the manner in which religious law is allowed to interfere in matters which are, to a Western mind, purely secular. In Islam, it should be remembered, nothing is regarded as solely worldly ; the whole operation of daily living is assumed to be covered by religion, and to be controllable by the laws laid down in the Koran and the books of Traditions. In practice this view has had, in modern times, to be much modified ; and in Mesopotamia, as part of the Turkish Empire, an adaptation of the French Code Napoleon had long been in operation for the trial of purely civil cases. But more personal affairs, such as marriage, inheritance, status and so on continued to be regarded as religious matters, and to be dealt with under religious law ; and thus the system of double courts came into being, dealing respectively with civil and criminal or with religious cases, and independent of each other.

The present Department of Justice in Iraq owes its inspiration to the work of Sir Edgar Bonham-Carter, who was appointed senior judicial officer in Baghdad after the occcupation of the city by the British in 1917.

Afterwards associated with him was Sheikh Mustafa al Alusi, a legal official of great experience in matters of Sunni or orthodox Moslem law, who had once held the high office of Qadhi of Mecca. In 1920, Sheikh Mustafa became the first Minister of Justice in Iraq. Under the system evolved by them courts were created for both civil and criminal cases, with a final joint Court of Appeal, the latter taking the place of the old Court of Cassation at Constantinople, which had been the final court of appeal throughout the old Ottoman Empire.

At the present time the lowest courts on the civil side are the Peace Courts, or Courts of Small Causes, no Peace Court judge having the power to try cases in which a larger sum than 750 rupees (about £50) is involved. Directly above the Peace Courts come the Courts of First Instance, which have the power to decide civil cases up to any sum; an application in revision or appeal lies from them to the Court of Appeal.

On the criminal side the lowest courts are those of the Magistrates, graded into three classes; serious criminal cases are committed by the magistrates to the Court of Sessions. The decisions of the Court of Sessions are submitted as a matter of course to the Court of Appeal, and the convicted person has the right to state his case in writing before that court, and may be called before it to explain his defence in person. The Court of Appeal sits in Baghdad; there are courts of sessions and courts of magistrates in all administrative divisions, courts of first instance in Baghdad and nine other large towns, and peace courts throughout the country. In the case of a criminal condemned to death, the sentence has to be considered and confirmed by the King.

On the religious side, the Sunni, or orthodox Moslem, law is based finally on the writing of the founders of the four great schools of law, all of whom flourished under the early Abbassids. Every Sunni Moslem professes one or other of the four schools. It was this final fixation of Moslem law by the fathers, and its powerlessness in consequence to adapt itself to modern conditions, that was largely responsible for the creation of an outside civil code and the restrictions of the functions of the religious courts.

Shiahs recognize none of the four Sunni schools of law, and their methods of decision are based upon their own code. Under the Turks, who were Sunnis, only Sunni courts were permitted, and thus the Shiahs could not in practice bring their religious cases into court at all; and they were compelled to adopt the procedure utilized by the non-Moslems. In the case of the latter, all questions of marriage, divorce, personal status or inheritance were, and still are, decided by the accepted head of their community, who later applies to the civil courts for authorization to make his decision binding. An appeal against such decision, as also against a decision of the Sunni religious courts, lies with the Court of Appeal. In the case of the Shiahs, a separate system of religious courts has been set up for them since the British occupation, the Court of Appeal being again the final authority. It is proposed eventually to create a Court of Cassation in Baghdad to take the place of the old court at Constantinople, and to act as a final court of appeal from all courts, civil, criminal and religious.

After the British occupation the duties of judge or magistrate were shared between the British and Iraqis, a commendable effort being made to offer posts to as many as possible of the latter; difficulty arose, however, through the poverty of legal knowledge in the case of the Iraqis, and ignorance of the Arabic language in the case of the British. The Baghdad School of Law, almost the only school in Iraq in pre-war days which possessed a reputation for the quality of its training, was reopened in 1919, the teaching in it being for the first time conducted in Arabic instead of Turkish.

Considerable headway has since been made in the matter of the provision of trained Iraqi lawyers, and British personnel is, under the new Government, confined to the higher rungs of the ladder.

On the whole, the administration of justice in Iraq must be pronounced a success, although there is a suspicion abroad that it is neither so thorough nor so impartial at the present time as it was two or three years ago. The uproar over the Mesopotamian question in England, and the consequent anxiety of British officials on the spot to hurry forward the creation of the native administration has tended to undue haste in the discharge of gifted foreign judges and their substitution by native ones. Iraq suffers at the present time from a desperate attempt to make her run, as an independent modern State, before she has shown her ability to walk; and this is bound to have a deleterious effect on such a department as that of justice, which above everything else depends upon stability and experience.

On the other hand, the improvement compared with Turkish times is marked and genuine. The work of the Courts, formerly conducted in Turkish and therefore quite unintelligible to the bulk of the litigants, is now carried on in Arabic; the honesty of the judges and magistrates is, generally speaking, above suspicion, whereas in Turkish times a judgeship was almost a recognized step from poverty to at least comparative affluence; and much of the complication of Turkish law has been abolished, and cases are now heard promptly and settled reasonably quickly. By reducing the number of the courts and increasing the remuneration of the judges, the whole social status of the latter has been raised.

Closely connected with the administration of justice is the political organization of the country. Iraq is divided into fourteen provinces ("liwa"), sub-divided into a number of counties ("qadha") and small country and borough districts ("nahiyah"). The head official in each nahiyah is a mudir, in each qadha a qaimakam, and in each liwa a mutassarif, except in the case of Baghdad liwa, which is administered by a special official who also controls the city of Baghdad.

The organization of the Iraq police was originally closely connected with that of the Iraq Levies, who are native Arab, Kurdish and Assyrian soldiers enlisted under the British flag. The institution of the Levies dates from the early days of the British occupation in the war, the first formation being the section at Nasriyah, known as the "Muntafiq Horse." As the British forces moved up country, various small bodies were enlisted from time to time, who were used as guides, guards for the lines of communication, and in other semi-military capacities. After the Armistice their duties became more responsible, and for the first time they were used for police work on a large scale. Meanwhile, the need of an Arab militia for purely military purposes was beginning to be recognized, and in March, 1919, the Levies were reconstituted as a fighting force, and the police organized as a separate body.

Separate police forces had in the meantime been formed in individual towns as the British occupation proceeded, but it was found extremely difficult to get a good class of recruit for the rank and file, and almost impossible in the case of the officers. The Turkish police had enjoyed a very bad reputation, and even to-day the public prejudice against the local police is very great. There were additional difficulties experienced in building up the force, such as the unwillingness for the local policeman to be given sufficient authority to proceed against an European offender ; and, above all, the universal habit among the civilian population of carrying fire-arms. A lucrative traffic in arms is conducted through the Arabian ports by European business interests, and from Arabia they penetrate easily to the far wealthier tribesmen of Iraq. Regulations were issued after the Armistice forbidding the carrying of arms without a licence ; but they are almost universally ignored, even in the towns, and indeed until public security can be assured by the disarming of the tribesmen, it is asking too much of the ordinary citizen to suppose that he will not take the precaution of keeping himself armed against an emergency.

The police force now forms a single body, with headquarters in Baghdad. In some of the provincial divisions the local detachments are organized as a joint town and country force ; in others the town police are organized as a single force, the detachment serving the country outside being separately controlled by the political administration of the district. This is a necessary procedure in the wilder districts, where the official responsible for maintaining the prestige of the Government must be able himself to call upon all available force at a moment's notice. The railway police force, though a part of the regular force, is confined in its responsibility to the railway system. The whole service, officers as well as men, now consists mainly of Iraqis, who, when their difficulties are taken into account, must be admitted to be fairly efficient. Some decrease in efficiency has been noticeable since the departure of the previously strong English element, but in a force so young and inexperienced this would appear to be inevitable. The force contains men of all religions, which is in itself a very hopeful sign. A regular Criminal Investigation and Secret Service bureau is maintained, but it is questionable whether such an institution is capable of being manned entirely by local people, at any rate without some sort of permanent foreign assistance.

Crimes of violence are not, perhaps, as numerous as might be expected under the circumstances. Certain districts of Iraq, from their accessibility to both Asia and Europe and from their freedom from too rigid police control, have long been regarded as a haven of refuge by the disreputable and the vagrant. Eastern people of these classes travel farther afield than is generally realized. It is not uncommon in the courts in Baghdad to find Arab or Indian petty criminals against whom convictions can be traced in half the cities of Asia.

There appear to be quite large classes of the wandering gipsy variety, who are as well known and as little desired in Shanghai or Vladivostok as they are in Basrah and Bombay. Before the World War a number of bands of undesirables had their head-quarters and their refuges in the land of the rivers; but the energy of the new police force and the British secret service officers associated with it has probably done something towards uprooting these evilly-disposed persons.

The problem of the registration of aliens in general will always be troublesome in a country surrounded on two sides by wild and undeveloped neighbours, and on a third by desert. It is possible even now for anyone to cross the frontier almost anywhere without the knowledge of the authorities, and to remain hidden from them in the country itself, and it is not easy to see how the adequate policing of the frontier could be undertaken except upon a large and expensive scale. On the whole, the police give extremely little trouble or worry to visitors, and the passport regulations are very lenient compared, for instance, with those in use in Syria, where the French authorities insist on passports being carried and inspected even on train journeys within the country itself. The freedom of movement permitted in Iraq, though perhaps tending to allow undesirable characters to accumulate in the cities, may be said to have justified itself by the lack of annoyance from perpetual official inspection, and by the general contentment of the travelling population. Competent observers have been heard to assert that not a little of the trouble which the French have encountered in their administration of Syria has been due to the petty tyranny of the Syrian police.

A department of Government which is based upon Moslem law and which has no counterpart in any European country is that of Waqaf, or Pious Bequests, which is important enough to enjoy the status of a separate Ministry Briefly, it is possible under Moslem law to bequeath property to Providence directly, the property being legally assumed to be the possession of the Almighty, and the interest from it being due to some pious object nominated by the testator ; this object must be laid down in the deed of gift. The department of Waqaf exists to administer all properties of this nature, and to see that the terms of the deed of gift are carried into execution ; should, in the course of the years, the charity nominated to receive the interest either cease to exist or cease to need the money, the department has the power to apply it to other pious uses at its own discretion, but the actual title to the land can never be alienated from the name of the Almighty. The Waqaf department is responsible for the upkeep of mosques, religious schools, certain religious charities, and other institutions of a pious character ; it thus has a dual function, of guarding religious buildings and institutions and of administering the very large number of estates which have in the course of the centuries been donated to pious uses.

Under Moslem law the provision of worldly support for one's family ranks as a pious object ; and the advantage of using the facilities offered by the Waqaf for this worthy cause began to be recognized in very early days by the Moslem public. The property can be safely tied up, out of reach either of thieves or of a possibly predatory Government ; some small portion of the interest from it can be devoted to a pious object, the maintenance of a mosque or a sick-bed ; and the bulk devoted to the equally pious object of providing for the necessities of one's descendants. In the turbulent times of the later Middle

Ages, the Waqaf offered practically the only safe plan of tying up family property, and it was very generally used for that purpose. It follows that, in all Moslem countries, the Waqaf departments have grown extremely wealthy, sometimes being the largest single landowner in the country.

In Iraq the Waqaf properties are very numerous both in town and country; but under the Turks, by whom the properties were administered direct from Constantinople, corruption was rife, the minor officials and workers were underpaid and of poor quality, the income disappeared largely in overhead expenses, and, as a consequence, practically nothing was available either for pious works or for repairs. In 1917 most of the Waqaf properties in the towns were in such a state of dilapidation that it had become a habit with the people to refer to any ruined building jokingly as "Waqaf." Much the same held true of the country properties. Some of them were leased at quite inadequate rents, others had fallen into complete disuse; out of all the valuable town sites and river gardens that the Waqaf owned, sufficient money could not be found even to keep the mosques in a reasonably good state of repair. The mosque officials were poorly paid and consequently dishonest, and the state of the buildings, even in Baghdad, was so disreputable as to amount to a public scandal.

Since the British occupation the change in these conditions has been as remarkable as, considering that the Waqaf is a purely Moslem institution, it might have been unexpected. There have never at any time been more than two British employed in the department, and for the greater part of the time there has only been one; yet in the last six years the Waqaf properties in town and country have been overhauled, the salaries of all the officials have been raised (and in some cases as much as 200 per cent.), large building contracts have been carried out, the mosques have been restored, some of them extensively, and, above all, the revenue has gone up by leaps and bounds. As an example of what sound business management can accomplish, the following figures, covering the Waqaf revenue for a period of five years, are worth attention :

ORGANIZATION OF THE EXECUTIVE 243

Year.	Revenue (in Rupees).	Expenditure (in Rupees).
1917-18	304,089	288,901
1918-19	455,726	399,735
1919-20	1,370,439	1,058,320
1920-21	1,670,886	1,312,191
1921-22	2,916,601	2,903,596

Much of the expenditure, it should be remembered, is entirely unremunerative, being in the nature of religious, social or educational work ; the cost of the first college of the new University of Baghdad, for instance, is being entirely met by Waqaf funds. In addition, the disreputable condition of the mosques, which will be remembered by any Englishman who happened to visit Baghdad as a soldier in the war, has now been very largely remedied, and the exteriors at least of all the places of worship are now presentable. In many cases this work of reconstruction has involved labour of a really complicated nature, including the repair of foundations and of the large and heavy domes which are a feature of some of the mosques.

The Waqaf properties in the city of Baghdad itself have been transformed in a most remarkable manner, and a large proportion of the new building which has taken place in the city since the Armistice has to be credited to the department. Constructional work of the most varied type has been successfully undertaken, including the building of shops, offices, houses, flats, coffee shops, theatres (for the Waqaf, though religious in foundation and in aim, draws no fine distinctions where business is concerned), and the new college for the University, in itself perhaps the most ambitious building attempted in Baghdad since the days of the Abbassids. The Waqaf possesses its own building department, employs its own architects, builders and workmen, and aims at being a model, as well as a successful, State employer.

The success of the Waqaf department under one British supervisor is an interesting example of what can be done in Iraq by business methods and with the absolute minimum of foreign control. British assistance is vital to the Iraq Government, because it cannot hope for some years to be able to command the services of a sufficient number of well-educated local men ; and it is a notable fact that a British official, left alone in a department with no aid beyond that of local subordinates, will almost invariably make a better job of his task than if surrounded with British subordinate personnel. The high expenditure of the Mesopotamian administration under British control has not been so much in evidence in the civil service of the country itself, where the British employees appear to study the question of economy with extreme solicitude, as in the political and military services of the British themselves ; it is not against the Serai that the accusation of extravagance can be brought, so much as against the Residency and General Headquarters. The pity of it all has been that, if the British taxpayer really desired to be generous with his money in Mesopotamia, it could have been put to so much better use by the Serai than by the other two homes of officialdom. The money, for instance, that was wasted on Daurah and Kirind camps by General Headquarters might alone have been sufficient to have carried into execution a fairly extensive irrigation scheme, and thus helped towards putting the country upon a paying basis. When the British taxpayer thinks of his money, thrown (in the words of the popular English press) into the deserts of Mesopotamia, he might remember that the Arab has benefited less than the British army and civil officials placed there by the authority of the British taxpayer himself. The outstanding financial success of the Waqaf administration shows what might be done in Mesopotamia with careful business management ; but the British taxpayer cannot expect careful business management unless he takes the precaution of placing in positions of responsibility only careful business managers. To assume that Mesopotamia is a bad investment and is incapable of material development merely because a great deal of British money has been wasted there (an assumption which has frequently been made in the British press, and even by British public men), is unfair both to Mesopotamia and to the British servants of the Government of that country, who have made so unprecedented and so loyal an effort to make it, at the earliest possible time, self-supporting.

The department of State which, more than any other,

ORGANIZATION OF THE EXECUTIVE 245

has given serious concern to the organizers of the new Iraq Government is that of Defence. At the time of the coronation of the King, the Iraq army was only in its infancy, and it has been largely the creation of the new national Government.

Under the terms of the mandate by which the kingdom was created, the mandated country is prohibited from making war outside its own borders; and, although the mandate has now given place, at least in theory, to a form of complete independence, it is unlikely that Iraq in practice would be allowed to go to war as long as British troops are resident in the country. The Iraq army is, therefore, confined in its duties to home service; and no serving soldier can, on his present engagement, be taken for service outside his native land. Owing to the disinclination of the Iraqi to remain for long periods at a distance from his home, the serving soldier in practice has to be retained as far as possible in his own neighbourhood; an arrangement with very distinct disadvantages from a military point of view. The main garrison is housed in the old Turkish barracks in Baghdad.

The first steps towards the formation of the new national army were taken in the autumn of 1920, when Jafar Pasha al Askari, who had previously held high rank with the Arab army of the Hedjaz, was appointed Minister of Defence. The first recruit enlisted in Baghdad in June of the next year, and recruiting was for some weeks extremely brisk; a bad type of man was, however, obtained, and in the autumn recruiting figures dropped very low indeed. The higher rates of pay of the British Levies, and the obvious attractions of the Imperial service not unnaturally had an adverse effect on the chances of the new force; but early in 1922 the pay of the new army was raised to correspond with that of the Levies, and at the same time the British authorities agreed to refrain from recruiting Arabs. Recruiting for the Iraq army has since been steady, and a better class of man has been attracted; but the period of service is short, and the problem of training an army bristles with difficulties in a country where desertion is easy and where there are far more inducements for the adventurous young tribesman, who should form the backbone of a national army, to soldier with his tribe rather than with the Government.

Both the discipline and the appearance of the new army were at first very bad, and the soldiers themselves were treated with ridicule by the people, comparisons between their condition and the smart turn-out of the Levies, or even the police, being frequent. In 1922, however, a marked change for the better became noticeable, and a general smartening and tightening up of discipline was everywhere apparent; for so young and inexperienced a force, raised, not under the excitement of a national war but under peace conditions, their progress must now be considered very creditable. They went into action for the first time in 1922 at Anah, in the course of a small disturbance which threatened to spread among the tribes of the district; and their behaviour on that occasion elicited the praise of both the Iraq and the British authorities. They have since taken over responsibility for certain areas of the country.

The new army consists at present of infantry, cavalry, horse artillery, transport and medical services; it has been trained largely on the British model, and British officers and non-commissioned officers have served with it at various times as instructors. It uses an adaptation of the familiar British khaki as its uniform, and Arabic translations of British military textbooks as its theory of work. It offers promotion for commissioned officers up to the rank of full general ("Amid"), and an ordinary serving soldier is eligible for promotion to the commissioned ranks if he has served two terms of enlistment with credit.

The army is interesting to the student of languages as the first in modern times in which Arabic is the accepted language of command; many modern military terms have no counterpart in Arabic, and in some cases words have had to be adapted from Turkish or English, or even specially invented.

Presumably the new army is intended eventually to take over full military responsibility for the whole country from the British, together with the legacy of the great British military cantonment of Hinaidi; in the meanwhile the division of authority between the local Ministry of Defence and the British General Headquarters remains undefined. The development of the young army will be watched with interest, alike by the student of war and by the British taxpayer.

CHAPTER XVI

MONEY, WATER, FIELD AND ROAD

*" What do the people of the Jehun river know of the value of water ?
Ask those wearied in the sun."*—SA'DI.

PERHAPS the most important of the purely financial departments of the new Government is that of Customs and Excise. In a country where direct taxation is difficult and unpopular, recourse must be had as far as possible to indirect means of raising the revenue ; and the money likely to be derived in any given time from the Customs assumes an almost disproportionate importance in the eyes of the careful Minister of Finance.

The department of Customs and Excise is more largely staffed by Englishmen in proportion to its size than any of the Iraq Government bureaux ; this is necessitated by the fact that trained and reliable local officials are rare, and that it is imperative, whatever happens to other Government services, that the direction of the Customs should lie in honest, trained and capable hands. The chief duty of the department is the collection of custom dues at the three principal centres of Baghdad, Basrah and Mosul. A system is in operation by which payment of the duties is made at one or other of these centres, the goods being forwarded there from the frontier, under security, for duty payment. Baghdad is by far the largest export centre, and is also slightly ahead of Basrah as an import centre ; much of her export trade is, however, in reality, re-export. In the early autumn Basrah's export figures advance very considerably owing to the date season ; for the banks of the Shatt-al-Arab, the estuary on which Basrah stands, form one of the largest date-producing centres in the world. The increasing consumption of dates tends to make the future of this trade, by far the most important single industry in Iraq, extremely hopeful ; on the other hand, Iraq has lost considerable ground in recent years by her failure to adopt modern methods of grading and packing, and, unless her trade is organized on a better footing in the immediate future, it is to be feared that she will be left behind in the world's markets by Tunis and other more wide-awake date centres.

The bulk of Iraq's exports, including grain, the production and export of which is being carefully fostered by the authorities, go to the United Kingdom, Arabia coming second on the list; most of the imports also are drawn from Britain, though India is a very close competitor. Nearly all the re-exports go to Persia. The Persian trade is, however, tending to fall off, partly owing to the opening of the Caucasian railway route by Russia, which proved a great enemy to Baghdad trade in the few years that it was in operation before the war; and partly owing to the growing poverty and chaotic political condition of Persia itself. Until the rehabilitation of Persia takes place—a matter which may easily take twenty years—Baghdad can hardly hope to depend for her future prosperity upon the Persian trade.

The Iraq customs figures for the year ending 31st March, 1924, were as follows: Value of imports, Rupees 181,484,113; of exports, Rupees 42,101,228; of re-exports, Rupees 93,690,107. The figures thus showed a trade balance for the year against Iraq of Rupees 45,692,778.

The customs and excise department is organized as a directorate, with two collectorates; the latter are served by three deputy collectors and a number of assistant collectors. The principal exports are dates, liquorice and cereals; the principal imports, textiles, sugar, fuel-oil and petrol, carpets and liquors; the principal re-exports, textiles, liquorice, sugar and carpets.

The department derives a considerable portion of its revenue from its excise functions. A spirit named araq is distilled in the country from dates, and has a large local sale; and there is a considerable trade in imported European liquors, in spite of the strict Moslem injunction in favour of teetotalism.

Taking spirits alone, the consumption of araq as against imported spirits is in the proportion of five to three; but no beer is brewed locally, and the heavy consumption of both beer and wine has to be met entirely by importation.

MONEY, WATER, FIELD, AND ROAD 249

The bulk of the beer consumed comes from Japan, with Germany a good second. The drink trade has grown enormously since the British occupation, and the British authorities have done little or nothing to discourage it.

The bulk of the tobacco used in the country comes from Kurdistan. The local people smoke, as a rule, either locally made cigarettes or the large water pipes familiar throughout the Near East. Locally made cigarettes are far cheaper than those imported from Europe, and are generally fresher. Many European visitors or inhabitants smoke them, though, generally speaking, their use is an acquired taste. A fair number of local men prefer to roll their cigarettes, and there is a heavy import of French-made cigarette paper. Of late, imported machine-made Egyptian cigarettes have made some headway. A large number of shops stock tobacco or cigarettes in one form or another, and the number of annual licences in Baghdad alone is between two and three thousand.

An important branch of the work of the excise department is the licensing and general supervision of the country river craft, in which is done a considerable portion of the up-country trade. The Euphrates is used solely by native craft, but the Tigris is navigated as far as Baghdad by more than one British steamship company. The traffic between Basrah and Baghdad used to be extremely profitable, but it has been greatly diminished by the opening of the railway, and by increased competition in other ways. The native boats do a considerable trade from Baghdad to points farther north, both on the Tigris and on the two Zab rivers. The rather clumsy, though picturesque, boats are ably handled, and, as usual with sailors, some of the most entertaining company in Iraq is to be found among their owners and crews. They live to some extent apart from the general population, townsmen or tribesmen, and in certain cases pass the whole of their lives on their boats.

The importance of irrigation in Iraq can hardly be overestimated. On the proper control of the two great rivers, and on the proper distribution of the water which, uncontrolled, is capable of doing such immoderate harm to the countryside, depend the prosperity and the future of the country. Like Egypt and Australia, Iraq must be in a position to place her surplus water where she needs it; without water, her fertile soil becomes a hot and sandy waste; with water, a veritable garden.

It would thus appear a self-evident fact that the only means of permanently reviving the ancient prosperity of the land was by the re-creation of the irrigation system; but it cannot be said that either the Turks or the British have accomplished a great deal in this direction. In both cases, the failure to handle the problem has been caused, not by lack of the will, but of the means. The re-creation of the irrigation system is bound to cost money; from where is this money to come? The British, it is true, tackled the same problem in Egypt and made a financial success of it; but in Egypt they had the moral pressure of Europe behind them, their Imperial responsibilities were not then so heavy, and, above all, they were a great deal wealthier as a nation than at the present day.

The cost of irrigating Iraq is not a figure to be lightly faced. It has to be borne in mind that it is not only irrigation itself which is needed, but protection; Iraq not only needs an extra supply of water at certain times of the year, but she needs protection against an over-supply at others. The huge floods which desolated the country in the spring of 1923 show only too well what the people have to expect under present conditions in a year of high water. Before any attempt can be made to direct the water of the rivers where it is most needed, very large new escapes and cut-offs must be constructed to enable the flood-time water to be drawn off from the upper reaches of the rivers. In addition, the Hindiyah Barrage, itself a heavy work, is only one of several such that will have to be undertaken if a genuine irrigation project is to be carried through to its conclusion.

Moreover, it has to be remembered that it is not altogether proved that the material rewards would be commensurate with so heavy an outlay. It is believed by many authorities, including so eminent an expert as Sir William Willcocks, that the whole country was never under cultivation at any one time, and that, in fact, there is not sufficient water available, even with careful irrigation, to ensure more than a certain portion of the whole area

MONEY, WATER, FIELD, AND ROAD 251

being adequately fertilized. The great wealth of ancient Mesopotamia is thought by some investigators to have been founded largely on international trade, and to have been independent of agriculture except as a secondary means of livelihood. This latter theory is perhaps doubtful, but it is at least possible; and it would be unwise to undertake the project of reclaiming Mesopotamia from the desert unless it could be overwhelmingly proved that the return would be likely to justify such an expensive step*

The estimate for the reconstruction of the irrigation system before the war amounted to £24,000 000, a sum which would probably be considerably exceeded under post-war conditions. It is an aggravating thought, but almost certainly a justifiable one, that the British Government has probably thrown away more money in Mesopotamia since the Armistice than would have covered the cost of this great work, which might not only have brought back her ancient prosperity to the land of the rivers, but would have opened up to the Empire a new source of raw material in the way of cereals and cotton, and would have ensured a supply of orders for the British engineering industry during the desperately bad years which followed the " boom " of 1919. If the work could have been begun reasonably soon after the Armistice, it would almost certainly have prevented the rebellion of 1920, and thus saved the huge expense of suppressing it; for no people realize the value of water more than the Arabs, and the undertaking of this great work by the British would have struck their imagination and secured their loyalty. It has been perhaps the most irritating feature of the British occupation that, after such high expectations, so little has actually been done towards the material restoration of the country; and if Iraq is for the future to face the world as a small independent State with practically no material resources, it is difficult to see how the vast engineering works which are required can ever be undertaken. Thus the brilliant chance which the British had of restoring an ancient country and opening up for the world a new agricultural belt would now appear to have been completely lost.

* On this point see " Irrigation in Mesopotamia," by Sir William Willcocks.

Sir William Willcocks's scheme of irrigation depended, roughly, on the construction of two large " escapes " from the upper Euphrates and the upper Tigris respectively, on the lines of those in use in former times, and serving to draw off all surplus flood water and store it in two large desert lakes. Other channels would draw the water from these lakes as and where needed, and any surplus would be emptied again into the rivers lower down, for use in the lower reaches. At various points in the rivers dams and regulators would be built, and independent systems of canals controlled from them. Navigation would be as far as possible superseded by railway communication, thus leaving the rivers entirely available for irrigation purposes. The present very grave danger from flooding would be eliminated, and the towns and countryside made secure.

It need hardly be said that very little indeed of this great project has ever been carried into execution. The Hindiyah Barrage on the Euphrates, which controls the water supply of the most prosperous section of the country, was constructed before the war by a British firm to the order of the Turkish Government ; and sanction for it was only obtained owing to the extreme urgency of the situation caused by the complete silting up of one arm of the Euphrates itself. The construction of the Barrage saved Hillah and its wealthy environs from complete extinction ; for many of the cultivators had already begun to move westward to the other arm of the Euphrates owing to the drying-up of the Hillah channel.

Since the construction of the Barrage, no work of any but minor importance has been undertaken either by the Turks or the British. A Directorate of Irrigation was set up after the Armistice, but it has been continually hampered by the indefiniteness of Government policy, and severely starved of funds ; for although a fair amount of British money has always been available in Mesopotamia for the construction of camps, Residencies and Government offices, very little reaches the constructive departments of the administration who could obviously make the best use of it. In the way of irrigation, nothing has been done by the British or the new Iraq Government except the repair of the Barrage and the construction of river banks and minor canals; and already the new area of fertile ground which was made available by the construction of the Barrage has proved insufficient for the settlers.

Demands for new canals continue insistent; but, without embarking on a really comprehensive scheme of irrigation, it is no longer possible to draw more water from the Euphrates than is now being taken. The canals served by the Barrage even now have at times to be " rationed "; that is to say, water is directed into one set of canals at a time, the others remaining dry until their turn comes. It is difficult to see how the country can be further developed without the carrying into execution of some fairly comprehensive irrigation scheme.

An interesting branch of the activities of the Irrigation Directorate is the Training College in Baghdad, designed to make good the shortage of trained engineers and mechanics in Iraq. The College now accommodates nearly a hundred students, and the creation of a fully qualified local staff, though far from easy in view of the low state of general education in the past, is rapidly proceeding. In the summer of 1924, an irrigation project of some magnitude was sanctioned by the Iraq Government, in the shape of the so-called "Asfar Concession." Briefly, the proposals of the concessionaires consist of the immediate development of certain small "trial areas" on the Diala and Euphrates rivers, for commercial agriculture. Should these prove successful, the concessionaires possess the right to inaugurate a large scheme, involving the damming of the Diala river, and the diversion of the flood waters of the upper Euphrates into an existing desert lake. Both these great works would control a network of canals, which would in turn irrigate very large areas now lying absolutely desolate. The scheme is interesting, apart altogether from its bearing upon the agricultural regeneration of Mesopotamia, because it is the first example in the East of a large work of this nature being attempted, not by a Government, but by private enterprise.

In the matter of finance, the Department of Agriculture has been scarcely more fortunate than that of Irrigation. Agriculture in Iraq for the last six centuries has been conducted in a manner hopelessly crude and wasteful;

and the first step towards placing the agriculture of the country on a sound modern footing must take the form of the methodical education of the cultivator in modern methods. Fortunately, the department has been in both able and sympathetic hands since its inauguration, and a cautious but wise policy of making sure of the existing methods of agriculture used locally before suggesting improvements has been continually followed. Thus the department, though active, remains small, and in view of the influence which it has obtained throughout the country, over the conservative and suspicious cultivator, extremely cheap.

A notable difficulty in the improvement of the condition of the cultivator is the uncertainty of land tenure. Until the cultivator can be assured of permanent occupation, it would appear useless to expect him to show much interest in implements and improvements which, however much they may increase his output in the future, cost a good deal to introduce in the present. The land system in Iraq is throughout in a chaotic state, and will need very firm control from the central authority before it can be righted. An important Egyptian cotton-producing concern was recently prevented from locating in the country by the fact that it could not obtain land except on short leases. In a new country, crying out for development, a conservative land policy is little short of iniquitous, but unfortunately it would appear that no merely local Government is likely to be strong enough to risk the displeasure of the large landowners for many years to come. A grave evil is the large extent to which the system of absentee ownership has grown; many of the country estates are owned by residents of the big towns, who rarely or never visit their possessions. But this class has considerable political influence, and for a local Government to risk offending them for the sake of doing justice to the powerless cultivator would appear to be, at any rate for the present, impossible.

Considering the difficulties met with, the results attending the efforts of the Agricultural department must be considered fairly satisfactory. Grain is now being exported from the country in increasing quantities; the cultivation of cotton is being carefully, and not unsatisfactorily, fostered ; wool is being exported in rapidly increasing quantities, and silk and flax are receiving consideration. Mechanical cultivation is making some headway. The chief agricultural danger is the locust pest, which annually completely covers the northern area of the country. Steps have been taken by the Department of Agriculture to combat the evil, but the authorities are handicapped by the prevalent scarcity of Government funds, and by the fact that the breeding grounds of the locusts are not situated in Iraq territory.

One of the most successful accomplishments of the Agricultural department in Iraq has been the creation of the Governmental experimental farm at Rustam, near Baghdad. Here may be found examples of every kind of plant used in Iraq, or likely to be of use there, growing under the observation of trained experts. In crops of which the Government is attempting to acclimatize a superior quality, the farm handles the sale, at cost price or even less, of Government seed, carefully selected with a view to results ; propaganda on behalf of new staples, such as cotton, is conducted from the farm, and the practical results to be expected are demonstrated on the spot. The Government breeding of silk-worms, carried on at Bakubah, is also practically a branch of the work of the farm. An agricultural college is now being built on an adjacent site, and the future training of the Iraq agriculturist on modern scientific lines will be carried out there. Incidentally, help in the popularizing of cotton among the cultivators has been extensively given by the Baghdad branch of the British Cotton Growing Association, which maintains a ginning plant of its own in Iraq.

One very gratifying result of the work of the Agricultural department has been the confidence bestowed upon its officials by the local farmers and cultivators. In no industry are the habits of rigid conservatism and suspicion of improvement so deep-rooted as in that of agriculture ; and if this is true, as is generally admitted, of a Western country, it is doubly so of the Middle East, where the habits of the cultivator have probably changed very little since the days of Abraham. That the Iraq cultivator is not, however, indifferent to modern methods once he realizes their practical advantages may be seen by the enthusiasm with which the petrol or oil-driven pump has been received along the rivers, where it is rapidly replacing the various old-fashioned forms of replenishing the canals from the main streams. That the officials of the department have succeeded in engaging the attention and the confidence of the cultivator is evident from the mass of inquiries which it receives from all parts of the country. Needless to say, the advice offered is by no means always followed; it is certainly flattering that it should even be asked for.

A point on which emphasis is often laid in England in any discussion on the prospects of Mesopotamia, is the question of the supposed shortage of labour. It is frequently said that, even if the country were fully developed from an irrigation and agricultural standpoint, there would not be enough available labour in it to till the ground. In point of fact, there is an almost inexhaustible recruiting ground for labour in the deserts of Arabia; and it is indeed probable that the migration of Arabs northwards, a movement which has gone on since the dawn of history, and which certainly shows no sign of abatement, may in the future, given a prosperous Mesopotamia and Syria, take the form merely of a migration of labour. Mesopotamia as a country does not stand alone; it is closely and irrevocably connected with both Arabia and Syria, and the total population of the deserts which lie on the edge of it is probably a good deal larger than is usually believed. In any case, in a part of the world where the rate of infantile mortality is several times what it is in Europe, there should be no fear, given modern medical and sanitary supervision, of any shortage of population.

After irrigation and agriculture, the most important task of the Government on the constructional side is the development of the means of communication. In very ancient times Iraq, as we have seen, was covered by an intricate network of roads which served, with the larger canals, for the transportation of both the passenger and goods traffic of the country. In the time of the Abbassids, Baghdad was directly connected with Arabia, Syria and the borders of China by a system of main roads as daring in their conception as that of the Romans in the West;

and the remains of many of these ancient roads are in use to-day. In the years preceding the World War, the Turks had made some effort to revive the road system of the country, and many of the bridges crossing gullies or canals had been repaired or reconstructed ; and the advent of the Baghdad Railway from the capital to Samarra, the first link in a chain destined to connect Iraq directly with Constantinople and Europe, seemed to herald the dawn of a new period of local transportation development.

In spite of the great development of the railway system during the World War, these dreams have not been fulfilled. Indeed, in some ways, the transport system of the country is worse to-day than it was ten years ago. The Baghdad Railway has not even yet reached Mosul ; and many of the roads and road bridges have been completely destroyed by the war.

The reconstruction of the latter is one of the aims of the Department of Public Works, an active branch of the administration, though one labouring under the common disability of lack of funds. The department is very largely the child of the British army, and for some time after its creation its whole attention was devoted to executing and keeping in repair works required for army use. After the rebellion of 1920, and the decision of the British Government to hasten the creation of a local administration, the department was finally severed from its military parentage, and has since been under the control of the Ministry of Communications and Works.

Considering the small amount of money at its disposal, a good deal of progress has been made by the department in the improvement of road communication. It has wisely made no effort to encourage large schemes of new construction, but has confined itself to the provision of reasonable road surfaces on routes connecting the principal centres. The most important works of this nature recently completed have been the opening of a road serviceable for motors from Baghdad to the Persian border ; the completion of the road from Shergat (the northern terminus of the Baghdad Railway) to Arbil, work on which was commenced by the Turks before the war ; the new approach road to the environs of the holy cities from the south ;

the commencement of a new road eventually designed to connect Basrah and Fao, the money for which is being raised locally ; and the construction of a new two-way bridge across the creek in the most congested part of Basrah. An effort has also been made to put the important Baghdad-Aleppo road in working order, and a fine piece of road along a portion of the route is in process of construction by tribal labour ; but a very large number of bridges still await reconstruction, owing to the shortage of funds.

The work of the Public Works Department is by no means confined to the construction or the care of roads. Three new and important schemes for the supply of water to the towns have recently been prepared by the department ; that at Mosul, financed by the municipality, has been already completed, as also has a smaller but similar one at Arbil ; the third is intended for Basrah, but the financial position of that city is not strong enough to allow of its execution at present. Several important new schools have been built on behalf of the Ministry of Education, notably the extremely handsome Awainah school in Baghdad, and similar erections at Amarah and Kut. Other important constructional works under the supervision of the department include the Maude Memorial Hospital at Basrah, the King's pavilion on His Majesty's estate north of Baghdad, and the completion of the handsome little suburb of Alwiyah, originally designed in 1919 for the British officials of the Government. It is interesting to note, incidentally, that the contractors for the schools and the Memorial Hospital were an English firm domiciled in Iraq. The designs for the new University of Baghdad were also prepared by the department, but the actual construction of the one college now completed was undertaken by the Ministry of Waqaf.

One of the most troublesome tasks confronting the department has been the keeping in repair of the many bridges of boats that cross the two great rivers. With the exception of railway bridges, there are hardly any large permanent bridges in the country at all ; and the whole of the very considerable traffic of Baghdad, which is divided into two unequal portions by the Tigris, has

THE OLD TURKISH BRIDGE AT BAGHDAD

THE SHRINE OF THE IMAMS AT SAMARRA

to be conducted over two one-way boat-bridges. The construction of a permanent bridge in the city has been urged on countless occasions of recent years, and the idea has the personal support of the King; but, though the new bridge would probably pay for itself in a very few years (for the upkeep of the present boat-bridges is abnormally heavy), it has not been found possible up to now to finance its construction. Such a bridge does not offer any very grave problems from an engineering point of view, and could be both designed and constructed without any increase of the engineering facilities now at the disposal of the Government; it is merely a question of ways and means. The bridge would undoubtedly prove an immense boon to Baghdad, for it would tend to draw to the city all the traffic passing from Syria to Persia, for the purpose of crossing the river in comfort; and, in addition, the city would be saved from a crisis such as occurred in the summer of 1923, when both the boat-bridges were put out of action by the abnormal floods. Before the war Baghdad possessed one single-way bridge of boats only, another one being in operation some miles north of the city; both were destroyed by the Turks before they retired, and the two bridges now in use were constructed by the British army. There is, in addition, a bridge of boats at Mu'adham, four miles north of Baghdad, and another at Amarah, as well as a number of structures across the Euphrates at various points.

The Department of Public Works has also been responsible for the installation of several electric lighting plants. The municipal lighting plant at Kirkuk was laid down by the department; and the interesting scheme to light the famous Shiah shrines of Kerbela and Najaf by electricity, the money for which has been promised by rich Persian and Indian pilgrims, is being prepared by it.

The position of the railways, which have only recently been taken over by the Iraq Government, has been largely misrepresented in the English press and Parliament. The origin of the railway directorate was the sudden growth of railways in the Basrah area which immediately followed the British occupation. The directorate was formed as a separate department under military control in 1916, and from that year to the Armistice some 1,000 miles of track were laid, much of which was afterwards dismantled. The first line to be built outside the Basrah harbour area was the metre gauge route from Makinah (Basrah) to Nasriyah, part of which still forms the main line. The construction of the Qurnah-Amarah narrow-gauge line soon followed, to be shortly afterwards dismantled. Other new construction followed as the British army advanced up country, including the metre gauge lines from Kut to Baghdad East, from Baghdad East to Baqubah and the Persian border, and the standard European gauge line from Baghdad West (where it connected with the German Baghdad Railway) to Hillah. The Baghdad Railway was meanwhile extended from Samarra, where the Germans had left it, to Tekrit, to Baiji and eventually to Shergat, close to the ruins of the Assyrian city of Assur, where the terminus still remains, Shergat being connected with Mosul by motor convoy. Narrow-gauge lines were also constructed for military purposes from Baghdad South to Fallujah, on the Euphrates, and from Hillah to Kifl, and in 1918 it was decided to extend the Basrah-Nasriyah line through the Euphrates valley to Hillah, and to convert the Hillah-Baghdad West section from standard to metre gauge. In 1920 through trains ran for the first time from Makinah to Baghdad West, on what has ever since been known as the main line. This line was cut and severely damaged during the rebellion of that year, and all traffic between Basrah and Baghdad diverted to the Tigris valley, travelling between Basrah and Kut by steamer, and thence by rail to Baghdad East. In 1921 the railway system was for the first time considered from a business instead of a military point of view, with the result that the Baghdad East-Kut, the Hillah-Kifl, and the Baghdad South-Fallujah lines were dismantled. In 1922, further economies and changes occurred. The station at Baghdad South was closed, all traffic on the left bank of the Tigris being concentrated at Baghdad North, and on the right bank at the twin standard and metre gauge stations at Baghdad West. A branch was constructed from the main line to Hindiyah Barrage, and continued the next year to Kerbela, thus tapping at last the wealthiest districts in Iraq. A new line was constructed to Khanikin town, and, in 1924, the branch from Quaraghan to Kingerban was continued to Kirkuk. This line it is intended eventually to carry forward to Mosul, after which the present Baghdad-Shergat broad-gauge track, which serves the northern town, will be abandoned north of Samarra, unless some scheme is evolved in the meanwhile for the completion of the Baghdad Railway. Recently large reductions have been effected in the staff of the administration, which had grown to abnormal proportions under military control.

The mileage in operation is now approximately 780, of which 187 are standard, and the remainder metre gauge. By way of concentrating the administration, new repair shops were commenced in 1922 at Salchiyah, a few miles north of Baghdad West station. On completion of the building, the whole of the repair and stores work will be centralized there, and the present workshops at Baghdad West and Shaiba (near Basrah), together with the stores at Makinah, closed down. A train ferry connects the metre gauge systems on either side of the river just north of the city of Baghdad, and through freight traffic is booked via the ferry between Basrah and Khanikin, on the Persian border.

The Iraq Railways are completely without working capital, and consequently can only undertake such extensions and replacements as can be paid for out of revenue. Their equipment was largely imported from India by the British army authorities, and is old and unsuitable for ordinary traffic. For some time there was considerable confusion and inefficiency in the management, but of late this has been eliminated, and for the past two years the railways have made a very striking effort to perform their normal functions with efficiency. Naturally, no money can be spared for " show," and the stations are of the most primitive description; but the new corridor passenger stock, imported from England, is noticeably good and even luxurious, and though the travelling is slow, it is reasonably comfortable. Freight traffic has gone up by leaps and bounds, and is conducted with reasonable speed and security. With the possible exception of the Palestine Railway, the system is certainly the best managed in the Middle East to-day.

The postal, telegraphic and telephone services in Iraq are controlled by a single department of the Government. All three services originated in their present form in the necessities of the invading British army, though an independent British telegraph and postal service had been in operation in Baghdad for many years, and in the old days the British authorities used to maintain their own camel post across the desert to Damascus and the Mediterranean. The present postal service is efficiently directed, and the telegraph department has gained the rare distinction of actually earning a revenue. The services now are very largely locally manned, and the change-over from a staff of British and Indian personnel was an extremely difficult matter, particularly in the telegraph department, where the operators had to be taught a code in a strange language. In its external arrangements, the Post Office works in conformity with the rules laid down by the Postal Union, and in operation in other parts of the world.

The postal administration has to its credit the success of the automatic telephone installation at Basrah. It cannot be said that telephones as a whole have proved a successful innovation in Iraq; the standard of service has been low, the instruments have been mostly of second-hand army pattern, and nothing has been done to interest the local subscriber. The telephone books are printed in English only, and the system is thus largely unintelligible to the local population, who consequently can hardly be blamed if they have not taken to the telephone with any great enthusiasm.

In Basrah, however, the operation of the automatic exchange is excellent, though the slump in trade of the last two years has naturally resulted in a falling-off in the number of subscribers; efforts are now being made to attract the local population, and Basrah has dreams of developing into the most up-to-date telephone centre in the East.

The greatest postal triumphs associated with Iraq have been, however, only partly due to the initiation of the post office authorities. The Baghdad-Cairo air mail, now famous all over the world, was inaugurated as an experiment by the Royal Air Force, principally for military and technical reasons. On these grounds it has probably justified itself, but its utility to the general public has already been practically eliminated by the institution of a motor mail service across the desert from Damascus to Baghdad. This service, running weekly in each direction, connects Baghdad directly with the Mediterranean, and thus with Western Europe. During the first complete year of operation the cars carried 35,000 lbs. of mail matter, no mean achievement when it is remembered that the enterprise was quite experimental, that over 450 miles of the route consists of desert country, and that the company operating the cars is a commercial concern, not subsidized in any way by the Government. It is gratifying to be able to add that the company is a British one, though the cars used are American.

A minor public service of some interest is the Fire Brigade maintained by the civic authorities of Baghdad. This again was originally instituted by the British army, and the chief officer is still an Englishman; the subordinate officers and the men are now all Iraqi, and a motor fire-float is maintained on the Tigris in addition to the motor-engines on the streets. Grave difficulty is sometimes experienced in the case of a bad fire in Baghdad owing to the low level of the water, which has to be pumped from the river, sometimes over a considerable distance. Bad fires are fortunately rare, though always possible; several outbreaks in the last few years have spread with alarming rapidity, aided by the extreme congestion of the city. A minor duty of the Brigade is rescue work in connection with the collapse of old houses, a frequent form of accident in Baghdad, and one which is responsible for a number of deaths annually. The Fire Brigade is perhaps the most popular of all the State or municipal services with the local public, and always possesses a long waiting list of would-be recruits; a distinct tribute both to the interest of the work and to the English chief officer who has controlled the fortunes of the little Brigade from the time of its inception until the present day.

CHAPTER XVII

HEALTH AND EDUCATION

"Opportunity flies, O brother,
As the cloud that quick doth pass;
Oh, make use of it! Life is precious,
If we let it go—alas!"—HAFIZ.

PERHAPS the most interesting Government departments in Iraq are not those dealing with the administration of the country or its constructive works, but those whose aim is purely social. The departments of Public Health and of Education are ever, from the very nature of their work, in direct touch with the people. Other departments may have to organize the people, to make them work, to move them about in bodies from place to place, to superintend their morals, or to teach them to defend their country; these departments merely have to shepherd them. Consequently a more human as well as a more interesting note is struck by the labours and the personnel of these two bureaux.

The supervision of public health officially commenced in 1919, when an English Secretary for Health was appointed. Under the first Iraq Government a Ministry of Health was created, but considerations of economy compelled its reduction to a directorate, functioning as a part of the Ministry of the Interior.

Probably no country in the world needs sanitation more than Iraq. Covered with ancient ruins, peopled by a largely nomad and semi-nomad population, entirely ignorant of the laws of health, and the prey of epidemics which could be almost wholly eliminated, the country seems eminently suitable for the display of modern medical skill. Unfortunately shortage of money, here as elsewhere, prevents the problem being approached in anything but the most perfunctory manner; but considering the very small proportion of the Iraq Budget that is allotted to the health services, the organization which is at the service of the public is remarkably complete. It may be said with truth that there is no longer any need for any man, Iraqi or foreigner, to be ill unless he wishes. Facilities for investigation and cure exist everywhere. Twenty-six hospitals and a large number of dispensaries are now in operation in the country, and the large towns possess separate hospitals for the treatment of women and for cases needing isolation. There are pathological, X-ray and Pasteur institutes in Baghdad. The central medical stores depôt for the country on occasion supplies orders from neighbouring countries, and not infrequently despatches medical goods as far afield as Teheran. A small factory for the manufacture of vaccine lymph exists at Amarah, thus doing away with the previous necessity of importing it, at considerable expense, from India. In a country like Iraq, subject constantly to the smallpox scourge, a ready supply of lymph is an absolute necessity.

Many romantic stories are associated with the work of the health department, particularly in the country districts. One day news came to the British authorities from a party of officers on tour that a powerful sheikh of the Anizah in the Syrian desert was lying mortally wounded. A passing aeroplane was ordered to locate him and bring him to Baghdad for treatment. The aeroplane landed at the sheikh's settlement, the potentate was tenderly but unceremoniously bundled into the machine, and a few hours afterwards was safely in bed in a Baghdad nursing home. His wounds were attended to, the gangrene which threatened to bring about his death was overcome, and in due course he recovered and returned to his people. One day some months later, a British aeroplane was forced by engine trouble to descend for the night in the Sheikh's country. At dusk a score of tribesmen suddenly appeared on camels, and without further warning took up their station in a circle round the aeroplane and its English passengers. The Englishmen could not speak Arabic, and the Arabs could not speak English; and at dawn the Arabs stole away again, as silently as they had come. Later the English discovered that they had been sent by the grateful and friendly Sheikh, in order that the stranded machine and its passengers might come to no sudden harm in the treacherous desert night.

On another occasion a sheikh on the Kurdish border was bitten by a wolf, together with thirteen of his family and followers. The sheikh had heard of the British medical men in Baghdad and of the great work they did; and he made up his mind to make the journey to the city, taking with him his daughter, who was also one of the victims of the wolf. The old man and his daughter on arrival were taken in hand by the Pasteur Institute, and were shortly afterwards sent back home cured; the remainder of the victims, who had not come to Baghdad, died.

It is very hard, indeed, to put a high enough value on the medical work which is being done, under the very greatest difficulties, in Iraq. For centuries such medical work as has been undertaken at all has been the prerogative of the missionary, usually overworked, and with a variety of other duties. The quack doctor, a danger, even in a Western community, possesses in Iraq enormous influence and a corresponding power for doing evil. In a country whose two principal scourges, diseases of the eye and diseases of sex, lend themselves so admirably to specious amateur treatment, the position of the quack doctor, among an ignorant and superstitious population, becomes impregnable. He speaks the language of the people, knows their habits and their prejudices, and has his consulting room in the bazaar, that is, in the most accessible place to the public; there is no need for his patients to risk the publicity of repairing to the hospital, which even in more advanced countries the common people are not uninclined to shirk.

The evil that the quack doctor does is twofold. He makes a large income out of the credulity and faith of his patients; and he fails altogether to cure them, or at best effects only a partial cure. Those who have taken a hand in the great battle against the quack doctor in Western countries, with the force of the law and public opinion on their side, can best appreciate the difficulties in tackling the enemy in a semi-Oriental country, where ignorance and religious prejudice still exercise great influence over the common people. The evil in Iraq appears to run in a vicious circle, for it is useless to legislate against the quack

HEALTH AND EDUCATION

doctor unless a sufficient supply of efficient professional help is assured; and Iraq at present does not possess more than the beginnings of such a supply. The quack doctor, it is to be feared, will continue to flourish until the growth of material prosperity brings a higher standard of education and better facilities for the local training of medical students. Most of the diseases chronic among the Iraqi public are due to dirt and ignorance of the requisite remedies, and would yield readily to really comprehensive medical methods. Sanitation, or rather the lack of it, is at the bottom of a great deal of local illness, especially in the towns. It is difficult for Western people to realize how much they owe to modern sanitation, and to what an enormous extent that science has developed in the last century. Baghdad is probably only about a hundred years behind London in her sanitary knowledge; but that hundred years makes all the difference. All the Iraqi cities, including one of a quarter of a million population, are completely innocent of drains, and until the last decade an efficient and wholesome water supply was quite unknown. The degradation and dirt of the dwellings of the poorer classes are quite indescribable. The prevalence of sand-storms in the hot weather, and the heavy rains in the winter, tend equally to make the unpaved and undrained streets of the big towns nearly intolerable; and the chronic state of congestion of the latter, with their higgledy-piggledy mass of houses almost on top of one another, would appear to make them powerless to stand the attack of any infectious disease whatever.

Iraq is not, however, such an unhealthy country for residence as the casual traveller might be inclined to judge. Against the evil sanitary conditions has to be set a singularly healthy climate, whose brilliant sunshine sterilizes the crowded lanes and dilapidated houses of the cities. If the climate of Baghdad was as unkind as the climate of London, the population must certainly become liable to death in a week. For six months in the year one can bathe with comfort; for seven sleep at night in the open air. Even in the hottest months the nights remain relatively cool; and the low humidity serves to make the climate of Baghdad bearable at a temperature twenty degrees higher than that at which New York, for instance, becomes almost intolerable. In Basrah and the southern districts of the country, the climate is, however, both hotter and more humid, and therefore a good deal more trying and dangerous; it is less, in fact, characteristic of Mesopotamia than of the Persian Gulf, notoriously one of the most unpleasant places in the world in the hot weather. Malaria and heat-stroke attack native and foreigner alike, and dysentery, enteric and cholera are common, the latter being usually introduced from India. Plague also occurs at times in Basrah, being drawn from the same source. Sand-fly fever, a peculiar disease of a few days' duration, thought to be caused by the bite of the sand-fly, is exceedingly common throughout the country districts, and most strangers who remain any length of time catch it. Another equally common, though more annoying, complaint is the Baghdad boil, which occurs in the form of a sore on the face, hands or arms. Baghdad boils will frequently remain six months or more without healing, and invariably leave a scar. Almost all native children have them, and the scar on the face which follows them is extremely common.

The ordinary chronic diseases of Europe, tuberculosis, typhus fever, smallpox and diarrhœa are common throughout Iraq, the latter being mainly responsible for the very severe infantile mortality in the country. Additional and, on the whole, more serious plagues are the eye diseases, such as trachoma and other forms of conjunctivitis, which amount in Iraq to epidemics. So terrible have been these scourges in the past that it is estimated that over 75 per cent. of the population of Baghdad have at some time been affected with eye trouble. In 1920, out of a large number of people examined by the ophthalmic officials of the Government, 44 per cent. had permanently damaged eyesight, and 12 per cent. were blind in one eye. Indeed, blindness in one eye is so common as to excite no remark among the population. Among the children at school in that year, it was found that 10 per cent. had permanently damaged vision. At the present day three per cent. of the population of Baghdad are estimated to be quite blind, making a small army of something like 7,500 blind persons in the streets of the capital city alone.

It will readily be seen that there is practically no disease present which would not disappear at the touch of wide-reaching medical attention. Unfortunately, lack of Government funds and a complete ignorance among the general public of even the idea of publicly supported hospital charities makes such general attention difficult. For instance, the question of ophthalmic treatment has been tackled by the authorities with commendable perseverance, and at times with notable success; but lack of the necessary funds prevents anything more than the fringe of the problem being effectively covered. The ophthalmic department was opened in Baghdad at the new General Hospital in 1919, the same service being afterwards extended to Basrah. In Baghdad alone there are now four additional centres, and nearly four thousand patients a year are attended at the General Hospital, and 4,500 at the branch centres. In the other big towns and the desert centres practically nothing is done, in spite of the known urgency of the problem, simply because the money is not available. Trachoma is as prevalent among the tribes as in the towns; and the tribal quack doctors have a peculiarly cruel and ineffective way of treating the disease, which results in very great pain to the patient, and probably in eventual blindness. Whereupon the poor unfortunates, in their ignorance, accept their burden as an " act of God." In the Near East, the shoulders of Providence must needs be broad, for He is asked to take the blame for the results of His peoples' carelessness, as well as of their sins !

It is not easy to see how the Iraq Government, with limited resources and heavy responsibilities, is ever to make an adequate effort to place the preservation of public health on a really sound foundation. And yet the problem is a most urgent one. Of what use are schools, roads and railways if the vitality of the people is sapped by dirt and disease ? The re-creation of the country must depend, in the first place, upon the creation of a better population, and at present the resources of the Health department are quite unequal to such a task. No country in the world stands more in need of generous outside assistance in medical matters than the land of the rivers.

In addition to the eye scourges, a variety of other

grave and special problems engage the constant attention of the administration. The appalling death rate among infants is a serious matter in an undeveloped country needing increased supplies of labour. The spread of sexual diseases in the cities, gravely increased in the last decade, is a matter with which the officials have constantly to battle, though fortunately they are confined more or less to the town, the tribesmen being as a rule clean and moral in their mode of living. The risk of epidemics through the presence of thousands of foreign pilgrims at certain times of the year is another matter of serious concern to the officials. Stringent precautions are taken at the frontier stations, especially Khanikin, where a large quarantine station, built by the Turks, is in use. Apart from the risk of his introducing infection, the pilgrim frequently presents a difficult problem through the condition of his ordinary health. Some pilgrims, exhausted by their long and painful journey, and overjoyed to be at last on the holy ground of the sacred places, will cheerfully lie down to die in the streets, only later to be brought by the police to the nearest hospital in a state of general collapse. Such cases, which are numerous in the pilgrim season, are made the more difficult by the mental attitude of the patient, who, though possibly only a young man, has no desire whatever to live; and the problem resolves itself into the prevention of a perfectly healthy individual, in the throes of spiritual intoxication, from committing suicide. So strong is the force of religious persuasion upon imaginative and stunted natures.

What may be termed a side issue of the pilgrim traffic, from the medical point of view, is the importation of dead bodies from various Shiah countries for burial in the holy cities. Najaf claims, perhaps correctly, to possess the largest cemetery in the world; and the number of bodies imported every year for burial is surprising. A form of import duty was charged by the Turks on this traffic, and the charge is still made; it is not, however, as infamous as it sounds, because the pious desire on the part of hundreds of Persians to be buried in the vicinity of the holy cities involves the Iraq Government in considerable expense, and it is only right that the relatives of the dead should help to meet it. Careful precautions have to be taken with regard to the quick removal of the bodies, and their burial has to be supervised; and, in spite of the duty at the frontier, the " dead pilgrim " traffic is probably one of the least remunerative branches of the Government's activities. The tax in Turkish times gave rise to a story current in Baghdad for many years, but almost certainly apocryphal. The story told of a Persian gentleman who, wishing to have his grandmother buried at Najaf, and anxious to avoid the tax at the frontier, cut the old lady up into a number of small pieces, and smuggled her into the country by parcel post. In due course he himself repaired to Najaf, collected the parcels, put the old lady together again, and buried her in the odour of sanctity with all due respect and ceremony.

The collection and compilation of vital statistics are dealt with by the Health Department. This service, so important to a country organized and run on modern lines, is extremely difficult and elusive to maintain. A moderately complete registration of deaths is obtained without trouble in the larger cities, because by law it is impossible to procure permission to bury without a properly attested death certificate. The law applies equal compulsion to birth registration, but it is extensively and continuously evaded; among a people to whom any form of registration implies taxation and military conscription, this is hardly to be wondered at. In the days of Turkish conscription, it was common for a child to remain unregistered for ten years after its birth, and thus to escape the operation of the military service law, because when called up it was already several years over age !

The medical arrangements of several independent Government departments are under the direct control of the Health service, including those of the Iraq Railways and the Iraq Levies. The new national army, on the other hand, maintains its own health service. In the face of many difficulties, with slender financial resources and with little or no encouragement either from the public in Iraq or in England, the British health officials have performed a notable service in the organization of so complete and efficacious a department. Apart from the direct value of their work, one of the most striking testimonies to their labours has been the influence which they have obtained over their own local subordinates. A notable instance of this occurred during the disturbances in Kurdistan in 1922, when for many weeks the British superior personnel had to be withdrawn from the country, and the local officials left to carry on the work. So conscientious a view did the latter take of their duties that they even compiled, and sent to Baghdad, careful and regular returns on the lines of those previously used by their superiors, although they had received no request to do so ! No review of the work of the Health Department, however brief, is complete without a reference to the travelling dispensary, which works among the tribes of the Middle Euphrates. The dispensary has the equipment approximately of an army field unit, and is in a position even to undertake minor operations; it is worked by an Iraqi staff, supervised by an Englishman. The dispensary is the first of its kind, and much of the work performed is at present of an experimental nature; if its success is proved in the difficult task of caring for the health of the tribes, others will be established as the necessary funds are forthcoming.

If the body of the Iraqi is the especial care of the Directorate of Health, his mind is equally the care of the Ministry of Education. For the first time in seven hundred years the children of Iraq are now being offered the rudiments of an ordinary education; for the first time in modern life the human capabilities and possibilities of the people are being explored in the light of present-day knowledge and present-day educational conditions. That the demand for education has been far greater than the Government, in the present straitened condition of the national finances, can possibly meet, is a most encouraging sign, and goes far to show that the people have not lost the tradition of the times when Baghdad could offer the finest higher education in the world.

For the last six hundred years the education of the Iraqi has been completely in the hands of the various religious bodies, either native or missionary. The little Moslem attended the school at the local mosque, where he learnt by rote the rudiments of his own language and of simple arithmetic, interspersed with long quotations from the

Koran. The little Christian or Jew went to the missionary or subsidized school maintained by, or on behalf of, his community, where his education depended largely on his own ability and willingness to remain long enough at school. In recent years the Moslems had begun to realize that the superior education of the Jews and Christians was proving a serious bar to Moslem assumption of superiority in the nation as a whole; and latterly even the mission schools had contained a goodly number of Moslem boys. The Turkish Government after the revolution had made some attempt to introduce public elementary education on the Western model throughout the Empire; but the teachers employed were ill-equipped and underpaid, and moreover the moral tone of the schools was such that respectable Moslem families hesitated to send their boys to school at all. Perhaps the most successful of the mission schools have been those established by the American mission in Basrah and the French Carmelite Fathers in Baghdad. Both schools have received a great impetus from the educational advancement of post-war days, and now rank practically as High Schools, and in both cases girls' schools are maintained. Religious instruction is given, but boys or girls of other than Christian creeds are excused from attending the religious hours. Though the curriculum of these and other privately-run schools does not agree in every particular with that laid down by the Government, the latter has proved its realization of their value by practically leaving them to their own devices. In cases where they apply for a Government subsidy, they are, of course, compelled to admit Government inspection. The educational system laid down by the British authorities after the occupation was largely founded upon that of Egypt, the country which is closest in affinity to Iraq of any maintaining a modern educational organization. Education was divided into elementary, primary and secondary, the series being of two years, four years, and four years respectively. Recently this system was revised in the light of experience, and the course now consists of four years elementary, two years primary and four years secondary training. The principal reason for the change was the accommodation of a great many children who leave and go out into the world after the elementary stage; in four years it is possible to give them at least the rudiments of such knowledge as may be of use to them in their own sphere. The primary course is now largely a consolidation of the elementary subjects, and is chiefly intended to enable a pupil to understand the more difficult work which will meet him in the secondary course. The latter is copied directly from the Egyptian model, and aims at the preparation of a boy for professional work, or for entrance to a foreign University.

There are roughly 120 elementary boys' schools now open throughout the country, and 24 girls'; with a proportionate number of primary and secondary schools. The technical school in Baghdad continues the work commenced by the Turkish technical school, but in a more efficient manner; and the teachers' training college in Baghdad, a new institution, is endeavouring to train local boys for the responsible work of becoming teachers to their own countrymen. It says a good deal for the enthusiasm with which the new educational facilities have been received by the people at large that admittance to the training college is now sought by boys in all parts of the country; and the institution normally contains far more country boys than town boys. The college is run as a boarding establishment, and some difficulty has been experienced in controlling a number of high-spirited boys drawn from every part of the country and from all religious communities; for there are resident Subbi and Yezidi pupils as well as Moslem, Jew and Christian. On the whole, however, the discipline of the school is well preserved; and if it succeeds in establishing itself, its influence on the formation of national character will be incalculable. Indeed, a common education throughout for all communities would seem to be the only method of breaking down the tribal and local loyalties which, however picturesque, are fatal to the creation of a real national spirit.

By far the highest average in point of the number of schools to population is claimed by Mosul, whose educational facilities are extremely numerous and varied. It is largely owing to her superior education in the past that Mosul has preserved in her citizens that spirit of alertness and enterprise which has made many of them so successful

THE NEW UNIVERSITY OF AL-AL-BEIT AT BAGHDAD

as men of business in America and other foreign lands. Men from the Mosul neighbourhood, and more particularly from the vigorous little village of Tel Kaif, are to be found in good positions all over the United States; though how the Tel Kaifis, who are notorious at home for their love of strong drink, manage to exist in " dry " America is one of the unsolved problems of the East. In the development of modern Iraq, Mosul will undoubtedly take a leading part, owing to the alertness and superior education of her citizens of all creeds. Not the least of the triumphs of the new educational regime has been the remarkable increase of patronage of the girls' schools. The first Government girls' school was opened in Baghdad in 1919 as an experiment, and not without a certain amount of fear and trepidation; at present there are three Government girls' schools in Baghdad alone, and so numerous are the applications that another three could be immediately filled, had the Government but the funds to open them. So far, there has been remarkably little disinclination on the part of fathers of families to allow their girls to attend school; and there is even the nucleus of a class of professional women who desire by training as teachers or nurses to help their sex to take their rightful place in the modern world. It is an interesting speculation to the outside observer in Iraq, as to how far the education of women can be prolonged without encountering the bitter opposition of the older-fashioned Moslem and his religious leaders.

The work of the technical school is perhaps more generally appreciated by the public at large than that of any other educational institution. The standard of work in Iraq in the trades practised by the people has sunk, in many cases, deplorably low; and it is both to raise the standard of crafts already in use, and also to introduce and teach the crafts of the modern West, that the technical school exists. Difficulty is often experienced with regard to the training of youthful skilled labour among the local population, for any system of apprenticeship is unknown and misunderstood; and it is not easy for the large engineering firms or the railways to procure the trained assistance they require. The technical school is doing a great work in instilling a sound theoretical knowledge of his trade into the young would-be tradesman, and in inducing him to accept a contract of sufficient length to make it worth the while of the railways or large firms to give him further practical instruction. A smaller replica of the Baghdad Technical School will shortly be opened at Kerbela.

One of the most interesting offshoots of the work of the Education Department has been the creation of the Government Book Shop in Baghdad. Originally founded for the purpose of importing and stocking books for the use of schools and students, the Book Shop has recently launched out into the business of general bookselling, and it now contains probably as interesting an assortment of books as can be found anywhere in the East. It has become a rendezvous of Baghdad society, both British and local, and the focus of such intellectual life as can be found in the City of the Caliphs; and, incidentally, it does a considerable business, and may be taken as a standing example of how a Government enterprise, at first started as a necessary luxury, can by good management be turned into a highly profitable institution.

The crown was put on the new educational regime in March, 1922, when King Feisal laid the foundation stone of the new University, which is being laid out on a site adjoining the River Tigris north of Baghdad. It has only been found possible to arrange for the building of one college at present, the funds for which have come chiefly from the Waqaf Department and certain private religious endowments. The first building, recently completed, is designed to form an integral part of the whole scheme, when the carrying into execution of the latter becomes a financial possibility. Every effort has been made to make the building a thoroughly sound and representative example of modern Arab architecture treated by an English hand, and the structure bids fair to prove a credit to its architect, and, incidentally, to the indomitable energy with which the King has pursued the task of bringing the project to fruition.

CHAPTER XVIII

INDUSTRY AND BUSINESS

*" O thou who goest empty-handed to the market-place,
I fear that thou wilt not bring back thy turban."*—SA'DI.

THE material and business possibilities of Mesopotamia have excited since the Armistice a large amount of discussion and controversy in both Europe and America. Before describing business conditions as they exist at the present time, it is perhaps necessary to indicate exactly what these possibilities are, and what use so far has been made of them.

The great industry of the country, so far as can be foreseen, must be in the future, as it was in the past, that of agriculture. The proper development of this is dependent, as we have seen, on irrigation and the introduction of scientific methods of work, as well as on a reasonable increase of transport facilities. The Euphrates Valley Railway has been responsible for a large amount of new agricultural enterprise in the country south of Hillah, and careful railway extension would unquestionably lead to corresponding agricultural effort elsewhere. But the great and crying need at the moment is irrigation.

The chief agricultural exports would probably be dates, liquorice, wheat, barley, wool and cotton. To the latter crop a great deal of attention has been given since the Armistice, owing to the increasing shortage of available supplies throughout the world. If it can once be proved that Iraq can grow large quantities of cotton of good quality, her economic difficulties will be very largely solved, for Lancashire would soon find the means to finance her irrigation schemes in return for the securing of a new source for the supply of cotton. Reference has already been made to the excellent work which is being done by the British Cotton Growing Association in Iraq, in an unofficial and unobtrusive way, for the development of cotton growing in the country.

With regard to the possible mineral wealth of Iraq, the public attention of the world has for some years been concentrated on the possibility of oil. In spite of the fact that experimental operations are in progress at several points just across the Persian border, there is as yet no certainty whatever that oil exists in Iraq in anything like the quantity that would justify its being worked, although petroleum does appear in many places, and has been utilized and marketed locally for many years. Crude petroleum also, in the form of bitumen, is present at several points, notably at Hit, the quaint little hill-town on the Euphrates, which is paved with asphalt drawn from the bitumen lakes at the back of the town. Bitumen has been worked by the local inhabitants for countless ages, and mortar made of it is mentioned in the book of Genesis as having been used in the construction of the tower of Babel. It was extensively used by Nebuchadnezzar in his reconstruction of Babylon, and it is possible that the supply in ancient times was more generous than it is to-day. The principal undeveloped oil-field is the Mosul area, to secure a concession for which there has been considerable competition.

It will thus be seen that the material future of Iraq would appear to depend principally upon the development of her agriculture, particularly of her ability to produce cotton. If those experts who believe that the great wealth of the old Mesopotamian civilizations was drawn, not from agriculture, but from international trade are right in their surmise, then it may possibly have to be admitted that the country can never support a population approaching that of ancient times on agriculture alone. But the prospects of the development of Baghdad as a great trading and marketing centre do not, at the present time, appear very bright. Persia is yearly sinking into a worse condition of anarchy, and, in spite of the local prosperity produced by the success of the oil workings of the Anglo-Persian Oil Company, her economic future would appear to be a poor one ; and in any case Russia, with the advantage of her considerable central Asian and Caucasian railway system, will, under normal conditions, be in a favourable position to compete with Baghdad for whatever Persian trade is going. If the whole of the late Turkish Empire from the Persian Gulf to Constantinople were under the control of one strong Power, prepared to build railways and develop the area as a whole, the favourable situation of Baghdad might again place her in a strong position as a trading centre; but as the capital of a small and struggling country, surrounded by customs barriers of her own and the countries adjacent to her, and with no control over her outlet to the Mediterranean, her business future would appear to be extremely limited. Her import trade has shown signs of increasing in the post-war years as compared with the pre-war period, but her export trade has remained, roughly speaking, at about the same level. Her facilities for trade have increased in some directions and declined in others; on the one hand, the closer British connection has brought improved communication and a large addition to the European trading community; on the other hand, the division of the late Turkish Empire into independent countries has tended to cut Iraq off from its natural neighbours of Syria and Asia Minor, and to impede the freedom of travel and movement which formerly existed. To travel nowadays, for instance, from Baghdad to Jerusalem, formerly two provincial towns under one administration, entails crossing two borders, with the consequent complications of passports, visés and permits; and commercial intercourse between Syria and Baghdad, once so intimate, has now almost ceased. Until the political situation in the Near and Middle East finally settles into some fairly permanent shape, the chances of Baghdad increasing her trade, or even recovering her pre-war position, would appear to be remote.

The most important foreign firms domiciled in Iraq are the banks, of which one has been established many years in the country and two have entered it only during and since the war. All of them are largely staffed by Jews, and in consequence enjoy the very numerous public holidays which are the prerogative of the followers of that faith. As they also close on Moslem public holidays and English bank holidays, the employees can hardly be said to suffer from overwork. Indian money, based on the rupee, is universally used throught Iraq except in the districts adjacent to the Syrian border, where Turkish gold and silver (lira and mejidie) are still current. Turkish gold is still sometimes used for large transactions in the bazaar among local people of the non-banking variety, and it can always be purchased at the money changers; Persian money is also accepted at times in the bazaars, especially in the holy cities or at Khadhimain.

The principal business firms in the country are British, some of them of wide connections and reputation. The largest retail store in Baghdad is owned by a French firm, and Egyptians, Syrians, Canadians, Americans and Australians are all represented among the business houses in the country. There are several local business firms of considerable standing, and a few Anglo-Iraqi companies have been established since the Armistice, financed by British and local capital jointly, and registered in the country. There are four daily papers in Baghdad and one in Basrah; one each in Baghdad and Basrah are published in English, as well as in Arabic. The Government maintain three weekly papers, published at Mosul in Arabic, at Kirkuk in Turkish and at Sulamainiyah in Kurdish.

The largest developments in business since the war have been in the motor and catering trades. The rapid growth in the use of automobiles is partly attributable to the lack of other modern means ot transport; for the railway system is still very incomplete, and the only serious rival to the motor is the camel. Several hundred " taxis " are now registered in Baghdad, but the title is a courtesy one, for the taximeter is unknown; the taxis are largely used for cross-country work, and run regularly as far afield as Aleppo, Damascus and Teheran. Various makes of car, chiefly American, are in use. Difficulty is sometimes experienced in the matter of repairs and spare parts. The official car of the British High Commissioner is a Crossley, while King Feisal is usually seen in a Lancia. Heavy lorries are in use, but not in any great numbers, owing to the bad state of the roads and the high price of petrol, due possibly in part to the monopoly maintained by the Anglo-Persian Oil Company.

INDUSTRY AND BUSINESS

The carriage of heavy goods by road is still chiefly done by camel, and much of the light portering by donkey. The Near Eastern donkey or ass is much larger and stronger than the European variety, and will carry considerable loads without flinching. Cycles and motor-cycles are not much used. For one thing, the bad condition of the roads is against them ; moreover, the country Arab is frequently mounted and never leaves his horse, and the town Arab does not venture very far away from his own city or suburb.

The local manufactured articles are few, and generally of poor quality. Shoes, textiles and various articles of local attire are made locally, and an industry of copper pot making is established in Baghdad ; and the peculiar tiles used in the adornment of mosques and other prominent buildings are locally made. The unique silverwork of the Subbis has already been mentioned. Such small industries as have been established by European firms or individuals are almost entirely locally manned.

Of the large towns, Baghdad is by far the biggest and most important. Its present population is estimated at a quarter of a million, and it is growing fairly fast. The next largest town is Kerbela, one of the holy cities, and an established centre of local trade ; its population is possibly 80,000, and in the pilgrim season it is greatly augmented. Basrah and Mosul are the only other towns of any size, though there is a large number of prosperous small towns, of which Najaf and Khadhimain (the latter an outside suburb of Baghdad), are probably the wealthiest. Both of them, as places of pilgrimage, do a very large retail trade in their bazaars ; the bazaar in Khadhimain has recently been rebuilt, and is now one of the finest in the country.

Practically all the major operations of business or finance are conducted from Baghdad, and the head-quarters of most of the big firms, local or foreign, are placed there. Baghdad's great retail bazaars, though not equal in picturesqueness to those of Aleppo or Damascus, are justly famous ; and her wholesale bazaars and khans, though less obvious to the eye of the visitor, handle a very considerable business. A large number of shops and stores on Western lines have sprung up recently outside the bazaars, especially along the new main street ; and a few of these are the equal in the quality and variety of their stock, though not in size or magnificence, to those of Europe or America. It is probable that there are too many retail shops in Baghdad for the needs of the population. There is a noticeable tendency on the part of the local man of all classes who has saved a little money to speculate in a shop of his own. Arabs dislike working for other people, and will prefer to earn less as their own masters than enjoy a higher wage in the employ of a firm; and there is in consequence a distinct trend in Baghdad towards a surplus of small general shops and a scarcity of shops containing goods of an exclusive or technical nature. Auctions are a common feature of the life of the great bazaars, and they are taxed by the municipality; there are a few local auctioneering firms operating on a more considerable scale, and there is one English firm. The electrical and other technical trades are largely in the hands of Indians, who however, are being forced out to some extent by the competition of the local man, as the latter begins to learn the intricacies of the trade. Some of the office staffs in the big business houses are Indian, due to the difficulty experienced in procuring good local men in competition with the Government, many of whose departments are probably over-staffed. Many business houses in Baghdad possess an entertaining variety of nationalities on their pay-roll, and it is not uncommon to find an English "chief" presiding over a staff of Jewish, Indian and local Christian clerks, and employing Arab and Persian coolies in the basement and an Afghan watchman at the door.

The amusement industry in Baghdad is confined to the hotels and restaurants, the larger clubs, the Arab theatres and the cinemas. The latter are mostly in the hands of the local Christian element, and, considering the difficulties, the programmes are creditable. They have, however, largely failed to capture the local population, and depend chiefly for their earnings on the soldiers, both British and local, and the Europeans. In Baghdad a British military band is frequently engaged to play in one or other of the cinemas.

The Arab theatres are merely cheap editions of the Cairene theatres, and occasionally one of the well-known

THE UNCOMPLETED BRIDGE AT MOSUL

Cairene "stars" pays a personal visit to Baghdad. The actresses are usually Jewesses; no Moslem women are allowed to appear in the theatres. The entertainments generally take the form of what the Americans call " continuous vaudeville "; Arab audiences like variety and do not care for the continuity of an ordinary play. Some of the individual work is good, but a second-rate Arab theatre is one of the dullest things in the world. Baghdad audiences are fairly critical, and if the entertainment fails to please them they will cease to pay any attention to it, and will amuse themselves by talking, smoking, or even going to sleep. On the other hand, a popular artiste will receive an immense ovation, and will probably be able to fill a theatre for some weeks at prices nearly as exorbitant as those of the West End of London.

The hotels and restaurants are largely the creation of the post-war trade boom. They owed their inspiration to the crowd of Russian refugees who poured into the country from Persia during the early part of 1921, and for some time their gaiety was notorious; since then they have settled down to more work a day conditions, and there are several hotels in Baghdad now that offer comfortable, if expensive, accommodation to the traveller. There is still perhaps a tendency, natural in a country where the tourist traffic is as yet infinitesimal, to cater more for the "diner-out" than for the resident. In addition to the European hotels, there are in Baghdad a large number of Arab hotels or khans, doing business on the usual Near Eastern plan of letting empty rooms to visitors or residents, to furnish according to their tastes; they come under municipal inspection, and are reasonably clean.

The work of the retail tradesman in the great bazaars is perhaps as strenuous as anywhere in the world. The goods are left unmarked in price, and the skilful shop assistant relies on his wits to get as high a price for each article as he can; success in this battle of brains necessarily requires great knowledge of human nature, and an ability to put to instant use an exact judgment of what a particular customer will be prepared to pay. In addition the Baghdad retailer has to struggle with a language difficulty unknown elsewhere in the world, except possibly in New York.

Arabic and English are the joint business languages of the city, but Persian, Tel Kaifi and Hindustani are in constant use. A shopkeeper handling a popular line, such as watches or cheap clothing, must be prepared to haggle in any of these five languages, and, to be on the safe side, in Kurdish, Turkish and Armenian as well. It is not uncommon to hear all of these languages spoken during a short stroll through the bazaars. French can be heard at times, and, though a good deal more rarely, Russian and German. The grasp of human psychology displayed by some of the shopkeepers is even more remarkable than their gift of tongues. The man who can, in the course of half-an-hour, play upon the susceptibilities of a British Tommy, an Assyrian mechanic, an Indian babu, an Armenian refugee, a Persian pilgrim and a gaping Kurdish countryman, and sell something to each and all of them, seems to deserve a more prominent stage for his abilities than a stall in a Baghdad bazaar.

Almost as great a variety of racial type can be seen on the railways or among the employees of the big firms as in the bazaars. Under army control, the junior officials on the railways were mostly soldiers, and the staff mainly Indian. Gradually the Indian staff were replaced from the bottom upwards by local men, and the British soldier-officials by Indians; the latter are now, in their turn, being replaced by natives. The present guards are chiefly Assyrians, the porters and linesmen Arabs, and the executive and office staffs local Christians; engine drivers may come from half-a-dozen races. The same diversity is noticeable in the industrial plants in Iraq and the neighbouring countries, especially in the depôts of the Anglo-Persian Oil Company. It might be hoped that the intermingling of the various races and communities in industry would have a decided effect eventually in consolidating the nation, except that the East has seen the same sort of process occur before, with precisely opposite results. Eastern races appear to retain the ability to mix on an equality, and yet never to intermingle, in the most baffling manner; there are Arabs and Persians who have been neighbours in Baghdad for centuries, but the Arabs still remain Arab and the Persians Persian. Taking a long

INDUSTRY AND BUSINESS 285

view, it would appear that race is stronger than environment, in spite of the apparent exception to the rule in the case of the United States of America, a country which, however, has yet its history to make.

It cannot be said that the indolence which is commonly reported in Europe as a characteristic Near Eastern vice is conspicuous in Baghdad. The working classes work long hours with little or no complaint; and some of the tasks they are asked, in these times, to undertake, are done with surprising skill when their complete lack of education and experience are taken into account. The Arab is on the whole more talkative and less industrious than the Kurd, and less enterprising than the local Christian, who will cheerfully risk the whole of his savings in a single throw if he thinks that it will advance his prospects. The Arabs, with notable exceptions, make bad business men, and are completely careless of the future; it is not uncommon, for instance, for a man to purchase a large town property and commence to build on it, only to have to pause later because he has run out of money, and cannot meet his contractor's account.

By local custom, labour is paid by the day, but the British army introduced the system of paying by the month, an unfair proceeding which gives the employer the advantage of retaining a large sum of money in his possession, while depriving the poor employee of his earnings for a long period. Most of the labourers employed by the British military authorities are penniless the last two weeks of every month. Some of the larger British firms pay by the week. There is as yet little sign of labour organization or of the rise of "class consciousness," though efforts have been made to transplant trades union ideas from India. The Iraqi is, however, both too ignorant and too easy-going to pay much attention at present to such points, and the country is not sufficiently populated to make unemployment a serious problem. The Arab is a faithful worker if his interests are studied and he is courteously treated, but he resents bullying and slave-driving; most of the tragedies on railways or public works in Arab countries, in which an Englishman or other European is secretly murdered, are due to this cause. The local man's worst faults, from an employer's point of view, are his tendency to petty theft and his volubility ; nobody, even an Italian, enjoys talking more than an Arab, and on the smallest provocation he will desert his work to indulge in a polititical argument or a piece of interesting scandal. The Arab weakness for " racontage," particularly of a salacious nature, is notorious ; fortunately, nobody believes the gossip, but the delight taken by Arabs of all classes in attributing serious secret vices even to their intimate friends is remarkable. The taste or lurid scandal is relieved by a pretty wit, which seems to be the birthright of every Arab ; the working man in patricular has a keen sense of humour, and the conversation of an " arabanchi " or horse carriage driver in Baghdad is quite as good in its way as the much boomed humour of the old Cockney cabman. But the latter would hardly dare to commit himself in public to such language as is habitually used even by youthful drivers in Baghdad.

Practically all the agricultural and industrial plant used locally is of an old-fashioned type, some of it reminiscent of the days of Noah. With such primitive tools it is remarkable that so much work is accomplished, but the hours worked are intolerably long. The country labourer toils all day and every day, except during the midday hours when the heat of the sun compels a respite ; the town labourer, even at fairly skilled occupations, frequently works ten or eleven hours a day, sometimes more. A bookbinder, for instance, may start work in the winter months at seven, eat his midday meal on the premises, and not leave for home before seven or eight at night. The conditions of labour in the European firms are better than those in the local firms, and the higher ranks of labour at times enjoy hours which would be envied in England. Clerks, accountants and office staffs in general have an extremely easy time of it, particularly since the war, when there has been a considerable amount of competition for their services. The conditions in the Government offices are decidedly enviable, for even a six-hour day is regarded as excessive in some departments.

A notable feature of business life in the last four years has been the improvement in the standard of shop and office property in Baghdad. Much of this has been due to the example set by the Waqaf department in their rebuilding schemes, and also to the introduction by the British army of electric light, which has not only enhanced the appearance of the streets at night, but has rendered possible an improvement in the interior elevation and decoration of the newer buildings. Many of the modern premises combine the old Arab style with a pleasing increase in elevation, made possible by the use of iron girders and other Western innovations; the girder has now almost supplanted the palm tree as the mainstay of the Baghdad house and shop architect.

A very real difficulty in the development of business in Baghdad has been the exorbitant rents demanded since the war by local house owners for even ordinary premises in the business quarter. In the matter of "squeezing" the unfortunate business man for the last possible penny of rent, the local Arab or Jew has nothing to learn from the ducal landed proprietors of London or the "realty millionaires" of New York. Even the violent slump in trade in 1922 has not served to qualify the local landowner's rapacity. An instance recently reported in a local paper will suffice.* A certain firm commenced business in Baghdad in April, 1918, holding a year's lease on their premises at a rental of approximately £74 a year, paid quarterly in arrears. For the six months April-October, 1919, they had to pay at the rate of £330 a year, still quarterly in arrears, but the following year they were compelled to pay no less than £790, all in advance, for a renewal of their lease. For the next period the owner insisted on a three-years' lease at a figure of £1,066 a year, which the firm, unable to find other premises, was obliged to pay. The building in pre-war days cost something like £850 to build; from the present occupier alone the fortunate owner has received approximately £4,400, and during the whole duration of the tenancy has paid £170 in taxes and £30 in repairs ! No wonder that a proportion of Baghdad landowners show a tendency to desert their native heath for the more healthy and pleasant resorts of the South of France !

* *Baghdad Times*, May 20th, 1923.

The same spirit of shameless profiteering has been shown in the field of private dwelling-houses. Rents have been forced up to ten, twenty and even thirty times the value of pre-war days; and the violent irritation caused by such evil conditions blandly put down to political causes. Baghdad itself has increased enormously in population in the last ten years, possibly by as much as one-fifth, but the increase of house building has been infinitesimal. An elaborate plan for the building of a new Heliopolis on the south side of Baghdad was entertained by a large English firm, but unfortunately abandoned owing to the political uncertainty of the country. If the new Iraq State can, in the course of five years or so, prove its stability, confidence will return and new building will automatically reduce the hold of the house and office profiteer. But five years is a long time to wait.

A notable feature of recent business conditions has been the revival of communication across the desert to Syria and Palestine. Passenger motor cars, organized by local enterprise, commenced to run to Aleppo in the spring of 1922, and by the ensuing winter a large and profitable clientele had been secured. In 1923 a prominent British firm established in Syria entered the field with a direct service between Damascus and Baghdad. By this route the latter city is brought within eight days of London, and the possibility of her re-establishing herself as a great distributing depot for Persia and the countries beyond is greatly increased. The problem of reviving the flow of freight traffic across the desert has, however, not yet been solved, partly owing to the customs difficulty, partly to the avarice of the tribal sheikhs, who, like the Baghdad house-owners, assess their services to the community at an exorbitant figure. Some business firm or group will no doubt eventually be able to demonstrate to the sheikhs concerned that a regular yearly income, even if moderate, is more profitable than an exorbitant " security tax " levied irregularly and occasionally. Once the sheikhs become convinced of the folly of their policy of killing the goose that lays the golden eggs, freight traffic may once more be expected to flow with fair regularity between the Mediterranean coast and Baghdad. At the same time, it should

INDUSTRY AND BUSINESS

never be forgotten that the commercial future of Baghdad depends principally on the development of the purchasing power of the people of Persia and the adjacent countries.

There remains one opening for business enterprise to consider, which may in the event prove to be the most profitable of all. Iraq as a country for tourists has almost unbounded possibilities. Not even Egypt herself can rival her in the richness and variety of her places of interest, in the weird beauty of her sunsets, or in the mildness and healthiness of her winter climate. Babylon, Nineveh, Kish, Ashur, Ur of the Chaldees, Baghdad—what other country in the world possesses towns with such appeal to historical romance? Once political security and reasonable travel facilities are assured, there would appear no limit to the possibilities of the land of the Tigris and Euphrates as a tourist centre. And, from a purely business point of view, if 25 per cent. of the profitable millionaire traffic which finds its way every year to the banks of the Nile could be diverted to those of the twin rivers, the financial problems of the little Iraq State would come a good deal nearer to a favourable solution.

The business prospects of Iraq may be summed up as reasonably hopeful, if not extravagantly rosy. Agriculture must always take the first place among the country's industries, with oil, international trade and the tourist traffic as reasonable possibilities. Baghdad will hardly, perhaps, offer chances of the foundation of big fortunes, (except to property profiteers), but, given reasonable security, should be able to provide sound incomes for her established business houses. Mr. Winston Churchill's dream of Baghdad as the " Clapham Junction of the air " is hardly likely to be realized in our time ; but for those whose feet are on the ground, the future of the city may be said to offer, granted political security, decided scope for personal initiative, and a reasonable return upon invested capital.

CHAPTER XIX

SOCIAL LIFE

*"Why should your fellowship a trouble be,
Since man's chief pleasure is society?"*—SIR JOHN DAVIES.

As Baghdad is at once the capital and by far the largest city in Iraq, the social life of the country, both local and foreign, tends naturally to centre there; Basrah, partly owing to its remoteness from the other large towns, partly to its natural geographical connection as a port with the Persian Gulf and India, has developed what is in many ways a distinct social atmosphere of its own. Indian life and Indian ways are much more strongly represented in the port town than elsewhere in Iraq, and even the European element of the population shows in its habits and manners the influence of long years of Indian residence. Baghdad, on the other hand, is at once more Western, more cosmopolitan and more national; her social life reflects her consciousness of her past history and of her present position as the capital of the New State. Practically the whole of the topical and critical Press, small monthly and weekly reviews, etc., emanates from Baghdad; and the usual bazaar tittle-tattle of an Arab town takes on there a graver and more responsible aspect, as befits the conversation of the national capital. The cosmopolitan aspect of society is increased by the fact that there is no European quarter in Baghdad, in the ordinary Eastern sense of the term; with the exception of the two small bungalow suburbs laid out for British officials and railway servants respectively, the European resident population is scattered all over the town.

This lack of a European quarter unquestionably tends to make Baghdad more attractive to the inquisitive European observer than an Indian or Egyptian city. Here Arab and Persian life can be studied at first hand, for it is impossible to reside in the city for any length of time without being brought in contact with local people, either as customers, employees or neighbours. There is probably a better understanding in Baghdad between the local population and the European element than in any other Eastern city ; and it was noteworthy in the rebellion of 1920 that, although Baghdad was for some weeks practically undefended, and although anti-European feeling on the political side ran extremely high, no effort was made in the city to molest the ordinary European population, who went about their daily business in the usual way. This understanding has been cemented by a certain amount of inter-marriage between the European and local elements.

At the same time, Baghdad enjoys none of the amenities of India or Egypt, and the Westerner contemplating residence there must be prepared to improvise his own amusements. There is no European theatrical entertainment except the cinema and the concert parties, usually organized by groups of British officers and soldiers in their plentiful supply of spare time ; several attempts have been made to organize small dramatic societies. Most of the entertaining is done at the various hotels and clubs, two of which, the Alwiyah in Baghdad, and the Basrah at Basrah, are excellent examples of the American " country club." Exclusive and expensive, and fitted with all the latest contrivances for arousing gaiety from the American bar and the Jazz Band to the Sunday afternoon " musicale," these and other clubs provide a rather hectic background for local English society, reflecting perhaps, the instability of Iraqi and Middle Eastern post-war conditions.

Of local social activity, there is probably more than in most Moslem centres, with the exception of Constantinople. Moslem ladies do not appear in public or receive gentlemen at their houses, though of late there has been a tendency to break the rigidity of this rule ; there is even in Baghdad a small but active " woman's movement," on the lines of those in Constantinople and Cairo. On the other hand, European ladies are welcomed at receptions held by Moslem gentlemen, and many personal friendships exist between Englishmen and their wives and local men of position. The King, in his desire to become a model Moslem ruler, sets a wide example in this respect, and his receptions include people of note without distinction of race or religion.

Dancing has been a post-war craze among the European element, and has also spread to the local population. It is even whispered that Moslems of high rank are to be seen indulging in this fascinating pastime in the privacy of their inner apartments, to the tune of a gramophone or a hired band. All the clubs hold frequent dances, which are well patronized, and some of the hotels do the same. A few of these hotel dances have led to a certain amount of searching of hearts, owing to the objection of Europeans to allowing local diners to watch their wives dancing; on the score, apparently, that in a Moslem country the Europeans cannot be allowed the same privilege.

The development of Hinaidi as a military centre, and the consequent withdrawal of much of the British military population from Baghdad, has tended to the growth of class consciousness among the Europeans; and there is now an officers' club in Hinaidi with ambitions to supplant the Baghdad clubs in exclusiveness, comfort and gaiety. On the other hand, there has been a certain tendency for the civil European community, both official and unofficial, to retaliate by joining hands with the local residents; a noteworthy example of this has been the successful inception of an Anglo-Iraqi club in Baghdad, to which many of the most prominent members of both the English and local population belong.

The social life of the English official in the provinces is a lonely one, but not altogether without compensations. Situated in some small town or village, possibly many miles away from any other Englishman, he must rely for his pleasures on his car, his shooting and the hospitality of local " notables " or the desert sheikhs. Many of these, particularly of the semi-nomad variety, lead a far gayer life than is sometimes realized in more civilized centres. The desert even possesses its own theatre, in the shape of the wandering troupes of " dancing boys " who are engaged to perform on festive occasions or on the arrival of an honoured guest; and considerable consumption of the forbidden " strong drink " is not unknown in the tents of the well-to-do. In addition, the desert chieftain must always be ready to welcome strangers round his " mejlis " coffee hearth of an evening; and desert life, though limited, cannot be said to be monotonous in the way that, for instance, English country life is monotonous. There is generally something "going on," even if it be only raiding, fighting, or gossip; and there are many duller places for guests than the tent or house of a country sheikh. On the other hand, the social life of a paramount sheikh is trying to the stranger, owing to the strictness and complexity of the etiquette, which would have been considered excessive in a Hanoverian London drawing-room; and a European guest, unless of many years' experience among the tribes, is apt to have his pleasure largely spoilt by the fear that he is ever on the brink of committing some unconscious indiscretion.

All Moslem society, both in town and country, is fatally compromised by the absence of women. The exclusively male atmosphere gives it a slightly puerile air, similar to that of an entertainment given by a group of schoolboys; the conversation, if kept on a high level, must be kept unpleasantly exclusive to the happenings of the outside world; and, if allowed to drop at all, tends instantly to descend to the level of semi-obscenity. Formal Arab society has thus something of the intellectual limitations of the commercial taproom.

The Jews of Baghdad, in the interior of their houses, differ very little in their social habits from the Moslems. Though their women are unveiled, they do not mix with visitors; and at an entertainment in a Jewish house of standing, the guests will be ranged with their hosts in one room or on one side of the balcony, while the ladies of the household will remain at the other. The Baghdad Jew is permitted by custom considerable laxity in his relations with the opposite sex, so long as his indulgences are confined to the house; a point of view exactly opposite to that of the European. The "sanctity of the home," a phrase embodying a sentiment which is revered in Europe even by the good-for-nothing, has little meaning for the Iraqi; but on the other hand it is only fair to remember that the European's tendency to seek pleasure in the streets appears equally shocking to the Easterner. A travelled Baghdadi will hardly ever fail to impress upon a European listener that what struck him most in the West was not the traffic or the grandeur, but the quantity of "loose women" to be seen everywhere. If Europeans condemn Baghdad life as immoral, they must in justice carefully consider the appearance of their own habits to Near Eastern minds. Such remarks, of course, apply only to a certain fraction of either the European or the Near Eastern population; and there are in Baghdad, as in London, hundreds of men and women who lead a happy and contented family life, untouched by spurious gaieties, and without the world being any the wiser.

Social life in local Christian circles naturally comes more directly under European influence, and is less characteristic in consequence. The Christian women at times affect European dress but more commonly retain the elaborate silk or cotton shawl over the head, which gives them something of the appearance of the old-fashioned "Lancashire lassie." The shawls are gaily coloured, and, in the case of ladies of wealth, of extremely rich design. Baghdad girls are pretty when young, but there is a tendency among the Christians and Jews to grow abnormally stout at an early age; this stoutness disappears later in life, and there are Christian old ladies in Baghdad hardly distinguishable from similar types in England. The Moslem women do not, as a rule, grow so stout early in life, possibly owing to the fact that their food is more simple and less "Europeanized."

All creeds and classes roughly follow the same regime in their manner of daily living. Early rising is universal; a light early meal of milk and unleavened bread is followed at mid day by the heavy meal of the day; a short rest is taken after this, lengthened in the summer owing to the extreme heat. A light or heavy meal is taken at sunset, according to taste.

In the case of the leisured classes, the morning or afternoon's labours will be interrupted by frequent resort to the coffee shop, which in Iraq forms the centre of all social life, and is the main resort for both business and pleasure. Some local business men of substance conduct the whole of their affairs in the coffee shop, merely repairing to their office to confirm in writing what has already been settled. A gentleman of leisure may consume, in the course of an afternoon in one of these resorts, a very large number of cups of tea or coffee, which will serve to sustain him until the next meal. In the evening, after supper, the coffee shop will again be visited, and two or three hours passed there before the time for retiring arrives. In the case of the working classes, a surreptitious visit to the coffee shop will be risked at least once during the course of a morning's work ; and the evening will invariably be spent there. This predilection for café life is induced partly, as in France or Italy, by the climate, which makes sitting outside a pleasure nearly all the year round ; and partly by the extreme dullness of home life for a population which is largely illiterate, and knows little of pianos, gramophones or illustrated magazines. The coffee shop is the forum, the sports room and the music hall of the Iraqi, the centre of his social life, and the scene of most of his leisure hours ; and even the theatre is but an offshoot of, and depends largely for its patronage upon, the universal " gahwa." *

Owing to the entire absence of a popular music trade in Iraq, the songs sung in the theatres are usually passed on by the audience via the coffee shops to their own circle of friends, office companions or family. In every group of the gilded youth of Baghdad will generally be found one who makes a speciality of attending " first nights " when a visiting " star " is expected to sing a new song, and of rapidly acquiring by rote both the words and the tune. His social popularity in his own set will depend upon his ability in this direction, so that his companions in their own particular coffee shop may be kept fully " up-to-date " in the newest ditties which are sweeping the town. A man of quick and retentive memory, and possessing ability as a topical singer, is much prized in his own social circle ; and there are cases in Baghdad of men who do little else to earn their living but wander from house to house, as amateur entertainers to amuse their friends. The profession of " nadhim," or " gentleman companion," was looked upon without dishonour in the days of Harun ; and even to-day some of the wealthy notables have a man of this type, who combines quick wit with elegance and social

* The Baghdad Arabic for coffee, and thus for coffee-shop. Cp. French, " café."

tact, and who is expected, in return for his keep, to aid his host in entertaining the latter's guests. In the case of a paramount sheikh or local ruler of consequence, such a man may exercise considerable political influence over the community, even developing into a kind of perpetual premier or grand vizier to his patron. Men of good birth who possess the requisite gifts do not hesitate to adopt this profession; and one of the best-known gentlemen of leisure in Baghdad at the present time spent his earlier years in this way at the court of a powerful ruler in the Persian Gulf.

The coffee shops resorted to by the lower classes are naturally less elaborate and refined, and there are some rather shady varieties retailing drink and drugs as well as non-intoxicants. There are a fair number of licensed drink shops in Baghdad, and drunkenness among the local population has unfortunately greatly increased since the increase of European influence. Many of the lower type of European hotels depend for their revenue upon the sale of intoxicants both to Europeans and to local people; severe measures have had to be taken at times by the police against abuse of their licenses. A great many European men, particularly when young and single, tend to drink more heavily in Iraq than at home, partly owing to the influence of the climate and partly to social loneliness and lack of the usual type of Western evening amusement.

There is a strong movement towards total prohibition in Iraq, but it is difficult to see how it could be introduced at present; the British military forces would almost certainly refuse to be bound by it, and, in addition, the drink trade brings in a large and useful increment of revenue to the sadly-empty national exchequer.

The cinema has hardly made the progress in popular estimation which might have been expected of so prominent a feature of Western theatrical life. Several causes contribute to this. The geographical isolation of Baghdad, and the consequent prohibitive expense of procuring first-class films, have prevented the development of a high standard of entertainment, with the result that the more intelligent portions of the community have become alienated from the cinema almost as soon as they have taken to it, and the only firm supporters are the coolies and the " street Arabs," who revel in the exploits of American cow-boys and "stunt" film heroines. In addition, the prohibition against Moslem women visiting places of entertainment makes a serious inroad into the supply of potential cinema patrons ; and this ban has not yet been seriously shaken, although one enterprising cinema in Baghdad provides special boxes, out of sight of the general audience, for Moslem ladies desiring to watch the entertainment in complete propriety and seclusion. It cannot be denied, also, that much of the usual type of Western film drama is repellent to better class Eastern taste, especially in the matter of the relations between the sexes ; for an Eastern mind will always place the worst interpretation upon these situations, and many films which seem innocent enough in the West appear in quite another light when seen in the East. It has often been suggested in recent years by European residents in the East that some kind of censorship should be exercised over the importation of films, and also of the modern type of illustrated weekly, so popular nowadays in London, which delights in finely-executed photographic studies of female semi-nudity ; but it is doubtful whether such a thing in practice would prove either possible or effective. The only remedy appears to be an improvement in European taste, coupled possibly with an increased interest in the East for her own sake, and a consequent increased respect for Eastern susceptibilities. It must be remembered that the " modern " spirit of entire lack of self-restraint, which at present holds the field in the West, is, rightly or wrongly, extremely repugnant to Eastern, and particularly to Arab mentality, which has from time immemorial placed great emphasis on the importance of courtliness, good breeding and outward decorum, to a degree which possibly would strike modern Europe as hypocritical. In spite, therefore, of the degree in which the Near East and Europe have approached each other in the last few years, the true Arab would unquestionably find more bonds of sympathy between himself and an early Victorian Englishman, than between himself and the restless, motor-cycling, jazzing Englishman of the present day. Western social life is a mere history of passing phases, and the restless, jazzing phase will probably disappear as quickly as the early Victorian ; but Arab social life has gone on in much the same old way since the time of Abraham (in many ways a typical Arab), and will, no doubt, go on in much the same old way for another equal period of time. This does not mean that the Arab is old-fashioned, in the sense that he refuses to use the fruits of modern invention and discovery. Far from it; any thing modern that is of use in his own particular sphere, from the rifle and the compass to the automobile and the fountain pen, the Arab will take to with avidity; but these acquisitions will not disturb the general even tenour of his way. An Arab merchant writing on an American portable typewriter is still an Arab and not an American; and so he will remain to the end of time. And what applies to the Arab in particular applies in general to the other communities in Iraq, who, with all their political and religious differences, yet retain the common Eastern desire for careful procedure and good breeding.

One result of this is an almost universal dignity, entirely lacking in the West except in the case of men of very marked strength of character, of the type of Mr. Gladstone or the great American President, Abraham Lincoln, who both possessed several traits strongly reminiscent of Arab character. An Arab is one of the few people who can look dignified in a Ford car; and the entry of the present King Feisal into Baghdad, not mounted on the traditional Arab steed, but sitting in an Overland " four," and still looking extraordinarily impressive, will not easily be forgotten by those who saw it. This dignity is the outward and visible sign of a spiritual poise, the result of a perfect conviction that the ways of the fathers, handed down for generations, are still the best ways; and that, so long as the ups and downs of the world are met with perfect composure, no very great harm can befall. Satirical Western writers not infrequently gibe at the " fatalism " of the East; but fatalism, after all, is at least half the truth of life, and if the restless activity of the modern West is admirable, the perfect restraint of the East is almost equally so. At least an Arab is saved the spiritual horror of " nerves," the fruit of that perpetual craving for excitement which is becoming so disturbing a feature of modern Western life.

Coupled in the Near Eastern character with the

admiration for a dignified mode of living is the universal distaste for heeding the importance of time. Time has become something of a fetish in the Western world; and the commonest excuse of to-day, when an unpleasant duty has to be faced, is that the individual concerned has "no time." Such an excuse would be futile in the Near East, for the boundaries of time are there completely ignored; and even the hour of an important engagement is frequently only vaguely indicated. An Arab will meet his business partner, not at three o'clock, but in "the afternoon"; an arrangement which may entail his partner's awaiting him at the rendezvous for anything from two to six hours.

Even the motor car is powerless to shake this universal refusal to be bound by the dictates of time; and a driver, say, on the Baghdad-Aleppo route will only guarantee the arrival of the car at its destination—"to-morrow—if God wills." This disregard for the value of time is a real weakness in Near Eastern character, due possibly to some extent to climate and historical environment; it is not at bottom an Arabic national characteristic, and is in strong contrast to both the teaching and the practice of the Prophet, who was extremely business like and practical in the execution of his daily duties, and whose admonitions at times bear a strong resemblance to the doctrines of Samuel Smiles, or a modern American "up-lift" leader.

A peculiar feature which must again be alluded to as affecting the social life of Iraq is the huge annual influx of pilgrims, chiefly Persian and Indian, to the holy places of the Shiah faith. The historical, political and medical features of these pilgrimages have already been touched upon; but their social influence is no less important. It cannot be emphasized too often that the presence of the holy cities, and the train of priests, holy men, mendicants, pious believers, criminals and outcasts which their presence attracts, constitute a serious menace to the security and to the general life of the country; and the social evils attending the pilgrimage are many and pressing. A fair number of unsocial trades, from the making of holy relics to prostitution, depend largely for their existence upon the pilgrim traffic, and the strain which they throw on the local police is severe, for, in addition to the responsibility of maintaining order and restraining pious fanaticism within reasonable bounds, the police have to tackle such evils as the infamous custom of importing young girls for sale in the holy cities in order to provide the pilgrim with his fare home. This nefarious business was openly carried on in Khadhimain, a suburb of Baghdad and one of the holy places, until quite recently, and even now unquestionably goes on surreptitiously ; and the fate of these young girls, brought down by their patron from some country village to the holy shrines, and condemned either to the house of a wealthy Baghdadi or to the " Red Light " district, is too terrible to dwell upon. This is only one of several evils which follow the annual influx of many thousands of poor, ignorant, dirty and backward people of all ages from some of the wildest parts of central Asia. Time, civilization and education may gradually deprive the holy places of some of their sanctity and influence ; but the strength of reactionary religious influences even in Western Europe and America shows what a slow process this must be. In the meanwhile Iraq will have to continue offering her hospitality year by year to thousands of poor and hungry pilgrims, and other thousands of corpses, intent upon either visiting or securing internment in the holy land that shelters the martyred Hosein and his father, Ali, the " Apostle of God."

CHAPTER XX

THE DAWN OF A TO-MORROW

"*The servants arrange, but God settles.*"—ARAB PROVERB.

THE second year of the existence of the Iraq kingdom started somewhat inauspiciously. The anniversary of the coronation was celebrated in Baghdad by various ceremonies suitable to such an occasion; and these included a formal call on His Majesty by the British High Commissioner, not in his capacity of tutor to the infant Iraq State, but as Consul-General of the British Crown. His arrival in the courtyard of the Serai was the signal for a violent nationalist demonstration, conducted, however, with great courtesy and no sign of personal animosity; and it was difficult for the High Commissioner, on so formal an occasion, to accept it as anything but an open insult. The delicate situation was further complicated by the sudden illness of the King, who was stricken that same night with appendicitis. The Council of State had resigned in a body the preceding week, owing to a local political crisis; and, in the absence of the King, there was for the moment no one at the head of affairs to gloss over the awkward incident of the affront, or to restrain the further activities of the jubilant Nationalists. The High Commissioner for once threw off the disguise of tutor, and boldly stepped into the breach as master. The leading nationalist offenders were arrested and exiled, and the two Baghdad nationalist newspapers suspended. These measures caused some ill-feeling and were much criticized, especially on the score that the High Commissioner had himself provoked the incident by his previous repression of all open expression of opinion, either in the market-place, in political clubs, or in the more reputable newspapers; and the Nationalists declared with some show of truth that, though they regretted the impropriety of the occasion chosen for their demonstration, it was the only possible means of making sure that their point of view was heard by the High

Commissioner at all. On the other hand, it is difficult to see how such a situation could have been dealt with by any but stern measures, and the sudden assumption of personal responsibility by the High Commissioner was, on the whole, generally commended.

This incident had the unfortunate, but perhaps natural, sequel of doubling the stranglehold of the authorities upon the national life. There had been some hope during the summer of the disappearance of the press censorship, and even of the odd plan by which political parties and clubs had to obtain licences from the Government, who thus retained the power at any time to break their political enemies; but any such hope had now to be abandoned. The authorities, possibly alarmed by the strength of the extremist movement, determined to re-double their precautions. Press telegrams either entering or leaving the country were subjected to a heavy censorship, and journalists to considerable official pressure; and, four years after the Armistice, the population of Iraq were still passing their daily lives under the shadow of martial law.

During the autumn the political situation became more complicated. In October the treaty between Great Britain and Iraq, designed to define the relationship of the two countries for a period of twenty years, and to some extent to supersede the mandate of the League of Nations, was published, and aroused a storm of protest in both countries. The treaty, which was a carefully worded document, involved in fact the assumption by Great Britain of all the exterior responsibilities of Iraq, both diplomatic and military, with a corresponding right to exercise control over her official decisions, and to claim a privileged position for British influence over that of other foreign Powers. Great Britain was to assist Iraq to obtain membership of the League of Nations—an outward and visible sign that the " tutorial " period of Iraqi national life was over—and to do her utmost to procure such foreign loans or financial assistance as she might require for the development of her territory. An important article secured the abolition of the Turkish capitulations in return for certain judicial privileges for European residents. Iraq agreed to observe tolerance towards the followers of all religions, and to recognize a law of antiquities which should allow the unimpeded research work of the nationals of responsible foreign Powers.

The point which struck dismay to the hearts alike of the British taxpayer and the Iraqi nationalist was the extreme length of the period of the treaty. Was Great Britain, asked the one, to be called upon to spend money for the defence of Mesopotamia for twenty years, without any visible return and without even possessing political control of the country? Was Iraq, asked the other, after having been promised her political independence, to be subjected for twenty years to the practical control of a foreign Power, exercised, not through the local Government, but through a High Commission? An immediate outcry arose in the English popular press for the evacuation of Iraq by British troops and officials and for the abrogation of all political responsibility for the country; while the Iraqi Nationalists declared bitterly, and with some show of truth, that the treaty was merely the hated " mandate " in disguise, and that in practice the whole government of the country would be assumed by Great Britain, who would, in fact, be in a position to pull all the strings. A compromise was eventually arranged, by means of which the original twenty years of the treaty were reduced to four. This was embodied in a protocol to the document published in May, 1923, and afterwards ratified by the representatives of both Iraq and Great Britain in the summer of 1924.

It had been proposed to hold elections for a National Assembly in Iraq during the autumn of 1923, based upon an electoral roll which had now, at long last, been prepared; but one of the leading Shiah *mujtahidin* issued a " fetwa," or bull, forbidding any Shiah to vote, on the score that the Government was, in practice if not in theory, not Iraqi but " foreign " and " infidel." Thus fifty per cent. of the Moslem population were, at one stroke, prevented from voting; and it soon became clear that the holding of the elections was out of the question for the present. Efforts were made by the King, by the High Commissioner, and by several influential local men to persuade the mujtahid to withdraw the fetwa; but the pontifical terms were onerous, including the immediate withdrawal both of the British mandate and the new Anglo-Iraq treaty, together with several other points which practically amounted to an assumption of the government of the country by the holy cities. The situation was somewhat clarified during the summer of 1923 by the banishment to Persia of the most intractable of the Shiah leaders, an action which, as was to be expected, provoked a storm of anti-British feeling in the latter country. Meanwhile, a Turkish agitation for the re-acquisition of Mosul had been offset, so far as Iraq was concerned, by the personal campaign of Arab propaganda conducted by the Amir Zaid, a younger brother of King Feisal; and the final decision of the question was left over, by the terms of the Turkish peace treaty, for later settlement between Turkey and Great Britain. The fact that Mosul is an Arab city, both in language and in sentiment should prove a decisive factor in the retention of the vilayet for Iraq, if the eventual decision is given on really impartial grounds, and freed from the influence of European trade politics.

In the spring and summer of 1924 a step forward was taken in Iraq's political history by the bringing together of a Constitutional Assembly of Notables, charged with the ratification of the Treaty with Great Britain, and the creation of an organic law for Iraq. The Assembly was opened with some ceremony by the King at the end of March. The future Constitution was discussed and laid down, and preparations were undertaken for the creation of a popular Parliament of two Houses, which should offer to the land of the rivers, for the first time in all her long history, the gift of representative government. Thus the phase of the actual rebirth of Mesopotamia as an independent state might be said to have reached its conclusion.

The situation in the neighbouring countries remained for the most part indeterminate and disturbed. Persia, in spite of the fact that she was receiving nearly £500,000 a year in royalties from the Anglo-Persian Oil Company, appeared to be sinking into a state of economic desperation, which grew worse every year; and her political situation, owing to the growing weakness of the central administration and the increasing power of the tribal chiefs, appeared more anomalous as time went on. It seemed indeed in 1923 and 1924 as if nothing could save Persia from the eventual intervention and control of some foreign Power, except a sudden and unlooked-for renascence of the national spirit. Meanwhile the corruption of the ruling classes was only equalled by the inefficiency of their rule; and it did not appear that the intervention of an American financial mission, which had been summoned to Persia in 1922 by the Persian Government itself, would be allowed in practice the necessary freedom of action and control which would alone enable it to carry out its suggested reforms.

In Palestine the antagonism between the Moslem and Christian Arabs and the local and foreign Jews who formed the backbone of the Zionist experiment, appeared to be coming to a head. The Zionist experiment had received the general support of America, but increasing hostility in England, the country most responsible for its inauguration and working; and it appeared extremely likely that sooner or later a compromise with the Arabs would have to be sought, less distasteful to them than the idea of a "Jewish National Home." Meanwhile the material organization of Palestine, especially in the important matters of roads and railways, remained far ahead of that of any of the countries released by the war from the sway of Constantinople.

The state of Syria was gloomy in the extreme. The French had shown little skill either in their interpretation of the instructions of their mandate, or in the pacification of a mixed local population; and even the Maronite Christians, who had been intriguing for French intervention in Syria for nearly forty years, began to express themselves as heartily sick of their bargain. The French authorities, annoyed by the Damascus incident, which had ended in the flight of Feisal, and equally perturbed by the action of the British Government in allowing that prince to seek, and afterwards to obtain, the throne of Iraq, imposed upon the unfortunate Syrians a militaristic regime which became almost intolerable. The police cordon was drawn so thick throughout the country, that passports were inspected and inquisitive personal details taken of passengers by train even in the interior districts of the country; and fair Syria, which even under the Turks had enjoyed a certain prosperity, languished under the heavy taxation and an administration that was almost Teutonic. The towns were filled with French soldiers, drawn from all parts of the globe; and so sacred was the person of the soldier that no civilian might walk on the pavement in front of a sentry on duty, but was compelled by law to walk in the street. Such was the paternal rule of the great Republic which, but six years previously, had been fighting with her back to the wall—"for freedom."

The Arabian country on the south-western border of Iraq was tending to come more and more under the influence of Abdul Aziz Ibn Saud, the Sultan of Nejd, whose romantic rise to power has already been alluded to. In 1924 he startled the world by boldly invading the Hejaz, capturing Mecca and driving King Hosein and the Hashimite family out of the country. Thus for the second time Mecca became a Wahabi possession. The future, however, will test Ibn Saud's power as a statesman even more than the past, for his successes have now brought him within the arena of world politics, and he cannot escape the responsibilities which such a position entails.

To the north of Iraq the disturbed territory of Kurdistan continued to give concern to both the British and Iraqi administrations in Baghdad; and it became increasingly difficult to see how law and order were to be guaranteed in a country which resolutely refused to come under the Government of Iraq, and which it was impossible for Great Britain to administer directly without prohibitive expense. It was hoped, however, that the increasing prosperity of Iraq would attract the attention of the avaricious and hardworking Kurd, and would in the course of time have the effect of inducing him to settle down to something approaching a peaceful existence. In 1924 Sulamainiyah was re-occupied by British and Iraqi troops, and became once more a part of Iraq. It was later visited by Lord Thomson, the first British Labour Minister for Air, in the course of his short visit of inspection to Baghdad.

Beyond the Kurdish country, and touching the boundaries of Iraq in the north and north-west, came the territory of the Kemalist Turks, whose future was at least as indeterminate as that of Iraq itself. The Kemalists had repudiated the Treaty of Sèvres, negotiated between the Government of Constantinople and the Allies, and had successfully set up a new national Government at Angora, the little town on the Anatolian Railway, which has appeared several times in the course of our story. The year 1922 had seen resounding victories against the Greek armies in Asia Minor, which had been completely driven into the sea; and for some time it appeared as if the new Government, under the inspiration of an undoubtedly able leader, Mustapha Kemal Pasha, was indeed about to inaugurate a new and more vigorous epoch for the Turkish race. But the vigour of 1922 appeared in the succeeding years to be relapsing into a mere struggle between local parties for the control of what was left of Turkey by the World War; and there was little evidence of any realization of the enormous responsibility which must be assumed by a Turkey really regenerated and anxious to play that part in the world to which her situation and her history entitled her. Something of a sensation was, however, caused early in 1924 by the final repudiation on the part of the Kemalists of the Caliphate, and by the banishment of the last Caliph from Turkey. This incident had, however, singularly little effect either in Turkey itself or in the outside world of Islam. Interminable negotiations for the securing of a final peace were only ended at Lausanne in July, 1923, by an agreement which appeared extremely generous to the Kemalists; but, in spite of this success, the future of Turkey in 1924 remained almost as uncertain as in 1918.

On the whole, then, it might be said that the situation in Iraq was at least as stable and as hopeful as that of her neighbours; and in some respects she appeared to have travelled further along the path of her political destiny than the other states in the Near and Middle East. An interesting rumour arose during the summer of 1923 that the controlling interest in the Anatolian Railway had been acquired by a British firm, who were inviting French and Italian financial collaboration. The rumour led to the hope that, after all, the Baghdad Railway might be completed, but this time under joint auspices and control; and that the overland route to India via Mesopotamia, so long a vision of enthusiastic dreamers, might at last become a reality. Meanwhile the growth of the motor and aerial traffic between Baghdad and the Mediterranean began to revive commercial relations between Iraq and the neighbouring Arab countries and Europe; and an increasing interest in Iraqi affairs began to be manifested in business circles in the great financial world of London. People who had learnt to know and love Iraq had at last some reason to hope that the material, as well as the political, future of the country was receiving the attention which it deserved.

The end of this phase in the long history of the land of Shinar was marked by the final retirement from the political field of Sir Percy Cox, the British High Commissioner who had borne the brunt of the actual creation of the new kingdom. In the days before the World War Sir Percy's reputation had rested upon the success of his ceaseless efforts to counteract anti-British influence in the Persian Gulf, and to secure to his own countrymen the fruits of three hundred years of adventurous national toil. He had lived to see those rival influences thwarted, one by one; and to watch the English power, through the course of the World War, attain to an eminence which completely outshone even the achievements of its own romantic past. He had negotiated the Anglo-Persian Treaty of 1920, which, however, had promptly broken down the moment his back was turned; and he had done more than any man to establish the infant Iraq State on a foundation of something like security, with a treaty agreement both with the King of the Hedjaz and the ever-watchful Ibn Saud, and with the assurance of the powerful support of the British people. He might well be excused the feeling that, after forty years of strenuous service, he was entitled to retire from the tumultuous scene, and henceforth, from the quiet of an English village, to watch the ever-changing drama of Middle Eastern life not as a possible combatant, but as a spectator.

And, with the departure from Mesopotamia of Sir Percy Cox, the practical creator of the new Iraq State, we may at the same time take our leave. We caught a first glimpse of Mesopotamia at the dawn of history; we have

SIR PERCY COX, G.C.M.G.

THE DAWN OF A TO-MORROW

followed her through her periods of brilliant civilizations, Akkadian, Assyrian, Babylonian, Persian, Alexandrian; we have seen the arrival of European influence, in the person of the Romans, and the long duel which ensued between the Eternal City and the local inhabitants of the country; we have watched the dramatic rise to power of the desert Arabs, under the challenging personality of the Prophet Muhammad; and we have followed the rapid creation and gradual decay of a Moslem civilization based directly upon the teachings of the youngest of the world religions. Finally, we have seen the centre of gravity shifted once more to Europe, and a second attempt, this time more successful, to extend European influence over the land which, so far as we know from our present incomplete knowledge of history, can truthfully claim to have been the cradle of mankind. Great names and varied personalities have flitted across our pages; Sargon, Hammurabi, Nabuchadnezzar, Alexander the Great, Trajan, Zenobia, Julian the Apostate, Heraclius, Ali the "Lion of God," Harun ar-Rashid, Hulagu Khan, Tamerlane, Suleiman the Magnificent; all men of vast influence, but of the most variegated type and culture, representing half the races under Heaven. We have touched upon some of the most decisive battles in Eastern, and even in world history, and noted the sieges of some of the most famous cities of mankind; and we have seen something of the strange play and interplay of national and racial forces, which act and re-act upon each other with the power and regularity of tidal waves. We leave the land of our story at the parting of the ways, derelict, but with the seeds of new life, barren, but capable of untold fruitfulness, hot, dirty and unkempt, and yet capable of arousing the loyalty of the most alien hearts. For whatever be the fate, in our time or in the dim and distant future, of Mesopotamia, she must always exercise a curious fascination over the minds of those who have once known, and either loved or hated her.

. . . . . .

And what of the immediate future? Does there exist any means of so assembling our facts that we may arrive at an accurate deduction of what lies before Iraq? Or must we end our story, as is the case with so many stories nowadays, with a large note of interrogation ?

In a sense the future of no land can be foretold except along the very vaguest lines. Even in solid, prosaic, civilized Europe states and kingdoms nowadays go up and down, disappear and reappear with an agility which almost takes the breath of the serious historian. We cannot tell with any degree of certainty how many of the present " Great Powers " will even be in existence fifty years from now. In the Near and Middle East the political prophet is on even more slippery ground. The various races and religions of that area are now so intermixed and sub-divided that it is almost impossible to foresee in what direction the people will tend, as the years go on, to settle and re-group themselves. But on three issues at least affecting the future of Iraq we may express an opinion with some degree of certainty.

It is fairly certain, in the first place, that the revival of the Arab national spirit, which we saw making its debut in the Wahabi victories a hundred years ago, is a genuine and a growing thing. The idea of nationalism, which was so strong in Europe in mid-Victorian times, has since spread to all parts of the world, and many of the extravagant racial hopes which were born of it seem destined to die before the world is very much older; but as the re-birth of Arab nationalism preceded most of these spurious outbursts, so it will probably outlive them. It would appear that Arab nationalism, and with it the religion of Islam, is going to become once more a world force, although it may be some years yet before it is strong enough to make itself felt; and with a healthy Arab nationalism may come a gradual rise to power once more of the Middle East as a political and cultural centre. In the second place, it is possible that the Turks may be able eventually to re-assert themselves over much of the countries which were wrested from them in the World War. There is a stronger feeling of sympathy with Turkish aspirations throughout the Near and Middle East than is realized, apparently, in Europe; and there can be no doubt that, if the European Powers concerned show themselves unwilling or unable to develop their new Middle Eastern interests in the way in which they have developed other parts of the world, the inhabitants of these regions would probably be inclined to prefer the return of the Turkish Government to the mal-administration of the various little states which are the fruit of President Wilson's Twelfth Point; and, whatever the counts which can be brought against the old Turkish administration, it was at least as good as those erected since the war. If the Turkish power does not revive (and many indications point that way), it is possible that it will combine with Arab nationalism to form a solid foundation for the creation of a modern Islamic civilization and culture.

This brings us to the consideration of our third issue, upon which it is possible to dogmatize with something approaching certainty. The day in which European power was paramount in the Middle East is passing, and passing fairly quickly. One European Power alone, Great Britain, has been able to retain her political position in these regions, and that only by the general consent of the local inhabitants; for Great Britain's international position and services are unique, and her influence has become so inextricably mixed with the other threads of Middle Eastern life, that the Middle East could not continue to exist, in anything like its present form, without her. But the old picture of the " patient East " trundling heavily along under the talented direction of the wise and hustling West is rapidly disappearing. Europe and America have no monopoly of the talents and energy of mankind; Asiatics are at least as strong, as resourceful and as clever as the inhabitants of other portions of the globe. Scientific training, the sole advantage possessed by the West, is now becoming worldwide. No advantage in technical equipment is now confined to Europe, but even the latest inventions soon reach the ends of the earth; Arabs drive motor-cars and Chinese manipulate wireless at least as capably as the citizens of Manchester or Chicago. Fifty years may easily see the East as well equipped and even as inventive as Western Europe and America; and the boasted superiority of the white man, himself sprung from the highlands of Asia, over the " Asiatic " may have been found but an empty dream. There can be no permanent monopoly of Nature's gifts, or of the rewards which spring from them.

And what of the future of Iraq? How do our three hypotheses affect the destiny of the land whose story has been the theme of this book?

It is almost certain that, as the years go on, Iraq will be drawn either towards the neighbouring Arab countries of Syria, Trans-Jordania or Nejd, or towards the Turks. Iraq can only continue to exist as an independent unit provided that she can obtain a strong and united national feeling, and, on the material side, the money with which to develop her natural resources. Sooner or later, if left to herself, she is almost certain to become the battle ground between the rival claims of Arab and Turkish nationalism; and here the powerful influence of the Wahabis, fostered by their ever-watchful chief Ibn Saud, must not be overlooked.

What, then, of the future of the European influence in Iraq?

Almost alone among the countries of the Middle East, Iraq both needs and desires some degree of outside influence and control. It has yet to be proved that a stable State can be built up at all in the land of the rivers, surrounded as it is by other countries, and inundated constantly by foreign and cosmopolitan influences. Iraq is, materially speaking, the most backward of the Middle Eastern countries, and she has in consequence the most leeway to make up. There is, as a necessary corollary, nothing like the same amount of opposition to European interference as exists in Egypt, in Syria or in India. The thoughtful Iraqi knows that he cannot at present stand alone, and that not only the painfully erected political structure of the new kingdom, but all the outward and visible signs of material civilization—railways, motor-cars, a stable currency and security for trade—must all disappear if the hand of the European is entirely withdrawn. And he does not want this to happen. The past fifteen years have taught him many things, and he is no longer content with the quiet life of the backwater. Domination by a great Power may have its disadvantages, but it also has its advantages; and the Iraqi landowner and working-man alike have had cause to bless the occupation of the country by British Forces and Western methods of business. It is a *sine qua non* of the success of the new regime, that the

British support shall not be withdrawn, either soon or suddenly.

And what of the British connection from the British point of view?

The main feature of the British connection is usually overlooked both by the British press and by British public men; namely, that it is not a new thing. It does not date from the World War, or from the private ambition of some British general. It dates back to the capture of Hormuz over three hundred years ago; it has gone on steadily increasing in momentum for at least a hundred and fifty; it may even yet have not arrived at a climax. The foolish and irrational policy of a " bag and baggage " evacuation entirely overlooks this fact, and thus tacitly ignores not only British interests in the Middle East, but also British duties; it is a completely suburban and ostrich-like point of view, quite unworthy of the journalistic aristocracy that advocated it. The Persian Gulf is one of the nerve centres of the British Empire; and Iraq is easily the most important country bordering on the Gulf. British interests and British duties alike forbid her frittering or throwing away her great position in these regions. Listen on this point to Sir A. T. Wilson, the chief representative of the Anglo-Persian Oil Company in the Persian Gulf, and a man who could claim, after a long experience as civil servant and man of business, to know more about the Middle East than any newspaper proprietor in London:

> " We have heard a good deal of the promises made by His Majesty's Government to the Arab-speaking peoples of the Near East; on the strength of these promises much British money has been invested in these regions, and those who have built up enterprises in this country on the strength of those promises are entitled, equally with the inhabitants of the country, to look to His Majesty's Government not lightly to abandon her self-imposed mission.
>
> " The British nation is doing in these regions a work which no other nation has ever attempted before, and by the doing of which we shall be judged in history. The early efforts of a handful of merchant

adventurers two hundred years ago has produced, like a stone thrown into a pond, an ever-extending circle of pulsation which at the present moment embraces the limits and affects the destinies of all Asia. Our Eastern responsibilities will, so long as we remain an Empire, increase and not diminish."

Whatever be the eventual fate of Iraq, the British connection will not, and should not, be broken for many a day. Responsibility of any kind cannot be repudiated without dishonour and eventual misfortune; and though the British of this generation are not directly responsible for a policy by which Great Britain has become the one solid and unshifting thing in the whole Near and Middle Eastern landscape, the one sure rock and shield of the timid and the oppressed, the one influence by which outside civilization may hope to reach so many remnants of great races that seem to have lost their way; yet they still remain the sons of their fathers, and they cannot refuse to accept the responsibilities, even when expensive or unpleasant, that the policy of their fathers has brought into being. Upon their fathers' policy in the Near and Middle East have been built up Britain's Indian dominion, and the great Eastern connections of the British mercantile marine; upon it rests the Empire, that majestic and unique creation which alone distinguishes Great Britain from any other inconspicuous island of the northern seas. The Empire is at once the symbol and the mascot of the British race; in it are embodied the hopes, the duties and the destiny of the British nation. It is impossible, at this late hour, to complain of its existence, on the score of the myriad unpleasant and expensive tasks which its presence brings in its train; and, if it were not impossible, it would be cowardly and petty. If Fate has willed that the British Empire must, to some extent, bear the burden of civilization in Iraq and the other countries bordering upon the Persian Gulf, the task cannot be evaded by the hypocritical contention that it does not come within the bounds of Imperial responsibilities; unless indeed the British Empire would wish to bear the brand of Cain. For, just as the world of Western Europe two thousand years ago rested upon Rome,

THE TOWER OF NIMROD NEAR BABYLON
SAID TO BE THE TOWER OF BABEL

so to-day does the world of the Middle East rest upon the British Empire. Such stability as does exist is only guaranteed by the security of the British name ; such fragments of law and order, refinement and civilization as remain, remain only because, and as long as, the seas of the Middle East are patrolled by British ships, and the forces of disorder on land are controlled by British men. If the British Empire should collapse, or if the British people should suddenly withdraw from its self-imposed task, the world of the Middle East must immediately sink back into that chaos from which it has been the work of three centuries to rescue it. There is no present alternative. To say that the hopelessly disunited millions of Asia—Indians, Arabs, Persians, Turks, Kurds, Afghans, Armenians, Jews—are as capable of finding their own political level and of achieving their own destiny unaided as the millions of Europe or America is simply to say that which is not true. The withdrawal of the British influence does not mean " independence " or " self-determination "; it means chaos, utter and complete, until some other Power arises to take up the burden thus thrown down. For there is not one single connecting link, one single unifying idea, between the myriad races and religions that form the jungle of the Middle Eastern world—except the actuality of the British Empire; upon that all the nations, all the faiths lean in common; it is the mortar which, surrounding and enveloping the bricks of every sort and shape, alone secures the building. Britain will refuse the extension of her Imperial task, will abrogate her responsibility to civilization, only at the risk of forfeiting the tolerance and respect of her fellow workers in the world, and the approval of her God. By the Empire, lives or falls Great Britain; upon the Empire rests the present structure of the Middle Eastern world. Like the Coliseum of old, the Empire stands as a visible symbol of the genius of an uniquely constructive nation; for, as the Romans built in stone, so do the British build in peoples. And if the building falls, then must the bricks fall with it.

> " While stands the Coliseum, Rome shall stand ;
> When falls the Coliseum, Rome shall fall ;
> And when Rome falls, the world."

APPENDIX

The following books are recommended to those readers who wish to pursue the subject further:

"The Land of the Two Rivers." Edwin Bevan. (Edward Arnold, London.)

"Rise and Fall of the Abbassid Caliphate." Sir William Muir, K.C.S.I. (John Grant, Edinburgh.)

"Short History of the Saracens." Seyyid Ameer Ali, P.C., C.I.E. (Macmillan & Co., London.)

"Baghdad under the Abbassid Caliphate." G. Le Strange. (Cambridge University Press.)

"Irrigation in Mesopotamia." Sir William Willcocks, K.C.M.G., F.R.G.S. (E. & F. Spon, London.)

"The War and the Baghdad Railway." Morris Jastrow, jun. (J. B. Lippincott, Philadelphia.)

"The German Road to the East." Evans Lewin. (William Heinemann, London.)

"The Arab of Mesopotamia." Official. (Government Press, Basrah.)

"Historical Mesopotamia." Various. (Times Press, Basrah.)

"Review of the Civil Administration of Mesopotamia, 1920." Gertrude L. Bell, C.B.E. (H.M. Stationery Office, London.)

"The Heart of Arabia." H. St. J. B. Philby, C.I.E. (Constable & Co., London.)

"The Insurrection in Mesopotamia, 1920." Lt.-Gen. Sir Aylmer L. Haldane, G.C.M.G., K.C.B., D.S.O. (Wm. Blackwood & Sons, Edinburgh.)

"Encyclopædia Britannica," eleventh edition (with extra volumes). (En. Brit. Co., New York.)

"My Campaign in Mesopotamia," Major-General Sir Charles V. F. Townshend, K.C.B., D.S.O. (Thornton Butterworth Ltd., London).

INDEX

	PAGE
Abbas the Great	104
Abbas, uncle of the Prophet	59, 63
Abbassid family	60, 62, 63, 66, 79
Abdul Aziz Ibn Saud. *See* Saud	
Abdul Wahab	117
Abu Bekr	43, 45–50
Abu Muslim	62, 67
Ælius Gallus	38
Aga Khan	76
Agriculture	253–56
Ahman Pasha defies Turkey	104
Akhwan Movement	227, 228
Alexander the Great	19, 25–26
Alexander Severus, Emperor	33
Ali	43, 45, 53–58, 66
Allenby, Lord	157
Amraphel of the Book of Genesis	19
Amusements	282–83
Anatolian Railway	127, 130, 307
Anglo-Persian Agreement	182, 308
Anglo-Persian Oil Company	138, 145, 278, 280, 284, 304
Antiochus III	29
Antony, Mark	31
Arab delegates from Muhammad visit Chroses and Heraclius	37
Arab Empire, break-up of	89
Arabs as business men	285
— bravery of	199–200
— characteristics of	39–42
— colonists	110
— democrats	198
— dignity of	298
— fatalism	298
— language	39
— love of freedom	39–40
— merchants	86
— rise of	38–51
Armenia	32
Armenian massacres of 1895	128–29
Armenians	206
Army	79–80
Artaxerxes	25
Artisans	214–15
Asiatics and Europeans	311
Assassins Sect	95
Assyrians	205
Augustus, Emperor	38
Ayesha, widow of the Prophet	45, 55
Babak	92
Babism	211
Babylon	19–23
Baffin	107

	PAGE
Baghdad, capture of	155–56
— chosen by Mansur as a new capital	68–71
— civilization	89
— Clapham Junction of the air	289
— customs	85
— democratic	79
— dress	83–84
— East India Company appoints a Resident	112
— founding of the city	68–71
— in the Golden Age	82
— invaded by Mongols	98
— luxury of	82
— society	85
— social life	290
— splendour of	87
— university	276 and *passim*
Baghdad Railway	127, 129, 130, 137, 143
Balfour, Earl	132
Bander Abbasi	106–8, 110
Barmecides family	72
Basrah	52 and *passim*
" Battle of the Camel "	55
Bel, Temple of	23
Bithynia	30
Blind	268
Bonham-Carter, Sir Edgar	235
Bookselling	276
Bridges	258–59
Buckingham, Duke of	107
Burmah Oil Company	138
Business	280–89
— during the Golden Age	86
Buyid family	95
Caliphs at the Friday service	83
— frequently treated with indignity	88
— power decays	94
Caracalla, Emperor	32
Carmathians	94, 95
Carus, Emperor	34
Censorship	232
Chamberlain, Joseph	132
Charlemagne	22, 71
Chesney, Col. F. R.	111, 125–26
Chess	74 (*note*)
Christianity official religion of the Roman Empire	35
Christians	204–206
Chroses II	36
Churchill, Winston	138, 289
Cinemas	296–97

INDEX

	PAGE
Climate	267–68
Coffee shops	294–96
Communism in Ancient Persia	92
Constantine, Emperor	35
Constantinople, foundation of	35
Costume of the people	196–97
Cox, Sir Percy	193–94, 216–17, 308
Crassus	30–31
Crusades	96–97
Ctesiphon	30
Customs and Excise	247
Cyrus the Persian	24
Daurah summer camp	184
"Dead pilgrim" traffic	270–71
Deir-az-Zoir	179–81
Delcassé, M.	132
"Devil Worshippers"	210–211
Dhari, Sheikh, murders Col. Leachman	190
Diocletian	34
Diseases	268–70
Divine right of kings	57
Dress of the people	196–97
Dutch East India Company	106–8
Dutch influence on Mesopotamia	108
E-anna-du, conqueror	17
Ea, the culture-god	16, 17
East India Company	107
"Eden" of the Bible	17
Education	272–76
El-Lil, the sun god	17
Eridu	16, 17
Ess, Rev. John van	199 (note)
Euphrates Valley Railway	126
Europeans and Asiatics	311
Eye diseases	269
Falkenhayn, Marshal von	156
Fatimides	94
Feisal, King	159, 169, 180–82, 223–34, 276, 298, 301, 305
"Field of Tens"	50
Fire Brigade	263
French East India Company	109
French in Syria	241, 305–306
French influence on Mesopotamia	108–115
Games	85
"Gentleman Companion"	295–96
German influence on Mesopotamia	127–42
Gipsies	92, 240
Girls, sale of	300
Goa	106
Gobryas, Kurdish general	23
Golden Age of Mesopotamia	65–87
Gordian, Emperor	33
Grey, Earl	136
Gwinner, Dr. von	131

	PAGE
Haldane, Sir Aylmer L.	201 (note)
Harran	31
Harun-ar-Rashid	65, 72–73, 82, 86
— letter to Nicephorus	74
Hassan	56, 58
Hedjaz	150
Heraclius	36–37
Hindiyah Barrage	250, 252
Hira	39, 48
Hisham	61
Hormuz	105, 107, 112
Hosein	56, 57, 58, 60, 118, 150, 151, 153, 164, 225, 226, 229, 306
Hulagu	98
Hummurabi	19–20
Imam	57–58
Industry	277–89
Iraq (Mesopotamia)	
— and Great Britain	313–15
— Arab country	51
— army	245–46
— as a Persian possession	101
— bright prospects before the War	143
— connection with Mesopotamia	11–12
— British expenditure in	183–86
— coming of the Arab	38–51
— coming of the British	103–20
— coming of the German	121–42
— coming of the Turk	88–102
— creation of the new State	216–34
— early history	11–51
— effect of the War	143–59
— extravagance in Mesopotamia	244
— future of	309–15
— Golden Age of	65–87
— influence on Mesopotamia	108–20
— mandate to Great Britain	166–67
— meaning of name	12–13
— people of	195–215
— population	195–96
— present administration	13
— rebellion of 1920	187–93
— Roman-Persian rivalry	27–37
— social life	290–300
— tourists' centre	223–39, 289 and passim
Irrigation system	16, 250–53
Islam, see Muhammadanism	
Ismail, Shah	100
Jafar	67, 72, 73
Jafar al-Motawakkil	93, 94
James I	107
Jawasimi pirates	110
Jenghis Khan	97
Jerusalem, capture of	157
Jews	202–204, 293
Jovian	36

INDEX

	PAGE
Judaism	33
Julian the Apostate	35–36
Justice, Courts of	235–37
Justinian	36
Karind, summer camp	184
Karkh	70
Kemalists	307
Kerbela	57
Khalid	47
Koran	76
Koweit	134, 136
Kufa	52
Kurds	201–202
Kut	147–55
Labour conditions	285–86
Lagash	17
Lansdowne, Lord	136
Law, A. Bonar	145
Lawrence, Col. T. E.	151, 225
Laws	235–37
Leachman, Colonel, murder of	189–90
League of Nations	164
Locusts	255
Lot, nephew of Abraham	19
Ma'adan Arabs	122
Magnesia, Battle of	29
Malik Shah	95
Mamum, son of Harun ar-Rashid	65, 74–76, 78, 82, 86, 90
Manchester Regiment	188
Mandæans	207–210
Mandate, Mesopotamia	216
Mandate system	166–68, 221
Mansur	65, 67–74
Marcus Aurelius	32
Mark Antony	31
Maude, General	154–58, 163
Medical work	264–66
Medina (Yathrib)	44, 45, 46
Mehemet Ali	118
Merwan	61, 62, 63
Mesopotamia, meaning of the name	12–13
Mesopotamia, See Iraq	
Messageries Maritimes	133
Midhat Pasha	103, 111, 119, 121–25
Mineral wealth	278
Mithridates	30
Moawiyah	54, 55, 56
Mongols	97–102
Moqanna, al	66
Motasim	91
Motawakkil	93, 94
Mubarak, Sheikh	134, 135
Muhammad al-Mahdi	58
Muhammad ibn al-Hanafiyah	60
Muhammad, life and teaching of	42–45
Muhammad sends delegates to Chroses and Heraclius	37

	PAGE
Muhammadan religion	40, 42–46, 52–64
Mujtahidin	176
Mustafa al Alusi	235
Mu'tazilites	76
Nabatæa	39
Nabopolassar	22
Nadir Shah	104
Najaf	57
Nasir, Caliph	97
Navy	81
Nebuchadnezzar	22–24
Nicephorus, Emperor, letter to Harun-ar-Rashid	73–74
Nippur	17
Nisibin	35
Nixon, Sir John	146
Odenathus	34
Oil in Persia	138
Omar	43, 50, 51, 54, 81
Omar Khayyam	95
Othman, Caliph	55, 56, 101
Ottomans	101
Palmerston, Lord	125
Palmyra	34
Parthians	28–32
Pergamos	28, 30
Persia, British troops in	183
— communism in ancient	92
— oil in	138
— royalty from Anglo-Persian Oil Co.	304
Persian Empire	24–25, 51
Persian invasions of Mesopotamia	50–51, 100
Pilgrim traffic	270–71, 299–300
Pious Bequests	241
Police system	238–39
Polo, Marco	99
Portuguese traders	106–7
Postal service	262
Public health	264–66
Railways	259
Rashid, Ibn	133, 135, 146, 227
Religions of Mesopotamia	33, 202–211
Rents	287–88
Revenues and taxes	81
Roads	256–58
Russian expansion in the East	114
Russian influence on Mesopotamia	127
Russian Steam Navigation and Trading Company	133
Saba	38
Sabians	207
"Sabians"	123
Saladin	97, 202
Samarra	91

INDEX

	PAGE
Sanitation	264
Sapor II	35
Sargon, founder of Akkad	18
Sassanian Kings	33
Sassoon family	161, 221
Saud, Ibn	117, 133–35, 141, 146, 151, 154, 226–29, 233, 306, 308, 312
Seleucia	27
Seleucus	27
Selim, Sultan	102
Sexual diseases	270
Seyyid Talib Pasha	226, 229, 230
Shalmeneser I	20
— II	20
Shammar	122–23, 183
Sheba of the Bible	38
Sheikh, position of	212–14
Shiah faith	52–58, 201 and *passim*
Siemens, Dr.	129
Sports	85
Subbis	207–210
Suez Canal	125–26
Suleiman the Magnificent	102, 103
Sulla, proconsul	30
Sumabi, Arabian conqueror	19
Sykes, Sir Percy	154
Syria	305
Tel Afar garrison put to the sword	183
Telegraph service	262
Thomson, Lord	306
Tiglath-Pileser I	20
— III	21–22
Timur (Tamerlane)	99
Tobacco	249
Tourists, Iraq as a country for	289
Townshend, Sir Charles V. F.	146, 148, 151–52

	PAGE
Trajan invades Armenia	32
Transportation	256–58
Tribal system	213
Tughril Bey	95
Turks in the Arab Empire	88–102
— decay of power	102–104
Ultimatum of Nicephorus to Harun	73–74
Ummeyad family	54, 55, 57, 61, 66
Valerian, Emperor	34
Van Ess, Rev. John	199 (*note*)
Vital statistics	271
Von der Goltz, Marshal	152
Wahabi creed	227, 228
Wahabis	117, 118
Waqaf	241–44
White Slave traffic	300
Willcocks, Sir William	139, 250, 251 (*note*), 252
William III, German Emperor	127–29, 149
Wilson, Sir A. T.	313
Wilson, President	164–65, 168
Women	84–85
Women, absence of in Moslem society	293
Yahya	72
Yathrib	44, 45, 46
Yesdigerd " the hapless "	51
Yezidis	207, 210–211
Yue-tshi Mongolian people	29
Zaid, Amir	304
Zenobia of Palmyra	34
Zionist Movement	305
Zobeida, wife of Harun	84
Zoroaster	24

BRISTOL : BURLEIGH LTD. AT THE BURLEIGH PRESS